The Great Web

THE GREAT WEB
The Form of Hardy's Major Fiction

IAN GREGOR

FABER AND FABER
3 Queen Square
London

First published in 1974
by Faber and Faber Limited
3 Queen Square London WC1
Printed in Great Britain by
Western Printing Services Ltd, Bristol

ISBN 0 571 08906 2

Chapter 4 is based on material prepared by the author for his Introduction to the New Wessex Edition of THE MAYOR OF CASTERBRIDGE © Macmillan London Ltd, 1974.

Map of the Wessex of the Novels and Poems drawn by Emery Walker for the Macmillan editions of the novels (Macmillan London Ltd).

To
Mark Kinkead-Weekes

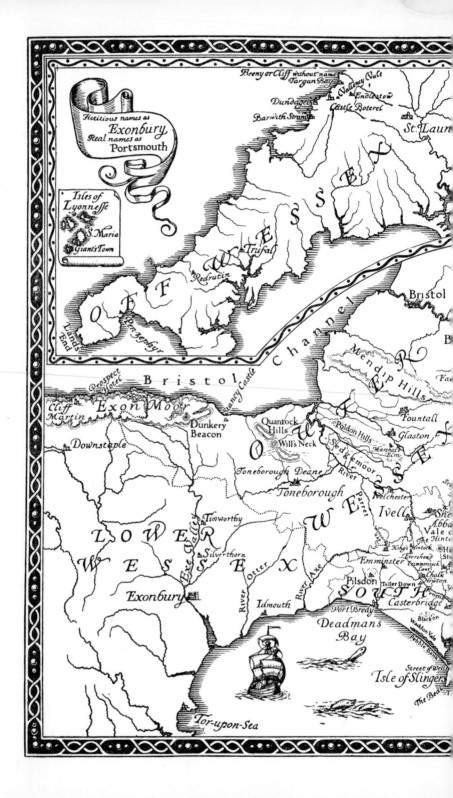

Fictitious names as
Exonbury
Real names as
Portsmouth

Isles of
Lyonnesse
S. Maria
Giants Town

Beeny or Cliff without name
Targan Bay
Valliney Vale
Endleston
Dundagel
Castle Boterel
Barwith Strand
St. Laur

O F F W E S S E X

Bristol

Trufal

Redrutin

Penzephyr

Lands
End

Channel

Mendip Hills

Fa

Bristol

Prospect
Hotel

Bristol Channel

Pency Castle

Exon Moor

Cliff
Martin

Dunkery
Beacon

Downstaple

Quantock
Hills
Will's Neck

Poldon Hills

Sledgemoor

O U T

Fountall

Glaston

Marnhull
Elm

W E S S E X

Toneborough Deane

Toneborough

Parret River

Ivell

She
Abba
Vale
The Hinte

L O W E R

Exe Valley

Tiworthy

Silverthorn

River Otter

River Axe

W E S S E X

Emminster

King's
Hintock
Evershead
Grimmerton
Lande
Challe
Newton

Hi
Sto

Exonbury

Idmouth

Pilsdon

Port Bredy

Teller Down
S O U T

Black on

Casterbridge

Wocton Vale

Deadmans
Bay

Pebble

Street of Well
Isle of Slingers

The Bea

Tor-upon-Sea

And yet their lonely courses formed no detached design at all, but were part of the pattern in the great web of human doings then weaving in both hemispheres from the White Sea to Cape Horn.

THOMAS HARDY, *The Woodlanders*

The chief factor in the thoughts of the modern mind concerning itself is the intricacy, the universality of natural law, even in the moral order. For us, necessity is not, as of old, a sort of mythological personage without us, with whom we can do warfare. It is rather a magic web woven through and through us, like that magnetic system of which modern science speaks, penetrating us with a network, subtler than our subtlest nerves, yet bearing in it the central forces of the world.

WALTER PATER, 'Winckelmann', *The Renaissance*

CONTENTS

ACKNOWLEDGEMENTS

While it is a pleasure as well as an obligation to be able to record an indebtedness to the work of others, it is not easy in a book which aims at a fresh reading of familiar novels to identify the various influences and insights which, over the years, have undoubtedly been active in shaping a critical account one likes to regard as largely personal. I have tried to keep in touch with most of the discussions which have taken place on Hardy on both sides of the Atlantic in recent years, and specific acknowledgements occur at various points in the book. More generally, if I had to name the books and essays which linger most in my mind, even though their interest in Hardy may now look very different from my own, I would include the following: John Holloway's chapter on Hardy in *The Victorian Sage* (1953); Douglas Brown's study of *The Mayor of Casterbridge* (1962); Raymond Williams's chapter on Hardy in *The English Novel from Dickens to Lawrence* (1970); Irving Howe's *Thomas Hardy* (1967); and, though written at an opposite pole to the present book, J. Hillis Miller's *Thomas Hardy: Distance and Desire* (1970).

I am grateful to Sheed and Ward for allowing me to reprint a version of Chapter 7, 'An End and a Beginning': *Jude the Obscure*, which appeared in *The Prose for God: Religious and Anti-Religious Aspects of Imaginative Literature* (1973), edited by Ian Gregor and Walter Stein; to Macmillan London Ltd., publishers of Thomas Hardy's novels and of Florence Emily Hardy's *The Life of Thomas Hardy, 1840–1928*, for permission to reproduce quotations; to the University of Kent at Canterbury for granting me a sabbatical term and for financing a visit to the Thomas Hardy Museum in Dorchester; and to members of the University secretarial staff among whom I would like to mention in particular Mrs. Muriel Waring and Miss Wendy Conway, who typed a difficult manuscript with fortitude and cheerfulness.

More personal acknowledgements bring home to me sharply the extent of my debt to friends and colleagues. Here my gratitude must go to Denis Donoghue of University College, Dublin and to Michael Millgate of University College, Toronto, who encouraged my progress with opportune invitations to lecture on Hardy; to Terry Eagleton of Wadham College, Oxford, for stimulating discussions; to John Goode of the University of Reading, who read the book in typescript and made useful suggestions; to Frank McCombie and Brian Nicholas who gave the completed book its first critical reading, and who, in most generously giving their time to correct the proofs, made their criticism quite invaluable to me. If I have failed to take advantage of suggestions made to me, the responsibility is wholly mine.

My special thanks, however, must go to Mark Kinkead-Weekes, with whom I have discussed literary matters in general, and Hardy in particular, for longer than he cares to remember, and to whom it gives me the greatest pleasure to dedicate this book.

Canterbury, 1973   I.G.

Preface

Some years ago I wrote an article with the title 'What kind of fiction did Hardy write?',[1] and though my thoughts on what might suitably appear under such a title have shifted a good deal since then, the question itself has continued to stay with me. The present book may be regarded as an extended meditation on the subject.

Contained within that question are two distinct, but related, interests. The first, obviously enough, is an interest in Hardy's novels, arising from the pleasure they have given me over the years, and indeed the recording and description of that enjoyment must be the first reason for a book of this kind. I have not seen any reason to challenge the generally accepted canon of Hardy's major novels, and seeing that my prime aim has been to define the nature of his achievement, I felt I could, with propriety, confine myself to examining those novels. I have been concerned not simply to bring out their individual nature, but to see them in relation to each other and to argue that, taken as a whole, the major fiction from *Far From the Madding Crowd* to *Jude the Obscure* constitutes a coherent imaginative journey.

The second interest is contingent upon the first, and it arises from the conviction that an attempt to give some account of the power of Hardy's fiction must involve a fresh look at some of the assumptions which underlie a good deal of contemporary novel criticism. We have said, it seems to me, too little about the nature of narrative itself, about the sense of a novel as a gradually unfolding process which builds itself up within the reader's experience; we have a tensed and wary relationship with 'ideas' in fiction; and on the relationship of the author to his work, we have been inclined to settle for a too simple distinction between the impersonal and the dramatised narrator. In consequence, running throughout this study of Hardy's novels there is an accompanying stress on the problems raised by a distinctive kind of fiction.

[1] *Essays in Criticism*, XVI, 3, July 1966, pp. 290–308.

It will be seen, even from this brief description, that the spirit in which this study has been undertaken, has been severely literary-critical in intent. If I have nothing explicitly to say about Hardy and his age, this should not be taken to imply that I am in need of persuading of the intimate relationship that must exist between the writer and the times in which he lives; likewise, if I have nothing to say about Hardy and his relationship with the writing of his contemporaries this does not mean I am in need of persuading that a novelist must choose from the literary forms that are available to him. These interests are tacitly present in all I have to say, but if I have chosen to keep them that way, this is partly because I feel such work has been adequately done elsewhere, partly because I considered such exclusions would enable me to focus more sharply on the distinctive nature of Hardy's fiction itself. What is a Hardy novel, what does it feel like to read, why does it take the form it does – these are the questions that shape what I have to say.

I
Reading Hardy

There is a famous stopping-place for critics of the novel in a letter which Henry James once wrote to the young Hugh Walpole:

> Form alone *takes*, and holds and preserves, substance – saves it from the welter of helpless verbiage that we swim in as in a sea of tasteless tepid pudding, and that makes one ashamed of an art capable of such degradations. Tolstoi and Dostoevsky are fluid puddings, though not tasteless, because the amount of their own minds and souls in solution in the broth gives it savour and flavour, thanks to the strong, rank quality of their genius and their experience. But there are all sorts of things to be said of them, and in particular that we see how great a vice is their lack of composition, their defiance of economy and architecture, directly they are emulated and imitated; *then*, as subjects of emulation, models, they quite give themselves away. There is nothing so deplorable as a work of art with a *leak* . . .[1]

A famous passage, in that it has not only given sharper definition to our understanding of James's sense of form in fiction, but it has been operative in creating an idiom for our discussion of fiction in general. 'Form alone *takes*, and holds and preserves . . .', the shaping idea is there, driving in the wedge hard and with ceremony, between art and the miscellany of daily experience, and seeing in form something to which justice can only be done in terms of physical possession. From this, it is but a short step to a sense of fiction as an organic whole, 'all one and continuous, like any other organism, and in proportion as it lives will it be found . . . that in each of the parts there is something of each of the other parts'.[2] Homogeneous in its nature, conscious of its artifice, consistent in its point of view, these are the marks by which we come to know and to talk about a James novel, and we have to

[1] *The Letters of Henry James*, ed. Lubbock, II, p. 246.
[2] 'The Art of Fiction', *Selected Literary Criticism*, ed. Shapira, p. 88.

take them all the more readily because James has himself indicated their significance. James, we might say, has not only written his novels, he has built into the writing of them how they should be read. The Prefaces are the formal extension of a process, already implicit in the novels themselves; they have, we feel, *already* been perfectly 'read' by their author, and the awareness of that reading becomes part of our experience of his fiction.

Where the Prefaces, together with the letters, have made their distinctive contribution is in the uncovering of some of the general assumptions upon which the particular readings are based, they have arranged for a set of novels to illustrate the art of fiction. And that art has, of course, been a pervasive presence in the general criticism of fiction in recent decades, a presence, even when it is not being consciously adverted to. Consider for instance E. M. Forster's sharp, influential book, *Aspects of the Novel*. Behind those seemingly artless chapter titles, 'Story', 'Plot', 'People', and so on, there is a Jamesian progress, as the postulant in search of the mysteries of fiction leaves behind him the flats of story, and arrives finally in the high ranges where pattern can be revealed and elusive rhythms are heard. In his own distinctive and unassuming way, Forster too reinforces the idea of fiction as an organic whole – his final analogue is with music – and these 'aspects of the novel' have become so much part of the current coin of criticism that, in citing James and Forster, we are only citing moments of influence, of persuasive coherence, not describing an argument consciously pursued.

When we come to look at Hardy's novels through the eyes of someone writing under that influence, this is how they appear:

James's rules were not cramping; they had as their object the liberation of his genius, and the extent of his liberation is best seen when we compare him to his great contemporary, Thomas Hardy. Hardy wrote as he pleased, just as any popular novelist does, quite unaware of the particular problems of his art, and yet it is Hardy who gives the impression of being cramped, of being forced into melodramatic laöcoon attitudes, so that we begin to appreciate his novels only for the passages where the poet subdues the novelist.[1]

[1] Graham Greene, 'The Lesson of the Master', *The Lost Childhood*, p. 50.

For Graham Greene the lesson of the master has been ignored by Hardy, a false notion of freedom has been aimed at, craft has had to give way to personal assertion. The result is that internal harmonies have been destroyed, and a deep divisiveness has been set up within the fiction, which can be described as a conflict between the poet and the novelist, or – more tellingly, perhaps – between the novelist and the sage.

It is not hard to see what it is in a Hardy novel which lends itself to this criticism. From a Jamesian point of view, not only has the novel developed a leak, it is distinctly porous. There is a number of quite definable interests running through it: the story-teller whose tales have the forceful simplicities of the ballad-writer, the social historian evoking and criticising the radical changes overtaking the rural economy of the south-west of England in the second half of the nineteenth century, the reader of Darwin, Mill and Schopenhauer, recording his troubled reflections. There are other interests too, but perhaps it is these that catch the eye most readily, and they catch it because they seem in no particular hurry to resolve themselves into an imaginative whole.

Nevertheless, separate and distinctive as these interests are, they do not seem to compromise, much less to threaten, the unity and coherence of the novels. The world of Hardy's novels is as undeniably present as the world of Henry James. Equally undeniably, it would seem to be constructed on very different principles, principles which make us think again about what we mean by the unity of a novel, by the presence of ideas in a novel, by the relationship between the author and his work. Put bluntly, we have to ask ourselves, what kind of novel did Hardy write? In attempting to describe it, we will have to ask what fresh emphasis will be given to those elements in our reading which Jamesian practice and precept has entered only in the margins of those critical accounts we customarily render.

If there is one element more than any other which has fallen on hard times, it is the element of story. When the story of a novel is mentioned it is as a preliminary ritual, rather like an acrobat hastily unrolling the mat upon which he is to perform his act. This is a pity because 'the story' is central to our experience of reading, and most novel readers warm to Wilde's observation, 'This suspense is terrible.

I hope it will last', however subtle, oblique and elegant its communication may be. What I am contending for is not that the critic should devote more of his time to relating the story, but rather underlining the fact that the experience of reading a novel is that of an unfolding process, a process which has implications not just for the psychology of reading, but for literary criticism. Precisely because it is a process, a novel looks and feels different at page 200 from how it looked and felt at page 100, whereas our methods of criticism incline to treat a novel as if it were a series of numbered paragraphs simultaneously present in the reader's mind. Every novel is only gradually exposed, and then it gradually recedes, as Percy Lubbock reminds us in the salutary opening paragraph of *The Craft of Fiction*:

> To grasp the shadowy and fantasmal form of a book, to hold it fast, to turn it over and survey it at leisure – that is the effort of a critic of books, and it is perpetually defeated. Nothing, no power, will keep a book steady and motionless before us, so that we may have time to examine its shape and design. As quickly as we read, it melts and shifts in the memory . . .[1]

In an attempt to support our fading memory we prefabricate a scaffolding upon which we can reconstruct our recollections, a scaffolding defined in terms of plot, character, setting, and so on. What we have also to remember is that these precipitates came to us gradually, as a process, and in isolating them, we should recall, as a complementary need, the dynamic which made them present to us.

These generalisations, which could apply to fiction in general, have a particular force when applied to Hardy, because for him the story, the process of revelation, is central to his fictional enterprise. His imaginative purposes require a heightened sense of anticipation and involvement, that peculiar kind of total involvement which is so much a part of a story's spell, and which was well described by a reader of *Jane Eyre* when that novel first appeared:

> We took up *Jane Eyre* one winter's evening, somewhat piqued at the extravagant commendations we had heard, and sternly resolved to be as critical as Croker. But as we read on we forgot both commendations and criticism, identified ourselves with Jane in all

[1] P. Lubbock, *The Craft of Fiction*, p. 1.

her troubles, and finally married Mr. Rochester about four in the morning.[1]

Hardy would have relished a similar reaction to his own novels.

While we must start by indicating this sense of involvement as a necessary preliminary in establishing the importance of story, it would not translate itself into a matter of critical interest, unless it raised an issue which affected Hardy's outlook as a novelist. Story, or more precisely plot, is mimetic of Hardy's metaphysic; in the plot the novelist makes, he finds an analogue both for the plots men make for themselves, and for the plots over which they seem to have no control. Hardy's ostentatious use of coincidence is the well-lighted junction where the lines of these various plots converge. Again and again his plot encourages us to ponder its links or its gaps, so that we can become aware of a process which is both leading us inevitably onwards, and yet is exerting a palpable design upon us. The effect is rather like that of being in a maze which involves us in getting out, and yet impresses us with how that exit will be effected. It is this duality of effect which is present in Hardy's references to fiction as being 'a precise transcript of ordinary life',[2] but also 'a tale . . . exceptional enough to justify its telling',[3] and 'the uncommonness must be in the events not in the characters'.[4] In other words, the pressure of the design is such that the reader is made continually aware that it is a story that he is being told, it has its own authenticity, its own fabrication: it is 'once upon a time . . .'. Consider the manner of our first acquaintance with *The Return of the Native*, *The Mayor of Casterbridge*, and *Tess of the D'Urbervilles*:

> A Saturday afternoon in November was approaching the time of twilight . . .
> One evening of late summer, before the nineteenth century had reached one-third of its span . . .
> On an evening in the latter part of May a middle-aged man was walking homeward . . .

These opening sentences all catch the classic cadence of the storyteller, the isolating precision of place and time, going along with a

---

[1] William George Clark, *Fraser's*, December 1849, p. 692, quoted by Kathleen Tillotson, *Novels of the Eighteen-Forties*, p. 19.
[2] *Life of Thomas Hardy*, p. 150.   [3] *Life*, p. 252.   [4] *Life*, p. 150.

generalised expansiveness, which will ensure our involvement as the design is gradually disclosed, an involvement which secures us as willing accomplices in the creation of 'make-believe'. What gives Hardy's sense of story its critical significance is that it is integral to his way of thinking, it silhouettes his metaphysic.

It is important that we grasp the dramatic existence of that metaphysic, and look at the way in which the ideas are present in Hardy's fiction. However much we may feel we want to italicise the ideas, they are an inevitable part of a developing text,[1] we come to them in the process of a particular narrative, and they take their place within that narrative. Nevertheless, their relationship can vary considerably. I would like to illustrate this by looking at two places in the Wessex novels, which have become something of anthology pieces in any discussion of Hardy's ideas. The first is from *Jude* and occurs early in the novel when Jude has been dismissed by the farmer for allowing the birds to eat his corn:

> Events did not rhyme quite as he had thought. Nature's logic was too horrid for him to care for. That mercy towards one set of creatures was cruelty towards another sickened his sense of harmony. As you got older, and felt yourself to be at the centre of your time, and not at a point in its circumference, as you had felt when you were little, you were seized with a sort of shuddering, he perceived. All around you there seemed to be something glaring, garish, rattling, and the noises and glares hit upon the little cell called your life, and shook it, and warped it.
>
> If he could only prevent himself growing up! He did not want to be a man.

What we notice about this passage is the shifting relationship of the

---

[1] I know that there is a persuasive school of current critical thinking which would give the word 'text' a much more comprehensive welcome than I do here, and by so doing, hope to make redundant such traditional categories as 'character', 'ideas', 'setting' and so on. The weakness of this position would seem to me that it identifies the text with the meaning of the text. The text, though obviously the controlling factor, only takes on life when it is realised in the reader's response, and it is in the structuring and communication of that response that we seek the support, though not necessarily the exclusive support, of categories which are precipitates from the text, such as 'character' and 'ideas'. Underlying this new claim for the pre-eminence of 'the text', I suspect the old mirage that literary criticism should aspire to the condition of science.

narrator to his protagonist. It begins with the narrator's sentiments being freely on loan to Jude; 'events did not rhyme quite as he had thought', the tone is that of someone who has had more experience of the ways of the world, and if Jude is 'sickened' we feel the narrator is also. But then the voice of the eleven-year-old boy begins to be heard, 'as you had felt when you were little', and the sentence concludes with that rather hasty, protective phrase, 'he perceived'. By that time the shift in feeling between narrator and protagonist has begun, the general indictment of the way things are has become submerged in the particularities of Jude's own self-pity, the narrator is aware of his obligations to this boy in this place, a boy recently clouted by an angry farmer for not doing the job he had paid him to do. The feeling is now completely the boy's, 'If he could only prevent himself growing up! He did not want to be a man.' The narrator has faded behind this intellectual Peter Pan, Jude has re-assumed possession of his dramatic imagination, and general reflections are returned to an individual mind. The shift of feeling, intimated in this sentence, is completed in the next, when Jude takes over completely: 'Then, like the natural boy, he forgot his despondency, and sprang up.' It would be as mistaken to read the passage in terms of that last remark, as it would be to read it in the spirit of the first, to counter a pessimistic outlook on the narrator's part, with an optimistic one.

What such a passage makes clear, and it is a representative one, is the continual dialectic of feeling that is operative between the narrator and his narrative. There is a constant impulse towards an inclusiveness of view, not through any calculating rhetorical strategy, but simply in the instinctual process of writing out the scene Hardy is moved to a point where his own voice has to be heard, then on to a further point, where he feels the challenging tug of his narrative, which, in its turn, will give way again and so on. The effect of this process is to make any extraction of ideas, however insistently they seek to claim our attention, false to the manner of their existence, which is a manner created out of a tension which is sometimes the tension between the narrative and the narrator.

It is the tension within the narrative itself that lies behind the second of my illustrations, perhaps the most quoted instance of the distorting influence of ideas in the Wessex novels. It is from an early chapter of *Tess of the D'Urbervilles* when Tess, accompanied by her young brother Abraham, sets out on the fateful journey in the early hours of the morning to deliver the beehives. Tess falls into a silent mood:

> Abraham talked on, rather for the pleasure of utterance than for audition, so that his sister's abstraction was of no account. He leant back against the hives, and with upturned face made observations on the stars, whose cold pulses were beating amid the black hollows above, in serene dissociation from these two wisps of human life. He asked how far away those twinklers were, and whether God was on the other side of them. But ever and anon his childish prattle recurred to what impressed his imagination even more deeply than the wonders of creation. If Tess were made rich by marrying a gentleman, would she have money enough to buy a spy-glass so large that it would draw the stars as near to her as Nettlecombe-Tout?
>
> The renewed subject, which seemed to have impregnated the whole family, filled Tess with impatience.
>
> 'Never mind that now!' she exclaimed.
>
> 'Did you say the stars were worlds, Tess?'
>
> 'Yes.'
>
> 'All like ours?'
>
> 'I don't know; but I think so. They sometimes seem to be like the apples on our stubbard-tree. Most of them splendid and sound – a few blighted.'
>
> 'Which do we live on – a splendid one or a blighted one?'
>
> 'A blighted one.'
>
> ''Tis very unlucky that we didn't pitch on a sound one, when there were so many more of 'em!'
>
> 'Yes.'
>
> 'Is it like that *really*, Tess?' said Abraham . . .

I have had to give a rather extended context for this episode, because it is necessary to see Tess's meditations on 'a blighted universe' as occurring in a particular scene where Abraham has his own part to play. My purpose in looking at this passage is not so much to absolve it from criticism – the usual form such criticism takes being that Hardy is burdening Tess with authorial reflections which she cannot support – as to suggest that these reflections are more obliquely authorial than is supposed. If we hear the author's voice more clearly than Tess's in her replies to Abraham, then I suggest the stridency is due not to 'the ideas' themselves, but to the place where they occur in the novel. If these same meditations had occurred not in Chapter 4 but, let us say, in Chapter 44 during Tess's stay at Flintcomb Ash, then we would have had little difficulty in assimilating them. We would have been able to do that because we feel that by that time Tess's experience might well have prompted such reflections. The reader could find room to manoeuvre his judgement in the gap between the narrator and his narrative. But, I suggest, that gap is present in the passage as it now occurs.

Tess's reflections are accompanied at every point by Abraham's, and, while he is not of course offering a contrary view, he is establishing, for author and reader, a sense of perspective. It is a perspective which creates a tone of gentle speculation, caught first in the whimsy of the spy-glass which would draw the stars nearer than Nettlecombe-Tout, then in the wryly humorous rejoinder, ' 'Tis very unlucky that we didn't pitch on a sound one, when there were so many more of 'em', and finally quite directly in ' "Is it like that *really*, Tess?" said Abraham.' The effect is not to counter Tess's remarks, but to give them a context where they can emerge as wonderings rather than as conclusions.

In these two passages from *Jude* and *Tess* I have tried to suggest some of the ways in which the ideas are present in Hardy's text, ideas for which no claim is made that they are dramatically embodied within a particular character, but which are rather created out of a tension either within the narrative itself as in the case of *Tess*, or, as in the case of *Jude*, between the narrator and the narrative. This is not a conflict, but a tension, because Hardy's kind of fiction dramatises a third-person consciousness, in which experience, and reflection upon experience, become an integral part of his imaginative act. The novel as an unfolding process, which I described earlier in terms of story, can in this way be seen to extend into its metaphysical structuring, so that the implied author exists neither as a mediator between his characters and the reader, nor as a dramatised consciousness taking a place with other characters, but as a distinctive presence existing alongside the characters, undergoing the same experiences as they undergo, reflecting upon them as they do.

The effect of this is that whereas in a James novel we feel the work has already found its finest reader in the author, in Hardy the reading is still in process, the narrator's reading being only as sharp and as fitful as our own. The novel lies open before us. It is this openness, this continuity of feeling which the author feels for the characters of his own creation, that gives us, in our turn, a continuity of feeling for the author, so that Hardy criticism often seems impelled to strike a note of personal testimony. For instance, we find Irving Howe in the middle of a good, but thoroughly orthodox chapter on *The Return of the Native*, appearing to feel that to do justice to the effect the novel makes he must turn aside from the main argument, and move into italics with the sentence '*here is a man who knows, who has seen and felt.*'[1] And more strikingly, largely because it happens to a critic whose practice is not associated with this tone, we find Dr. Leavis some years ago concluding a detailed analysis of one of Hardy's poems, 'After a Journey', with the remark: 'It is a poem that we recognize to have come directly out of life; it could only be written by a man who had the experience of a life to remember back through. . . . It is a case in which we know from the art what the man was like; we can be sure, that is, what personal qualities we should have found to admire in Hardy if we could have known him.'[2] Remarks such as these suggest how keenly the presence of the author is felt as a determining element in the quality of the work, and it is this transparent authorial self which gives unity and coherence to the diversity of impressions and the oscillations of feeling which characterise the novels.

Why we should have a continuity of feeling with the author, such as he, in his turn, has with his characters, is seen in a fine remark made by Virginia Woolf:

> The novels are full of inequalities . . . there is always about them a little blur of unconsciousness, that halo of freshness and margin of the unexpressed which often produce the most profound sense of satisfaction. It is as if Hardy were not quite aware of what

[1] Irving Howe, *Thomas Hardy*, p. 62.
[2] F. R. Leavis, 'Reality and Sincerity', *A Selection from* Scrutiny, I, p. 257.

he did, as if his consciousness held more than he could produce, and he left it for his readers to make out his full meaning and to supplement it from their own experience.[1]

Reading Hardy then becomes a way of reading ourselves, and we feel a summons both to enter the world of story and to understand what that story means.

Hardy himself understood this well when he described his novels as 'a series of seemings'. The notion of series brings with it an emphasis on the unfolding process of event; the notion of seemings the effort to find within the series a longer perspective, a hint of pattern. Taken as a whole, the phrase implies a seeking for a truth whose form is always provisional, whose dynamic is the tension between the story-teller and the sage, the author and the reader, a tension which, for Hardy, was the essential condition for the imaginative validity of the quest.

♣ II ♣

When we come to reflect on the relationship that exists between the kind of fiction Hardy writes and the substance of that fiction, we find an interesting correspondence. On 4 March 1885 we find Hardy making an entry in his journal:

> The human race to be shown as one great network or tissue which quivers in every part when one point is shaken, like a spider's web if touched.[2]

I would suggest that in that image we have a ruling idea in Hardy's development as a novelist, an idea which at once determines the shape of the fiction and its substance, as we can see if we follow out the line traced by the major novels from *Far From the Madding Crowd* to *Jude the Obscure*.

It is difficult to give in small compass any adequate sense of form – that will have to be left to the chapters that follow – but if the stress here has to fall on the substance of the fiction, perhaps enough can be said to indicate an overall movement in the interrelationship between the novels.

[1] Virginia Woolf, 'The Novels of Thomas Hardy', *Collected Essays*, I, p. 258.
[2] *Life*, p. 177.

To think of *Far From the Madding Crowd* (1874) is to think of the creation of Wessex, a pastoral world shot through with passion and violence which just manages to contain and subdue these disruptive forces. The title has its own pastoral acknowledgement to make, but it initiates us into a world where one worthy man is financially ruined, a girl is seduced and left to die in a workhouse, a middle-aged, respectable farmer becomes so devoured by jealousy that he shoots his rival and is confined for life as insane. 'Far from the madding crowd's ignoble strife, Their sober wishes never learn'd to stray . . .', the ironies are direct and poignant. And these ironies are rendered in the plotting, so that the book is driven on by those who think they can control their own plots, and those for whom the plot takes over. The first half of the novel belongs to the schemers, Bathsheba for Boldwood, Troy for Fanny and then for Bathsheba; the second half releases forces where the schemers are no longer in control, Fanny over Bathsheba, Boldwood over Troy. The book reaches its equipoise with the recognition by Oak and Bathsheba that our needs and our desires have to be found in 'the interstices of a mass of hard prosaic reality'; and if the limitations of those spaces put a limit on our plotting, they also safeguard us against the violence of our being plotted against.

Put in these terms, the book is made to seem much more sombre than it is, but the energy and colour which we associate with it emerges from its distancing, in that the narrator conveys his tale in terms of a backward glance which softens the outline of the conflict, and releases the geniality and humour of the rustics into the mainstream of the novel. And so we find Joseph Poorgrass, reflecting on Oak's marriage with Bathsheba, and being able to say by way of conclusion, 'But since 'tis as 'tis, why, it might have been worse, and I feel my thanks accordingly.' It is the first, and indeed the last time, that a character in a Wessex novel can look back upon events, and 'give thanks'. It is a mood which marks off *Far From the Madding Crowd* from the novels which were to succeed it, a mood which, in the end, allows Hardy to spin a tissue of circumstance which, while quivering in its detail, finally hangs together as a completed design.

With *The Return of the Native* (1878) the Wessex world is fractured, and it is the successive imaginings of the nature of that divisiveness that constitute the shaping spirit of the remainder of the Wessex novels. In *The Return of the Native* the fracture is seen at its sharpest, existing between a nature upon whose face Time makes but little impression, and the private history of man, disturbed by the conflicts of his own psyche. Hence that strangely bifocal impression the novel often makes on the reader, prompting him, if he is favourably disposed, to describe it as 'epic', if he is not, as 'portentous'. Eustacia Vye – Queen of the Night, or girlish daydreamer? Clym Yeobright – advanced thinker, or a mother's boy gone to seed? Diggory Venn – demonic visitant of the heath, or superannuated reddleman? The lines of the critical debate about the novel are familiar; what is less familiar is the attempt to locate the reason for these violent oscillations in feeling and presentation. If there is a blur in Hardy's vision in this novel, it is not because of an uncertainty in his attitude towards his characters, but because the basic conception of the novel – the dialectic between nature and man – is presented in terms which are too inflexibly opposed. The lines of communication between the conflict posed by 'Egdon' on the one hand and that posed by 'the closed door' of the Yeobright's cottage on the other, are too extended and they peter out. There is a huge ambition behind *The Return of the Native*; in some ways a greater ambition than behind any other of Hardy's novels, with the exception of *Jude*. For the first time the web of human doings becomes visible, but the spaces are too wide, we look for tissue and find vacancy.

In the next three of Hardy's major novels, the web is to be drawn into a finer and finer mesh. With *The Mayor of Casterbridge* (1885), he concentrates the epic dimension suggested by the heath, and the inner conflicts of the Yeobrights, into the life and history of one man. 'A Man of Character', the subtitle runs, but when we think of character in this case, we think not so much of individual traits, as of a massive authority which is both held in tight control and yet constantly vulnerable to forces which it fails to understand, forces which belong to the world of public event and to Henchard's own personal history.

The divisiveness of the public world can be located in its changing economy, man is no longer resident in a place where time makes but little impression. On the contrary, he belongs to a very particular place at a very particular time. 'Readers of the following story', the Preface begins, 'who have not yet arrived at middle age are asked to bear in mind that, in the days recalled by the tale, the home Corn Trade. . . .' That strikes the essential note in this novel: the mood may be one of recall, but it is dictated by the desire to recapture – with precision – the particulars of place, period and event. The novel belongs to a public world and, perhaps more than any other major English novel, it finds in a man's work the signature of his being. But the divisiveness in this novel finds expression not only in Casterbridge, in the conflict between Henchard and Farfrae, but within Henchard's own character also. The defeated Mayor looks into the pool he thought of drowning in:

> In the circular current imparted by the central flow the form was brought forward, till it passed under his eyes; and then he perceived with a sense of horror that it was *himself*. Not a man somewhat resembling him, but one in all respects his counterpart, his actual double, was floating as if dead in Ten Hatches Hole.

The form is, of course, the waxen effigy from the skimmity ride which the alienated in Casterbridge had set up to mock Henchard's affair with Lucetta. Occurring in this bizarre manner, the form arouses in Henchard a deep feeling of his own self-dislocation. But Lucetta's role exists only in the margins of Henchard's life, and it is in Hardy's next novel that he takes up in a very deliberate way the theme of sexual relationships and sees them as a further aspect of the economic and public world which he created and explored in *The Mayor*.

The Woodlanders (1887) was Hardy's favourite novel, and in one sense it marks the centre of his achievement. Although he was able to pursue individual strands with greater imaginative power and insight, it is in this novel that the whole web becomes fully defined, and we can see nature, work and sex shown as interconnecting. Of Marty and Giles we hear that 'their lonely courses formed no detached design at all, but were part of the pattern in the great web of human doings then weaving in both hemispheres from the White Sea to Cape Horn.' We remember that at the end of *Far From the Madding Crowd* Joseph Poorgrass was able to 'give thanks' upon the outcome of events, but with *The Woodlanders* and the novels which were to succeed it there can be no such 'end'; these novels are, in this sense, unfinishable, and their conclusions can be made up only out of 'a series of seemings'. Consider the final pages of *The Woodlanders*.

George Melbury, finding his daughter not at home, and then discovering a fragment of her dress in the man-trap, becomes alarmed as well as bewildered, and takes his workmen into Sherton Abbas to look for her. They find her reunited with Fitzpiers and planning to leave with him for a practice in the Midlands. Melbury wryly accepts her decision and rejoins his search party. Following a visit to a local inn they meet, on their way home to the woods, Marty South, now deserted by Grace, keeping her solitary vigil at Giles's grave. And so the novel ends with a variety of elements brought to no point of convergence. Grace and Fitzpiers are reunited at the Earl of Wessex Hotel, 'newly rebuilt to mark the arrival of the railway'; the woodlanders, out of place in the town with their 'much-stained' leather aprons, retreat into 'an antique tavern' where, for all their shrewd scepticism about what the future holds for Grace and Fitzpiers, they become lost in memories and anecdotes; Marty, now quite alone, speaks only to the dead.

There is here a network of strands which we can no longer isolate and identify as personal and public, passion and work, man and nature. In their interweaving, they hint at a greater design, like the trees which the woodlander sees gradually changing from 'an open filigree to a solid opaque body of infinitely larger shape and importance'. That body of larger shape and importance becomes, in Hardy's last two major novels, fully seen as the human body estranged from itself, and, inseparably bound to it, the social body, fractured by laws of its own devising. Conflicts lightly sketched in *The Woodlanders* can now be fully dramatised in *Tess of the D'Urbervilles* (1891) and *Jude the Obscure* (1895).

In one sense, *Tess* is an imaginative return to *The Mayor of Casterbridge*, in that, like that novel, and unlike *The Return of the Native* and *The Woodlanders*, it seeks to find within a single individual a complete expression for the author's vision. But where *Tess* goes much further than *The Mayor* – something made possible by the writing of *The Woodlanders* – is in recognising the continuities that exist between the individual self, finding in sexual conflict its most dramatic definition, and the social and economic conditions of the age. When we think of Tess as dispossessed, we can reflect on that moment on the railway platform when 'The light of the engine flashed for a second upon Tess Durbeyfield's figure, motionless under the great holly tree. No object could have looked more foreign to the gleaming cranks and wheels than this unsophisticated girl . . .'. Or, with equal relevance and propriety, we can think of another moment when, following her confession, Angel refuses to recognise her:

> 'The woman I have been loving is not you.'
> 'But who?'
> 'Another woman in your shape.'

But whichever sense of dispossession we think of, both senses come together when Tess, now Alec's mistress, faces Angel on his return. 'Tess had spiritually ceased to recognise the body before him as hers – allowing it to drift, like a corpse upon the current, in a direction dissociated from its living will.' In Henchard's case there is still a gap between the effigy and the self; in Tess's, they have become one. Dissociated from her will, she acts instinctively and with violence to remove Alec from her life, his body now being of as little consequence as her own. The public and the private strands are now inextricably spun, and the design is completed not by the President of the Immortals but by the police. As the law comes into view from behind the pillars of Stonehenge, Wessex, now fully and finally explored, fades into the light of common day.

The Preface to *Jude the Obscure*, directing attention to 'a deadly war waged between flesh and spirit', announces the last of Hardy's imaginings of the fractured world, but a world framed no longer by a remembrance of Wessex. It is the narrator's world, our world, and set within the madding crowd. In *Jude* we find carried to the furthest extreme conflicts which have been gaining in definition and momentum as Hardy's novels have continued: the self-estrangement of the individual, the clash with social institutions and, emerging out of this clash, an increasingly sharp sense of the needs of the present time. The seemingly inhuman conflict in *The Return of the Native* between man and nature has by the time of *Jude* come to be seen very differently. 'We must conform', Sue says. 'All the ancient wrath of the Power above us has been vented upon us, His poor creatures, and we must submit. There is no choice. We must. It is no use fighting against God!' To which Jude replies, 'It is only against man and senseless circumstance.' Of course, these feelings are explored in situations of considerable complexity, which shade and modify them, but what I would like to draw attention to in *Jude* is the way in which, with the framework of Wessex removed, the conflict passes directly into the very form which the novel takes. Hardy himself remarked on the novel being 'all contrasts . . . Sue and her heathen gods set against Jude's reading the Greek testament; Christminster academical, Christminster in the slums; Jude the saint, Jude the sinner; Sue the pagan, Sue the saint; marriage, no marriage; etc., etc.'[1] Although these antitheses are extremely powerful, we can feel a certain rigidity setting in, a web threatening to become a grid. With the power goes a new stridency, reflected in the way in which the journeys along the roads of Wessex are now replaced by the constant journeying by rail, with Egdon Heath just glimpsed from a passing carriage window. And each section of the book reinforces this sense of mechanical movement, the place names, 'At Marygreen', 'At Christminster', 'At Shaston', emphasising the rootlessness of characters now deprived of a coherent world. As in his first major novel, the conflicts within *Jude* seem almost too great to be contained, but as in *Far From the Madding Crowd*, though now writing in a very different mood, Hardy manages to encompass them and achieve a controlled coherence. And he does this because *Jude* is structured not simply in terms of biting contrasts, but more importantly, in terms of an unfolding process, in which Jude and his narrator gradually move away from a metaphysical condemnation of the universe, to a social condemnation of his particular society. It is not a journey which Sue is able to take, and when following the death of the children she returns to Phillotson, Jude reflects that they 'had mentally travelled in opposite directions since the tragedy: events which had enlarged his own

[1] *Life*, pp. 272–3.

39

views of life, laws, customs, and dogmas, had not operated in the same manner on Sue's.' The ultimate tragedy for her, and for Hardy too, is that she has forsaken her own self in a way that Jude never does. In that recognition, Hardy's understanding of tragedy has, like Jude's, become enlarged as his novels have continued.

Hardy's understanding of tragedy enlarged, but not necessarily his ability to communicate it, and *Jude* is a desperate victory. From *Far From the Madding Crowd* to *Jude*, his pursuit of the 'series of seemings' led him to an increasing scepticism about the coherence of his imagined world. The more he sought the truth, the more Wessex faded before his eyes; from being a region far from the madding crowd, it became a great landscape, an individual man, a group of woodlanders, a woman dispossessed, though at every stage he mined a deeper truth. By the time he came to write *Jude*, the web had become so finely drawn that his whole vision could be contained in the conflict between a man and a woman. Implicit in that relationship was his whole fictional world, which already lay beyond the frontiers of Wessex, and to which he could only put up a signpost, for imaginatively, he no longer had access to it. When Jude dies in a rented lodging, Hardy's fictional world is stripped bare.

♣ III ♣

'Form alone *takes*, and holds and preserves, substance . . .': James's view of form is insistent on clarity and stability, finding its strength in the sharpness of the demarcation line to be drawn between the experience which goes into the creation and the created object itself. It is a notion which relies, at least tacitly, on a notion of a reality which is antecedent to form, and of which that form is a copy. In Hardy, we find a notion of form, which resides in the structuring power itself, rather than in that which is structured, a sense of form seen not as a result, a shape, more as a process, a direction, a verb rather than a noun. Where James finds his key term in structure, Hardy finds his in story.

In the brief and necessarily schematic account of the novels which I have given, I hope to have indicated, at least in a general way, the manner in which 'the kind of fiction' which I described informs the substance of the novels, whether we think of them in isolation or in relation to each other. If a 'series of seemings' suggests an abstract description of this kind of fiction, then it finds, in the great web, its inclusive image.

It is an image which identifies a central element in what Hardy called his 'idiosyncratic mode of regard', so that the line to be drawn between man and man, man and nature is unusually fine. It goes on to suggest an idea of form antithetic to that which 'preserves and holds', in that a web can be thought of more as something defining space than as an object; it is a provisional design flung across the vacancy of miscellaneous experience. Moreover, the web makes us think simultaneously of the spider and its weaving, of the creator and the act of creation, and in the end, this is the experience we have in reading Hardy's major novels: for he created a kind of fiction which enabled him to convey, at every stage in his career, and with a remarkable purity and directness, both what mattered to him as a total human being, and the dramatic sense of the way in which it mattered.

2

The Creation of Wessex
Far From the Madding Crowd (1874)

Far From the Madding Crowd was the novel which Hardy's Victorian public wanted him to write again and again. It was a desire which did nothing to please the author, who felt himself typecast before he had even begun to explore his interests, and in the biography he remarks coldly that 'he had not the slightest intention of writing for ever about sheep-farming, as the reading public was apparently expecting him to do, and as, in fact, they presently resented his not doing.'[1]

The kind of appeal which the novel made to Hardy's contemporaries – an appeal made more poignant by the increasingly tragic tone of the later fiction – is expressed by Andrew Lang's review of *Far From the Madding Crowd* in the *Academy* for January 1875. The review is given edge if we remember that the publication of the novel came at a time when the agricultural unrest in Dorset had attracted national attention through the radical leadership of Joseph Arch campaigning for the rights of agricultural workers. Lang, taking the opportunity for a political comment, writes: 'the country folk in the story have not heard of strikes, or of Mr. Arch; they have, to all appearances plenty to eat and warm clothes to wear and when the sheep are shorn in the ancient town of Weatherbury, the scene is one that Shakespeare or that Chaucer might have watched. This immobile rural existence is what the novelist has to paint.'[2] For Lang the novel provides a version of pastoral deeply congenial to the conservative spirit, a spirit finding in remembrance of things past a sanction for the present, and in Hardy's title, idyllic celebration.

From the other side of the Atlantic 'the ancient town of Weatherbury' looked less pleasing. The young Henry James in a chilly review in the *Nation* would not have disputed that the novelist had painted 'an immobile rural existence', but wondered whether the

[1] *Life of Thomas Hardy*, p. 102.
[2] Quoted in Michael Millgate, *Thomas Hardy : His Career as a Novelist*, p. 103.

age still had leisure for such contemplation; and when there are so many other books besides novels competing for our attention, 'we are inclined to think that, in the long-run, (novelists) will be defeated in the struggle for existence unless they lighten their baggage very considerably and do battle in a more scientific equipment.'[1] If we must have versions of pastoral, then so far as James is concerned, Hardy's version is one that can be spared. The point is made plain in the kind of praise he accords to the novel: 'Mr. Hardy describes nature with a good deal of felicity, and is evidently very much at home among rural phenomena. The most genuine thing in his book, to our sense, is a certain aroma of the meadows and lanes – a natural relish for harvestings and sheepwashings.'[2]

It is common now to find James's view being cited as one of his less happy judgements, and certainly it is true that *Far From the Madding Crowd* is no longer treated with patronising indulgence. Commonly considered as the first of Hardy's major novels, its place seems secure within the canon. If, however, we feel the response made by Lang and James is no longer quite the response made by our contemporaries, this is not really because they view differently either the substance of the novel, or the mood in which it is written, but because we have developed more sophisticated notions about pastoral. For instance, we find a tough-minded critic like Albert Guerard – perhaps the critic who has done more than anyone to see Hardy's fiction in the light of the twentieth century – writing about *Far From the Madding Crowd* that 'at its best it creates a pastoral world of antique simplicity, a fitting background for the changeless drama of love and betrayal, of faithful shepherdesses and glamorous faithless soldiers.'[3] 'The changeless drama', 'the immobile rural existence', the perspective remains much the same and distance continues to lend enchantment.

My contention in the chapter that follows is that the creation of this particular pastoral, the genesis of Hardy's creation of Wessex, was a much more complex and precarious enterprise than these

---

[1] Quoted in Laurence Lerner and John Holmstrom, *Thomas Hardy and his Contemporary Readers*, p. 31.
[2] Lerner and Holmstrom, p. 32.
[3] Albert Guerard, *Thomas Hardy*, p. 74.

varied critical accounts suggest, and that we can already see in it the tensions which are later to characterise and define his whole fictional world. What changes is the deliberateness and self-consciousness with which Hardy explores Wessex in his later novels and with that, of course, goes a change of mood.

In *Far From the Madding Crowd*, Wessex is still largely an undiscovered country for Hardy, but he has already put his distinctive flag upon it. I say 'undiscovered' because we see Hardy beginning his career as a novelist with a succession of styles – the assumed political radicalism of the 'lost' novel, *The Poor Man and the Lady*, the melodrama of *Desperate Remedies*, 'the rural painting' of *Under the Greenwood Tree*; and then, with *Far From the Madding Crowd* completed, a turning away from Wessex to try 'a society novel' in *The Hand of Ethelbertá* – Indeed, it was only with the failure of that novel that he turned back to Wessex and began to contemplate its scope as a land of fiction. The confidence with which he talks in the 1895 Preface to *Far From the Madding Crowd* of envisaging 'a series of novels . . . requiring a territorial definition of some sort to lend unity to the scene' is very much a remark of hindsight. Nevertheless, it is a remark which draws on Hardy's instinctual response that in *Far From the Madding Crowd* he had created a world which would come to satisfy the needs of his imagination.

It was a world which was created in terms of dialectic, a dialectic which took a variety of forms. To begin with, a dialectic was inherent in the very idea of 'a fictional region' sustained over many novels. Writing of the creation of Wessex in his Preface to the novel Hardy remarks, 'the press and public were kind enough to welcome the fanciful plan and willingly joined me in the anachronisms of imagining a Wessex population living under Queen Victoria: a modern Wessex of railways, the penny post, mowing and reaping machines, union workhouses, lucifer matches, labourers who could read and write, and National school children.' Later he goes on, 'the dream-country has, by degrees, solidified into a utilitarian region which people can go to, take a house in, and write to the papers from.' 'A dream-country . . . a utilitarian region', the dialectic is caught here. Wessex creates within the reader an ambivalent response – so that he is self-consciously aware of the fictive, 'the fanciful plan', and yet at the same time, self-consciously forgets it, so that actually to go there, 'take a house in', seems a perfectly natural thing to do. The map which prefaces every novel expresses the feeling succinctly – the outline and contours wholly familiar, the places wholly fictive.

A dialectic present in the act of imagining itself is everywhere present in the particularities of that act. It is there in what we might think of as 'theme', in that conflict between passion and sobriety around which so much of the novel is structured. There is a moment in Troy's courtship of Bathsheba which, in a quiet and unobtrusive way, expresses that conflict exactly. In an impulsive moment, Troy presents Bathsheba with his father's watch.

> 'That watch has a history. Press the spring and open the back.'
> She did so. 'What do you see?' 'A crest and a motto.' 'A coronet
> with five points, and beneath, *Cedit amor rebus*. "Love yields to
> circumstance." It's the motto of the Earls of Severn. . . . It was all
> the fortune ever I inherited.'

Love and circumstance, the motto polarises a conflict at the centre of the relationship and, of all the main relationships, not only in that between Bathsheba and Troy. But the episode does more than that, it catches the controlling mood which colours our observation of that conflict. The motto is an element in a highly lit romantic scene, Troy's extravagant gesture is matched by the mysterious glamour of his past history. This sets the scene at one remove, the ironies are softened, and we are made as aware of the compassionate art of the story as of the moral theme which, momentarily, it lays bare.

If the dialectic is present in what I have called rather clumsily 'theme', it is equally present in 'scene', that vivid concentration of incident, which Hardy was later to call 'moments of vision'. The most memorable of these moments in *Far From the Madding Crowd* is Troy's wooing of Bathsheba by way of his sword display. It has been widely acclaimed as a masterly evocation of sexual fascination, and more generally, as evoking a state of feeling which eludes conceptual description either by the character involved, or by the author. What has been less noticed is that Hardy creates that state of emotional exaltation through the creation of its opposite, the precise discipline involved in the sword-drill itself. It is precisely because Troy is a soldier, a man who, in this matter at least, has mastered the art of an exact discipline, that he is able to release Bathsheba's feelings in the way that he does. There is no motto here as there is in the episode with the watch; we barely glimpse the 'theme', but it is there at the centre, contributing to the memorability of our impression. As in the watch scene we are aware, as part of our own response, of the encompassing art, of a heightened intensity of feeling which extends to the narrator as well as his characters.

It is perhaps the title itself which gives us the assurance that this tension is inherent in the whole of Hardy's conception of Wessex. As we have seen, for Lang and for James that title seemed to intimate an idyllic celebration, a passport to Arcadia. But when we think of a novel in which one character is financially ruined, a girl is seduced and callously left to die in the workhouse with her still-born child, a middle-aged prosperous man becomes so devoured by jealousy that he murders his rival and eventually is committed, as insane, to life-long imprisonment, and we go on to recall Gray's lines:

> Far from the madding Crowd's ignoble Strife,
> Their sober Wishes never learn'd to stray;
> Along the cool sequester'd Vale of Life
> They kept the noiseless Tenor of their Way.

then we have reason for thinking that if Hardy is celebrating pastoral life in his novel, it must surely be in the spirit of Samuel Beckett. If we say the novel does not read like this, then we are not returning to a pastoral mood, we are in fact being made aware that Hardy's art in this novel is more complex than most accounts would suggest. And to examine that art, to become aware of the form of this novel, is first to realise a genuine uncertainty about the tone of Hardy's title, and then to recognise that that uncertainty is a driving-force in the creation of his imagined world.

♣ II ♣

When *Far From the Madding Crowd* is viewed from within a pastoral perspective, the argument builds up in two, rather different, ways.

There is, to begin with, a classical emphasis on the preference of rural to urban values which finds its purest expression in a description like this:

> At bottom Hardy's story juxtaposes two different worlds or modes of being, the natural against the civilised and it insists on the superiority of the former by identifying the natural as strong, enduring, self-contained, slow to change, sympathetic, while associating the civilised with weakness, facility, modernity, self-centredness.[1]

This opposition between 'the natural' and 'the civilised', between nature and nurture, is crucial to the concept of pastoral; to apply it with this kind of directness to Hardy's novel is to see how remote it is from the particularities of that novel, remote both in the language employed and in the basic opposition implied.

The second way in which the pastoral argument builds up moves in a rather different direction and has behind it the canny empiricism of Corin in *As You Like It*: 'I know the more one sickens, the worse at ease he is; and that he that wants money, means, and content, is without three good friends; that the property of rain is to wet, and fire to burn; that good pasture makes fat sheep; and that a great cause of the night is lack of the sun.'[2] This is the realist version of pastoral, with the triumph of sobriety over passion, moderation over excess, work over play. It is the romance of Gabriel and Bathsheba 'growing up in the interstices of a mass of hard prosaic reality', and clearly this has a relevance to the novel in a way that the rural and urban conflict has not. But the trouble with the realist aspect of pastoral, so far as this novel is concerned, is that it leads into a moral interest which we feel was remote from Hardy's purpose. It is only a short move from emphasising 'hard prosaic reality' to identifying Oak's moral worth with it, and to seeing Troy's and Boldwood's weakness as the opposite. The novel then emerges as the moral education of Bathsheba in which she learns to reject the illusory world of Troy and accept the prosaic world of Oak. It becomes the story of the humbling of a spirited, vain and self-willed woman, and

---

[1] Howard Babb, 'Setting and Theme in *Far From the Madding Crowd*', *English Literary History*, 1963, p. 163.
[2] *As You Like It*, III, ii.

we are well on the way to seeing Bathsheba Everdene as a latter-day Emma Woodhouse.

What I think undermines these versions of pastoral, so far as Hardy is concerned, is not their particular emphasis so much as their methodology. In varying ways, they both aim at offering a total view, whether that view is thought of as the clash between 'two worlds' or as the overcoming of excess by moderation. One of the distinctive features of a Hardy novel is that it is 'open-meshed'; it contains many kinds of different elements, and we can only really get the sense of this if we see it, not as a pattern which defines itself, but as a gradually unfolding process. In this way we are better able to do justice to the impression that the novel is different things at different times. It implies a critical approach which doesn't so much re-view the novel, as try to record our sense of it as it unfolds in the process of reading it.

If, for example, we start from the dominant impression which the novel makes on the reader, then that impression would seem to be one of passion. Again and again we are made aware of surges of feeling, arising precipitately, and ransacking language for their expression. We have Oak to Bathsheba, 'I shall do one thing in this life – one thing certain – that is, love you, and long for you, and *keep wanting you* till I die.' Bathsheba about Troy, 'O, I love him to very distraction and misery and agony! Don't be frightened at me, though perhaps I am enough to frighten any innocent woman.' Boldwood to Bathsheba, 'I am beyond myself about this . . . I wish you knew what is in me of devotion to you; but it is impossible, that. In bare human mercy to a lonely man, don't throw me off now!' Troy about Fanny, 'This woman is more to me, dead as she is, than ever you were, or are, or can be. . . . But never mind, darling . . . in the sight of Heaven you are my very, very wife!'

These are the tones which sound throughout this novel and if the total impression made by the novel is not quite of this kind, the intensity of feeling which these assertions and pleadings expose is an integral part of the experience which Hardy is concerned to communicate: an experience of intense human vulnerability. And it is worth noting that it is Gabriel – the personification of self-possession and sobriety – who perhaps captures most exactly the anguished tone of them all in his phrase, 'I shall . . . *keep wanting you* till I die.'

An overwhelming desire to fill an unsuspected void within, unsought in origin, capricious and obsessive in its demands, unpredictable in its consequences – this is the kind of feeling which Hardy writes about, and it is there at the centre of *Far From the Madding Crowd*. It is not a feeling which offers itself for moral judgement, so that we think of it in terms of excess, reckless self-abandon. For Hardy, it is an inescapable part of what it is to be human, as likely to strike an Oak as a Troy, a Bathsheba as a Boldwood. If there is a distinction to be found between them, it lies in this, that alone of the four people, Oak recognises his vulnerability, 'having for some time known the want of a satisfactory form to fill an increasing void within him', whereas for Boldwood, women were 'remote phenomena', and Bathsheba had always 'felt sufficient to herself . . . and fancied there was a certain degradation in renouncing the simplicity of a maiden existence'. But whatever the distinctions and similarities between the various lovers may be, we feel that what is commanding Hardy's imagination is not the anatomy of emotional response, but the nature of passion itself, that imperious desire which seeks to drive the individual to live, as Boldwood does, 'outside his defences'. Absence and distance only inflame desire, so that Troy's visit to Bath helps to precipitate Bathsheba into marriage, Fanny's death serves to revive Troy's love for her, and Boldwood seeks to turn absence into possession:

> In a locked closet was now discovered an extraordinary collection of articles. There were . . . silks and satins, poplins and velvets, all of colours which from Bathsheba's style of dress might have been judged to be her favourites. . . . They were all carefully packed in paper, and each package was labelled 'Bathsheba Boldwood', a date being subjoined six years in advance in every instance.

Passion seeks to annihilate the obstruction of time, and just as our feelings are changed by that element so are our actions. The sending of the valentine is the most obvious example of an incident which we feel is not precipitated by man but rather overtakes him. And it is this which plays a very large part in the emotional structure of the novel, where the conflict is no longer between individuals but between man and his circumstances. Gabriel's sheep are destroyed, the great storm nearly ruins the harvest, the broken gargoyle washes the flowers out of Fanny's grave. It is true that for all these incidents we can make out a case for man's responsibility. Gabriel has failed to insure his sheep, his dog has been carelessly fed on raw mutton; the storm nearly brings disaster because repeated warnings of its impending arrival have been ignored; the gargoyle only needs to be turned in the other direction for the water to be directed away from the grave. But just as judging and discriminating about passion in 'moral' terms seems misleading, so here too in this series of events we don't feel that Hardy's imagination is actively engaged in seeking a response which shall adjudicate between blind circumstance and human failure. Behind the passionate encounters of individual with individual, of individual with event, we feel that Hardy is trying to communicate a sense of life, which cannot be adequately expressed by any individual, nor indeed by the human world.

This sense is most keenly apprehended in those moments of vision which are so characteristic a feature of Hardy's novels. Deriving from an intense human experience, they extend it, and then, disturbingly, move into a different dimension. We recall Oak suffering the destruction of his sheep:

> Oak raised his head, and wondering what he could do, listlessly surveyed the scene. By the outer margin of the pit was an oval pond, and over it hung the attenuated skeleton of a chrome-yellow moon, which had only a few days to last – the morning star dogging her on the left hand. The pool glittered like a dead man's eye, and as the world awoke a breeze blew, shaking and elongating the reflection of the moon without breaking it, and turning the image of the star to a phosphoric streak upon the water. All this Oak saw and remembered.

The pond, the moon, the breeze extend and crystallise Gabriel's emotion, so that his despair appears to inhere in them, the moon is an 'attenuated skeleton', the pool glitters 'like a dead man's eye'. The first impression is that this release has enabled Gabriel to come to terms with his emotion, so that 'a listless survey' leads into the pondered 'saw and remembered'. But while this may hint at the underlying movement of the passage, the striking thing about it is that Hardy has conveyed a change within his character, without that character consciously registering it.

There are many other scenes of a similar kind, perhaps most re-markably Bathsheba spending the night by the swamp, where she half realises its significance:

> The general aspect of the swamp was malignant. From its moist and poisonous coat seemed to be exhaled the essences of evil things in the earth, and in the waters under the earth. The fungi grew in all manner of positions from rotting leaves and tree stumps, some exhibiting to her listless gaze their clammy tops, others their oozing gills. . . . The hollow seemed a nursery of pesti-lences small and great, in the immediate neighbourhood of com-fort and health, and Bathsheba arose with a tremor at the thought of having passed the night on the brink of so dismal a place.

With that first phrase Bathsheba is coming back to consciousness, but we have been given in the malignant swamp aspects of her con-sciousness, which, as with Oak, lie quite behind her 'listless gaze'.

These moments, taken together with the crises of feeling which have precipitated them, combine to give an extraordinarily vivid impression of Hardy's ability to render 'unknown modes of being', modes which in this novel are deeply involved with human passion. What might be called the interior landscape of the novel is finely expressed in that moment when Boldwood stares at Bathsheba's valentine propped up on his mantelpiece,

> Here the bachelor's gaze was continually fastening itself, till the large red seal became as a blot of blood on the retina of his eye . . . 'Marry Me'. The pert injunction was like those crystal sub-stances which, colourless themselves, assume the tone of objects about them.

Oak's gaze, Bathsheba's gaze, and now Boldwood's gaze most dramatically of all, create for Hardy 'still moments' in which he can concentrate the passion that surges through this novel, a passion at once blinding and self-obsessed, 'blood on the retina of the eye', and then extending outwards, crystallising itself in the breadth of a landscape or in the particularity of a large red seal. It is this intense projection of feeling which is central to our experience of the novel, energising it, driving it inexorably forward from crisis to crisis, charging the narrative and giving us a first, and dominant, impression of the novel as it unfolds. If we feel this account gives a too intense impression of the novel seen as a whole, then we would be right, because the passionate element is continually set against a much more sober concern, whose effect is only fully seen when the novel is completed.

> Oak, his features smudged, grimy, and undiscoverable from the smoke and heat, his smock-frock burnt into holes and dripping with water, the ash stem of his sheep-crook charred six inches shorter, advanced with the humility stern adversity had thrust upon him up to the slight female form in the saddle. He lifted his hat with respect, and not without gallantry . . . he said in a hesitating voice:—
> 'Do you happen to want a shepherd, ma'am?'

This incident is a turning point in the novel, and we know that for this shepherd, at least, life will not be led in Arcady, but in the day-to-day routines and demands of a particular farm. As Raymond Williams has pointed out: 'Work enters Hardy's novels more decisively than in any English novelist of comparable importance. And it is not merely illustrative; it is seen as it is, as a central kind of learning.'[1] Work as learning, this is a counterpoise that Hardy offers to the demands of passion. Certainly, Oak finds in it an education. Given this perspective, the destruction of his sheep is not a capricious act of providence, it is the hazard which attends small capital farming which has been inadequately insured. There is a casualness in Oak, when we first meet him, which never recurs; Bathsheba's bailiff doesn't leave raw mutton for his dogs to eat, nor risk suffocation by forgetting to let sufficient ventilation into his hut. His proposal to Bathsheba has a theatrical casualness about it, which is reflected in her own lofty retort:

> 'Mr Oak,' she said, with luminous distinctness and common sense, 'you are better off than I. I have hardly a penny in the world – I am staying with my aunt for my bare sustenance. I am

---

[1] Raymond Williams, *The English Novel from Dickens to Lawrence*, p. 116.

better educated than you – and I don't love you a bit: that's my side of the case. Now yours: you are a farmer just beginning, and you ought in common prudence, if you marry at all (which you should certainly not think of doing at present), to marry a woman with money, who would stock a larger farm for you than you have now.'

Gabriel looked at her with a little surprise and much admiration. 'That's the very thing I had been thinking myself!' he naïvely said.

It is an exchange which reveals, in its light irony, the relationship that is to exist between love and work; the *naïveté* of both Bathsheba and Oak is exposed here in their assumption that they think they have come to terms with it. It is only when Oak appears before her again 'smudged, grimy, and undiscoverable from the smoke and heat', that this kind of language can begin to acquire meaning.

The life of the farm, the sheep shearing, the harvest, become inseparable from the development of the life of the individuals who work there, and in the interplay between the two we see further into the characters than they see themselves. During the storm Gabriel worked 'entirely by feeling with his hands', and we recognise in that, the instinctual movement that lies behind his love for Bathsheba, as well as the instinct which prompts him to do the right things to save the ricks. Oak is enabled to come to terms with his feelings in a way which neither Boldwood nor Troy can achieve, because he can find in the obduracy of work, in knowing precisely what particular situations demand, a self-forgetfulness, a wise passiveness. Gabriel may be urged by Bathsheba's pleading note into curing her sheep, but he only succeeds because he is able to employ a skill 'with a dexterity that would have graced a hospital-surgeon'. It is the impersonality of work, together with the support of the human community it necessarily requires, which Hardy uses as the counterpoint to the isolating self-absorption of passion. To understand the tension between them is for him a beginning of wisdom. 'The human community' which it involves is a more complex notion in Hardy than it is often thought to be, complex in the sense of the function it has in shaping the total novel. Certainly, it never manifests itself in the classic pastoral terms where the natural is pitted against the civilised, the one 'strong, enduring, self-contained', the other, weak, facile, self-centred. Within both of those worlds Hardy saw strength and weakness, but more important for him than registering these, was the conviction that the consciousness of such weakness and such strength was precisely the price to be paid for living when we do. It is only in the later novels that Hardy is to develop this theme; but even in this first creation of Wessex in *Far From the Madding Crowd*, if there is a weakness in the community it comes through 'insiders' like Troy and Boldwood, and strength is acquired through two new-comers like Oak and Bathsheba. Those who gather in Warren's Malthouse are indifferent to both. The locals have a different and highly distinctive role to play, one not associated with 'weakness' or 'strength', and different from that of a chorus of smocked innocents, to which they are frequently assigned.

'Yes; victuals and drink is a cheerful thing, and gives nerve to the nerveless, if the form of words may be used. 'Tis the gospel of the body, without which we perish, so to speak it.'

The authentic tones of Joseph Poorgrass sound out clearly in the Wessex air. 'The gospel of the body' is a gospel that has found willing converts in Warren's Malthouse, and though it is a message which would have a natural appeal to those who have, in Coggan's words, 'the most appreciative throats in the district', it has its part to play in the novel as a whole. It gives a sense of the warmth of human companionship, of the delight that the locals take in each other's company. And this has a subtle effect of providing for the reader's imagination a much more crowded background to the main action than is really the case; when we deliberately stop, we find that only some half-dozen characters are involved. This effect is obtained partly by the collective work they do at Bathsheba's farm, and here the sense of community comes home to us with considerable vividness:

The meek sheep were pushed into the pool by Coggan and Matthew Moon, who stood by the lower hatch, immersed to their waists; then Gabriel, who stood on the brink, thrust them under as they swam along, with an instrument like a crutch, formed for the purpose. . . . They were let out against the stream, and through the upper opening, all impurities flowing away below. Cainy Ball and Joseph, who performed this latter operation, were if possible wetter than the rest; they resembled dolphins under a fountain, every protuberance and angle of their clothes dribbling forth a small rill.

But the effect of community is perhaps best established by their talk in The Malthouse and in The Buck's Head. What we get from the apparently random collection of stories about love and deception and old age and change and superstition – stories which often act like distorting mirrors on the main themes of the novel – is the sense of a continuum of human experience which nothing can alter or shock. Like the element of work which is present in the novel, this affects our apprehension of the passion that exists among the main characters, softening it, unobtrusively distancing it. Our sense of this comes not so much from what the locals say as through their way of saying it. Their language has an exhilarating sense of play and humour, so that the reader's attention is shifted, momentarily disengaged from the action, he has a heightened sense of the medium which conveys it, and his reading response is altered as if he were to come upon italicised prose. Illustration is not difficult. Consider that moment in The Buck's Head when, with Fanny Robin's hearse standing outside in the gloom, Poorgrass is drinking with Coggan and Mark Clark, in an attempt to recover his drooping spirits. The conversation turns to religion, to the difference between those who go to Church and those who go to Chapel:

'Chapel-folk be more hand-in-glove with them above than we,' said Joseph, thoughtfully.

'Yes,' said Coggan. 'We know very well that if anybody do go to heaven, they will. They've worked hard for it, and they deserve to have it, such as 'tis. I bain't such a fool as to pretend that we who stick to the Church have the chance as they, because we know we have not. But I hate a feller who'll change his old ancient doctrines for the sake of getting to heaven. I'd as soon as turn king's-evidence for the few pounds you get. Why, neighbours, when every one of my taties were frosted, our Pa'son Thirdly were the man who gave me a sack for seed, though he hardly had one for own use, and no money to buy 'em. If it hadn't been for him, I shouldn't hae had a tatie to put in my garden. D'ye think I'd turn after that? No, I'll stick to my side; and if we be in the wrong, so be it; I'll fall with the fallen!'

In the context of the chapter the paragraph doesn't draw attention to itself, but if we pause we can see in it the multiple strands in Hardy's presentation of the locals and the way in which these are taken up into the pattern of the whole chapter. Colourful anecdotage is perhaps how we would describe our immediate impression, but then we see the anecdotage is being given weight by the incisive moral criticism which underlies it, in that Coggan is making fun of holier-than-thou attitudes. 'The letter killeth', 'love thy neighbour as thyself', these are the unspoken texts behind Coggan's criticism. And yet while that sense is certainly there, as soon as we use a phrase like 'moral criticism', we seem to be playing false to the whole tone of the passage, a tone which radiates humour as Coggan clearly enjoys his own ability in telling the tale. The humour is present in the artful paradox. To go to heaven is to betray 'our ancient doctrines', and those who go there are involved in shady collusion, 'hand-in-glove with them above'. Above all, it is present in the exuberance of the language, finding its climax in the mock-heroic pun, 'I'll fall with the fallen'. It is in making the reader feel this that Hardy reminds us of his *own* delight in the ability to tell a tale, and in that delight, his compassionate affection for human foibles. For Coggan, as for Hardy, telling a story is the mind in playful contemplation. Inevitably, this alters our distance from the narrative, which in consequence involves a shift in our attitude towards it.

We can best see the way in which this shift takes place by remembering Hardy's own description of himself as having 'an idiosyncratic mode of regard'. This enables us to get a sharper sense not just of 'story', but of the particular nature of the story which commanded his imagination. The scene of Fanny Robin's burial will provide us with both a meditation and an illustration.

Hardy prefaces his account of her burial with an authorial aside: 'It has been sometimes argued that there is no truer criterion of the vitality of any given art-period than the power of the master-spirits of that time in grotesque; and certainly in the instance of Gothic art there is no disputing the proposition.' In the last phrase we hear the confident note of the young ex-architect and, in taking Ruskin as his authority, Hardy is sure of his ground. Indeed, Ruskin's remarks on the grotesque – in *The Stones of Venice* particularly – cast considerable light on the way in which Hardy was using the term, and why it made its appeal to him. For instance, Ruskin associates the grotesque with man's need for play – a serious appetite in which man can express his nature with a freedom hard to come by in his pondered moments. A considered disengagement from the immediacies of experience is what Ruskin finds to be a distinctive mark of what he describes as the noble grotesque:

> . . . the master of the noble grotesque knows the depth of all at which he seems to mock, *and would feel it another time* (my italics), or feels it in a certain undercurrent of thought even while he jests with it.[1]

It is a description which both recalls the distancing effect of Coggan's speech and casts light on the nature of our reaction to such an episode as that of the gargoyle washing away the flowers, newly planted by Troy, on Fanny's grave. In that incident Hardy clearly expresses 'the depth of all' in the way that Troy, true to his nature, has ignored the fact that man is the slave of limit, but at the same time he wryly observes that Troy is theatrically anxious to cast himself as a victim of a cruel fate: 'He slowly withdrew from the grave. He did not attempt to fill up the hole, replace the flowers, or do anything at all. He simply threw up his cards and forswore his game for that time and always.' It is the appropriate curtain for his own melodramatic script. It is left to Bathsheba to make the silent criticism of Troy's action, and in so doing, to frame the episode for the reader. She 're-quested Oak to get the churchwardens to turn the leadwork at the mouth of the gurgoyle . . . and a repetition of the accident prevented.' The imaginative energy of the scene arises, as it did in the smaller incident of the conversation in The Buck's Head, from the criss-crossing of multiple strands, the self-dramatisation of Troy, the cool practicality of Bathsheba for whom the jeer of Troy's Providence is 'an accident' which could be prevented, and the delight of the author

[1] Ruskin, *The Stones of Venice*, III, Ch. 45.

at finding in his narrative a grotesque image expressive of these contrary feelings. We begin to see in Hardy's feeling for the grotesque not simply material for a specific scene or incident, but an instinctive 'tic' in the movement of his imagination. And if we pursue it further we come closer to the distinctive character of his fiction.

A passage in Ruskin's *Modern Painters* indicates where further pursuit would direct us:

> A fine grotesque is the expression, in a moment, by a series of symbols thrown together in bold and fearless connections, of truths which it would have taken a long time to express in any verbal way and of which the connection is left for the beholder to work out for himself; the gaps, left or overleaped by the master of the imagination, forming the grotesque character.[1]

The passage is suggestive of the centrality of the grotesque in Hardy's imagination, and if it is taken along with the remark of Virginia Woolf's which I quoted in my first chapter then the implications of the grotesque for Hardy's fiction in general become explicit. She is attempting to define the distinctiveness of the novels and says:

> . . . there is always about them a little blur of unconsciousness, that halo of freshness and margin of the unexpressed which often produce the most profound sense of satisfaction. It is as if Hardy himself were not quite aware of what he did, as if his consciousness held more than he could produce, and he left it for his readers to make out his full meaning and to supplement it from their own experience.[2]

Ruskin's 'The gaps left or overleaped', Woolf's 'the margin of the unexpressed', and both writers asking 'the beholder to work out for himself' and 'the reader to make out his full meaning' – it is clear that their response is to an element common in Hardy's work. So far as actually defining it is concerned, it is difficult to go beyond the terms which Ruskin and Virginia Woolf employ, but we can point to the different ways in which this element exists in the novels.

The first way is one which Virginia Woolf had in mind when she

---

[1] Ruskin, *Modern Painters*, III, Ch. 8, Pt. IV.
[2] Virginia Woolf, *Collected Essays*, I, p. 258.

talked of 'moments of vision', those scenes which suddenly seem to gather up the novel into an episode almost imagistically presented, so that it resists discussion in terms other than those which it proposes. It seems to intimate, in a line from one of Lawrence's poems, a 'sightless realm where darkness is awake upon the dark'.[1] The most dramatic instance of this in *Far From the Madding Crowd* is Troy's sword display before Bathsheba.

The second way takes us in a different direction. It involves the reader and forces him to contemplate a multiple sequence of meanings, which never merge, as they might in a novel of James, into a complex whole, but remain layered, finding in that form an interrelationship which gives us a meaning. But that meaning lies always just outside the novel, created in the reader's mind by the shape of the fiction he has read. What Ruskin and Virginia Woolf are responding to in describing the grotesque and describing Hardy's fiction is what he himself described as 'seemings', the resonances within his fiction. These acquire meaning when seen in relation to each other, when, in other words, they find a linear expression in plot, or what Hardy simply described as 'series'. And in the phrase 'a series of seemings' he offered a shorthand description of his fictional world.

The analysis so far has led me through a number of considerations towards a delineation of 'seemings'. What remains is to consider such isolated elements in the novel as passion, work, the role of the locals, not now for themselves, but as they act and react upon each other to define the processes of plot.

> The truth is that I am willing, and indeed anxious to give up any points which may be desirable in a story when read as a whole, for the sake of others, which shall please those who read it in numbers . . . the present circumstances lead me to wish merely to be considered a good hand at a serial.[2]

Hardy's remark to Leslie Stephen, made at the time when he was writing *Far From the Madding Crowd*, has not lacked quotation, but it has been invariably adduced in arguments about his general indifference to the art of fiction. Like so many of Hardy's *obiter dicta*

---

[1] D. H. Lawrence 'Bavarian Gentians'.   [2] *Life*, p. 100.

it seems to me to have an air of calculated wryness, which manages at the same time both to look disarmingly casual and yet to retain genuine point. There is a sense of course in which Hardy, at this stage in his career, is anxious to create an impression of a modest, adaptable author eager to please his influential editor, but there is also a sense in which the author, who was deeply irritated by being mistaken for George Eliot, had a very precise estimate of his own worth. But the remark has a significance for the criticism of Hardy which lies apart from these biographical reflections.

Hardy never felt that a fiction composed in numbers compromised his art – though he did on occasion resent the writing strain it imposed on him. 'The number' had for him something of the function of the gargoyle – it had its own sense of completeness, often lightly wrought, and yet it had continually to remind us of the larger design of which it was a part. Indeed, his total plot has a design which, in its ostentatious symmetry, has often reminded critics of a building, most notably Proust in the famous passage in *A la Recherche du Temps Perdu* when he talks of Hardy's 'stone-mason's geometry'.[1] Deep in Hardy's conception of the novel, and a source of its energy, is his sense of the tension between the unitary episode and the design of the whole; sometimes this is punctuated in terms of the individual number and sometimes it plays across it. To look at a number of such episodes in *Far From the Madding Crowd*, particularly if they occur at crucial moments, is to get a sharp sense of the actual life of the novel – sometimes it seems to take on quite suddenly an enormous vitality, and then at other times, with almost equal suddenness, it seems strained or fatigued. The constantly varying character of a Hardy novel, which I have described earlier in terms of a multiple sequence of meanings, has its correlative in the great variety of changes in imaginative energy which the narrative summons from the author.[2] I would like to have a look at three episodes in *Far From the Madding Crowd* with these reflections in

[1] 'cette géométrie du tailleur de pierre dans [ses] romans'. *La Prisonnière*, ed. de La Pléiade, III, 376.

[2] This of course would seem to account for the bewildering way in which Hardy can follow a good novel with a failure, and then unfalteringly return to a good one, and then repeat the pattern.

mind, because they help to define, not only where the achievement of this novel lies, but also its limitations.

Midway through the fourth instalment of the novel, Hardy begins a sequence of events which will bring together all the main characters and establish their relationships with each other. It is a sequence which continues into, and is concluded by, the next instalment. In the book it occupies Chapters 19 to 24. These linked episodes are: Boldwood's first proposal to Bathsheba; the fall and rise of Gabriel's fortunes, the first from his plain speaking to her about her flirtatious attitude to Boldwood, the second from his agreeing to return and save her sheep; the work of sheep-shearing followed by the celebration supper; and finally, Bathsheba's first meeting with Troy as she walks in the woods following the supper. Even so bald a summary serves to remind us of elements discussed earlier in this chapter; but what I should now like to insist upon is not so much the presence of these elements, as the way in which they are presented to us, the way in which they speak to our imagination. In other words, in a novel such as this, we cannot understand what we know, unless we also understand how we know it.

Passion, work, and the pastoral tale, all these elements are vividly put to work in this sequence, continually modifying and commenting on each other, the work of the farm providing the dramatic correlative for the emotional tensions generated between the characters. The setting for Boldwood's proposal, which begins the sequence of events, is the sheep-washing, and the mood is caught here:

> Boldwood went meditating down the slopes with his eyes on his boots, which the yellow pollen from the buttercups had bronzed in artistic gradations. A tributary of the main stream flowed through the basin of the pool by an inlet and outlet at opposite points of its diameter. Shepherd Oak, Jan Coggan, Moon, Poorgrass, Cain Ball, and several others were assembled here all dripping wet to the very roots of their hair, and Bathsheba was standing by in a new riding-habit – the most elegant she had ever worn – the reins of her horse being looped over her arm. Flagons of cider were rolling about upon the green.

It is a scene which is a kaleidoscope of moods: Boldwood, ill-at-ease, self-conscious, heedless of the sunshine and the activity about him, 'his eyes on his boots', Oak and his men immersed, literally, in their work and near them, Bathsheba 'standing by', very much the mistress of the farm, and, as the elegant riding-habit suggests, not really part of the activity, but aware of the possibility of being visited socially by the neighbouring farmer.

In the conversation that ensues, Bathsheba remains poised and very much in control of the scene, and her rejection of Boldwood's proposal is in formal and measured tones: 'I am afraid I can't marry you, much as I respect you. You are too dignified for me to suit you, sir.' It is practically the last time that Bathsheba is able to command these cool, self-assured accents, with the implied authority that she has over her farm and her own life. But the entry of Troy is to be delayed, while her relationship with Oak is to be taken up again and given fresh definition.

For the first time Bathsheba's authority is challenged, and challenged by Oak. It is a conflict which opens quietly, revealing the ease and fluency with which the scene moves between work and emotional tension:

> 'I wanted to ask you if the men made any observations on my going behind the sedge with Mr Boldwood yesterday?'
> 'Yes, they did,' said Gabriel. 'You don't hold the shears right, miss – I knew you wouldn't know the way – hold like this.'
> He relinquished the winch, and inclosing her two hands completely in his own . . . grasped the shears with her . . .
> 'That will do,' exclaimed Bathsheba. 'Loose my hands. I won't have them held!'

Oak 'in inclosing her hands completely in his own' is true to his own feeling for her, but it is a feeling which has been subdued to the discipline of precise skills. Bathsheba rejects that discipline, and with it the external restraint that seems to be an inevitable part of it, and she assumes for her personal conduct an independence of her farm and its demands: ' "I cannot allow any man to criticize my private conduct. . . ! Nor will I for a minute. So you'll please leave the farm at the end of the week!" "Very well, so I will," said Gabriel calmly.'

The next day reveals to Bathsheba that such feelings have only a tenuous life, that private conduct and public work are bound up with each other. Her sheep have got into the clover and are dying. Only Oak can save them and reluctantly she obeys the pleas of the men to summon him back, a summons he obeys only when her note makes it plain that she no longer wishes to assert her authority as employer over her appeal as a woman. 'Do not desert me, Gabriel' – her injunction is to echo throughout the rest of the novel, and whatever romantic appeal it may have for Gabriel himself, we are made to see that for Hardy the quality of Gabriel's responsiveness to Bathsheba is intimately connected with his skills as a shepherd Work is not just an occupation, it is knowing precisely what can be done, what cannot be done, or what to do when, and it is in a passage like this that we come close to seeing what was, for Hardy, 'the character' of Oak: 'Passing his hand over the sheep's left flank, and selecting the proper point, he punctured the skin and rumen with the lance as it stood in the tube; then he suddenly withdrew the lance, retaining the tube in its place. A current of air rushed up the tube, forcible enough to have extinguished a candle held at the orifice.'

Work seen in its particularity in this episode is formally celebrated in the next, and in the description of the Great Barn it receives its fullest definition:

> Standing before this abraded pile, the eye regarded its present usage, the mind dwelt upon its past history, with a satisfied sense of functional continuity throughout – a feeling almost of gratitude, and quite of pride, at the permanence of the idea which had heaped it up. . . . The lanceolate windows, the time-eaten arch-stones and chamfers, the orientation of the axis, the misty chest-nut work of the rafters, referred to no exploded fortifying art or worn-out religious creed. The defence and salvation of the body by daily bread is still a study, a religion, and a desire.

It is a passage written out of deep feeling and it has behind it Boldwood's indifference to the activities of the farm, Bathsheba's repudiation of Oak, and Oak's own skills as we have seen them employed in the sheep-curing. But Hardy's novel is continually moving forwards, and no sooner has he established the serene resolutions of the shearing in the Great Barn than we feel, moving beneath the surface, other forces at work. And Oak is made to feel them too. Looking at Bathsheba and Boldwood, 'Oak's eyes could not forsake them; and in endeavouring to continue his shearing at the same time that he watched Boldwood's manner, he snipped the sheep in the groin. The animal plunged; Bathsheba instantly gazed towards it, and saw the blood.' The defence of the body by daily bread may be a profound human desire, but it is not the only desire; the narrative having reached an emotional high noon with the shearing in the barn, the shadows begin gradually to lengthen.

Throughout the Shearing Supper that follows we are quietly made aware of a double exposure. There is a deliberate pastoral afterglow about the atmosphere in which 'The shearers reclined against each other as at suppers in the early ages of the world'. But if that sense of nostalgic artifice brings harmony, it also intimates discord. During the supper three songs are sung. The first is Coggan's, 'I've lost my love, and I care not'; the second is Poorgrass's, 'I sowed the seeds of love, It was all in the spring'; the third is Bathsheba's, 'For his bride a soldier sought her, And a winning tongue had he'. Oak, Bathsheba's valentine, Troy: the songs have a sombre echo. It would be false to the mood of the scene to stress it, but it is there in the margins. In what way it is there, Hardy helps us to see in a beautifully managed description as the songs are being sung:

> The sun had crept round the tree as a last effort before death, and then began to sink, the shearers' lower parts becoming steeped in embrowning twilight, whilst their heads and shoulders were still enjoying day, touched with a yellow of self-sustained brilliancy that seemed inherent rather than acquired.

'Embrowning twilight' catches the finely balanced mood, deep, relaxing, but darkening, cooling too. It is a movement which extends beyond the supper itself into the whole episode, which began with Boldwood's proposal under a bright sky and beside a sheep-pool full of the clearest water, went on to the Great Barn where 'the shearers knelt, the sun slanting in upon their bleached shirts, tanned arms', continued with the deep cross-lights of the supper, and concluded on that path in the woods where, 'By reason of . . . the interwoven foliage overhead, it was gloomy there at cloudless noontide', and where Bathsheba meets Troy for the first time. Boldwood comes into Bathsheba's life in full daylight, when she is surrounded by Oak and his men; Troy comes upon her at night, when she is completely alone.

'The man to whom she was hooked was brilliant in brass and scarlet.' Troy's attachment, unlike Oak's grasp, is not so easily resisted. The dazzle is brilliant, and light and shadow, as they have throughout the whole sequence, define the emotional mood: 'The lantern standing on the ground . . . radiated upwards into their faces, and sent over half the plantation gigantic shadows of both man and woman, each dusky shape becoming distorted and mangled upon the tree-trunks till it wasted to nothing.' The language of incipient threat, which has flickered through the passage, now comes into full use – and with the solidities of the Great Barn and the contentment of the Shearing Supper behind us, we move into a world which destroys these harmonies, so that the visible world would seem to waste 'to nothing'. With remarkable deftness Hardy, in the last sentence of the sequence, disengages our attention from the immediacies of Bathsheba's encounter with Troy, and reminds us in an authorial voice of the moment where we began: 'It was a fatal omission of Boldwood's that he had never once told her she was beautiful.' Laconic and poised, the remark cuts multiple ways: Boldwood's stiff proprieties, Bathsheba's vanity, Troy's easy charm – all are briefly held in the reflection, and the episode, as it has unfolded, has given us an anatomy of feeling which is also an anatomy of action.

The sequence is a remarkably successful one, and with an eye on later episodes in the novel, it is worth reflecting on the conditions for its success. Undoubtedly, one of the main conditions is its easy fluency, the way in which Hardy manages to juxtapose a whole variety of elements, so that without any sense of strain we can feel in a detail the presence of the wider plot and at the same time the sense of continual movement forwards. 'Movement', 'tension', these are the words we find suggesting themselves as descriptive of Hardy's effect, so that if we pause and isolate a particular passage as summarising a meaning, we are always in danger of failing to see how it is modified by the unfolding text. For instance, the paragraphs about the Great Barn, which have been so frequently quoted in accounts of the novel, take their proper weight only when we approach them through a consideration of the increasingly important part the skills of work are having to play in defining genuine feeling. As the description of the Barn fades away and passion begins to take over once more, the harmony it represents seems suddenly very limited and at the least precarious, though without in any way seeming less valuable. For instance, a sentence like 'the barn was natural to the shearers, and the shearers were in harmony with the barn' may be true to a mood in *Far From the Madding Crowd*, but the form the novel finally takes will reveal it as a sentiment lying only on the edge of Hardy's concern.

The second great communal gathering occurs when Troy takes the Harvest Supper as the occasion to celebrate his marriage to Bathsheba. In the serial version of the novel, the episode occupies the second half of the eighth instalment; in the book it runs from Chapter 36 to Chapter 38. It is an episode which falls into three sections. The first is Troy's wedding feast, which turns into a drunken revel – so that no one except Oak, is capable of saving the ricks from the storm; the second is Oak at work on the ricks during the storm, helped by Bathsheba; the third is Oak's meeting with Boldwood the following morning to hear that he has taken no precautions at all and that his harvest is ruined. The central episode, the storm itself, is, with Troy's sword display, probably the most vividly remembered chapter in *Far From the Madding Crowd*, and from the time of the book's first appearance it has always won the admiration of Hardy's readers. I feel, however, without wanting to detract from the quality of writing in that chapter, the fact that it has been singled out in this way may be symptomatic of an authorial unease which is beginning to enter the novel at this point of its development.

Unlike any of the scenes in the previous sequence which I discussed, 'the storm' is very much a set-piece, and it does not come as a surprise to learn that Hardy, in writing the chapter, was recalling a storm scene in Harrison Ainsworth's novel *Rookwood*. In accepting this indebtedness, however, I don't think it is necessary to adopt the accusing tone which Carl Weber employs in his biography when he writes of the debt having gone 'undetected' for sixty-seven years.[1]

[1] C. Weber, *Hardy of Wessex* (revised edition), pp. 90–1.

The mood of the two chapters seems to me quite different. Nevertheless, it is interesting that Hardy should be aiming for a big effect here, and if his literary memories of Ainsworth helped him, then, he felt, so much the better. It is not a big effect in the sense that it attempts a piece of 'bravura writing – Hardy's imagination is much too intensely engaged at this point for that – rather it is an attempt to shift gear, to give the novel a new tragic dimension. It is this which causes difficulties. In itself, the episode is admirable; in the context of the novel, it fails to find an adequate supporting structure.

It is not difficult to see Hardy's aim in this episode. 'Man', he writes, 'even to himself, is a palimpsest, having an ostensible writing, and another beneath the lines.' The revel and the storm are there to reveal, or at least to imply, what is beneath the lines. In the Great Barn, which only a few months earlier had suggested the harmony between the shearers and their place of work, we now have the effects of abandon and licence:

> The candles suspended among the evergreens had burnt down to their sockets, and in some cases the leaves tied about them were scorched. Many of the lights had quite gone out, others smoked and stank, grease dropping from them upon the floor. Here, under the table, and leaning against forms and chairs in every conceivable attitude except the perpendicular, were the wretched persons of all the workfolk, the hair of their heads at such low levels being suggestive of mops and brooms. In the midst of these shone red and distinct the figure of Sergeant Troy . . .

Later, on the ricks, we have Gabriel 'almost blinded, and he could feel Bathsheba's warm arm tremble in his hand – a sensation novel and thrilling enough; but love, life, everything human, seemed small and trifling in such close juxtaposition with an infuriated universe.' In both these extracts, we feel that the underlying emotion, however appropriate for the individual scene, is in excess of what we have been led to expect. In the first, the Great Barn appears as an illustration appropriate to another Hogarthian 'Rake's Progress', with Troy filling the title role as to the manner born. 'Red and distinct', Troy emerges as some demonic figure, rather than the vain and feckless philanderer we have been presented with earlier. There is the same excess in the scene with Gabriel and Bathsheba on the rick, so that we are moved to reflect that there is nothing in their particular relationship nor even, in Bathsheba's sense of failure in her relationship with Troy, which could find a dramatic equivalent in the storm. We feel that in both these episodes Hardy is trying for a deeper exploration of his characters, but if this is proving difficult it is not because of the essential mysteriousness of the characters, but because this particular novel cannot sustain this implied complexity. Its depth, in the sense that there is 'writing beneath the lines', is never far below its surfaces, and the climatic conditions in this particular creation of Wessex give no forecast of 'an infuriated universe'. Having said that, we have to go on to say that the power of the episodes is undeniable, though they lack that fluency of inter-relationship which was so marked in the earlier episode. What we feel has happened is that Hardy, driving on through his narrative, has reached a point where the exigencies of the novel are prompting a darker mood, but the emotional auspices under which it is being written are opposed to such a mood.

This is a conflict which is kept disguised for a little longer, because in the following episode Hardy is able to turn aside from the main plot and take up the story of Fanny Robin. This provides him with an extremely poignant coda to the previous episode, but it cannot really affect – other than at the level of plot – his exploration of Bathsheba's marriage with Troy. The whole development of the relationship between Troy and Bathsheba has provided Hardy with a problem. As distinct from Troy's wooing of her, the actual marriage takes place off-stage, and by the time she returns to Weatherbury Bathsheba is already 'listless' and seemingly disenchanted. With Troy's disappearance, following Fanny's burial, the main themes simply become atrophied. Throughout the next instalment (Chapters 48–51), Hardy is simply bound to the mechanism of his plot, in the sense that he can add nothing to what has gone before. The characters become cut-outs: Oak simply patient, Troy simply a villain, Boldwood simply possessed, and Bathsheba simply a passive register, a desolate victim. By the time we come to the third and last communal gathering, Boldwood's Christmas Party, we are in a world of pure plot, the gargoyle for the gargoyle's sake.

The titles of the chapters that follow suggest how intently Hardy is trying to give a feeling of brooding inevitability to his story – 'Converging Courses', 'Concurritur – Horae Memento'. But the resultant tension remains external to the scene, sombre background music covering up for the lack of inherent drama. The effects are strenuously worked for:

> The light from the pane was now perceived to be shining not upon the ivied wall as usual, but upon some object close to the glass. It was a human face.

and a little later:

> Troy next advanced into the middle of the room, took off his cap, turned down his coat-collar, and looked Boldwood in the face. Even then Boldwood did not recognize that the impersonator of Heaven's persistent irony towards him, who had once before broken in upon his bliss, scourged him, and snatched his delight away, had come to do these things a second time. Troy began to laugh a mechanical laugh: Boldwood recognised him now.

That Troy should now assume the role of 'the impersonator of Heaven's persistent irony', is suggestive of the strain in Hardy's writing here. When the pistol shot rings out a few minutes later we feel that it is all of a piece with 'the mechanical laugh', Hardy going through a series of gestures of burial for a plot which has died some time previously. The criticism of this final party is not that it is melodramatic – melodrama was an essential element in Hardy's imagination – but that it is *only* melodramatic, the actions having no resonance, having all been made before. It is a measure of how skeletal this party is if we recall that all those who were at the sheep-shearing are present again, but now they appear like actors who have suddenly had the lights turned upon them and stand embarrassed in costume and make-up.

If this scene is compared with the earlier episodes I have examined we are made aware of how crucial a concept plot is for Hardy – crucial in the sense that it is charged with a metaphysical significance as well as a literary one. The plot of the novel, for Hardy, is mimetic of the plot of the universe, and in his most successful episodes he makes the ironies of the one expressive of the ironies of the other. The interrelatedness of the episodes and the tension between them keep his plot running in such a way that it can both assimilate, and yet keep sharply distinctive, a wide variety of elements. Oak enclosing Bathsheba's hands in his own as she holds the clipping-shears, and then her breaking away, is such a moment and Hardy's masterly handling of it is typical of the mastery he shows throughout the entire sequence. A crucial change occurs in the second episode, the Harvest Supper and storm, where the force of the plot is taking Hardy into an increasingly tragic dimension, even though the mood of the plot is hostile to it. The effect is powerful but the rhythm has been badly checked. The last episode may be thought of as simulated action – an evacuation made to look like a final occupation. It is unquestionable that *Far From the Madding Crowd* has enabled Hardy to occupy Wessex in a remarkably effective way, but by the end of the novel he has been driven to its margins. To re-occupy it he must move into the centre, take stock of that moment in the storm-scene when 'the infuriated universe' broke into the action. And it is that centre which he is later to locate as 'the vast tract of unenclosed wild known as Egdon Heath'.

♣ III ♣

If *Far From the Madding Crowd* were to end with the death of Troy it would of course be a very different novel and a much less successful one. If, at the end of the novel, we have a sense not of diminishing power but of rounded satisfaction, that is a tribute to the way in which Hardy has successfully recaptured the mood of the earlier part, without compromising the tragic developments that have issued from it. The last two chapters are built around Oak; and the plot swiftly revives and takes on richer life.

Oak is now free to marry Bathsheba, he can fulfil his role as devoted lover, patience prevails over adversity, an Arcadian destiny for a pastoral hero. That is true, but only partly. For Hardy, 'in my end' is not quite 'in my beginning', and both Oak and Bathsheba have felt the power and the consequences of passion. And passion is now something that has to be set aside:

They spoke very little of their mutual feelings; pretty phrases and warm expressions being probably unnecessary between such tried

73

friends. Theirs was that substantial affection which arises (if any arises at all) when the two who are thrown together begin first by knowing the rougher sides of each other's character, and not the best till further on, the romance growing up in the interstices of a mass of hard prosaic reality. This good-fellowship – *camaraderie* – usually occurring through similarity of pursuits, is unfortunately seldom superadded to love between the sexes, because men and women associate, not in their labours, but in their pleasures merely.

Sobriety triumphs over excess, the moral hero justifies his charter. But it is just here in this speech that we can feel the pressure of the form of the novel, exerting itself *against* the story. It is this pressure which dissuades us from taking these reflections, for all their summarising rhythms, as giving a conclusion to the novel.

It is not that the remarks in their context are not fitting, but that they presume too much; they seek to make a universal truth out of a particular instance. Complacency, disdain, a dry judicial analysis, these are the tones of that speech and they don't reflect back happily on the passionate and exuberant life which so much of the novel has revealed. If this passage were to constitute 'a conclusion', we can see why Lawrence, for instance, felt that any relationship that Bathsheba might have with Oak could never touch her in the way that her relationship with Troy could. '*Camaraderie*' had little to do with that brief but distinctive moment, when Bathsheba moved unerringly to take Troy in her arms after he had been shot by Boldwood. It is not that Oak's reflections are ironically undermined, it is rather that the form of the novel has given us a vision which is more inclusive than the final narrative permits. The form finds an embodiment, as seems only fitting, in those who have witnessed the continuum of human existence, the locals, and it is the last speech of Poorgrass which guides us in responding to the general tone of the conclusion. 'A Foggy Night and Morning' is the title of the last chapter and Poorgrass's sentiments nicely articulate obscurity, promise and sober acceptance:

'Yes; I suppose that's the size o't,' said Joseph Poorgrass with a cheerful sigh as they moved away; 'and I wish him joy o' her; though I were once or twice upon saying today with holy Hosea, in my scripture manner, which is my second nature, "Ephraim is joined to idols: let him alone." But since 'tis as 'tis, why, it might have been worse, and I feel my thanks accordingly.'

' 'Tis as 'tis, why, it might have been worse', it is an empirical observation and, though he gives thanks, we feel it is rather to the tough obduracy of the *whole* plot, than to the happy contrivance of the ending. It is a last irony and one perhaps rather ruefully made by the author on his own work, as it has turned and twisted in his hands, in this first creation of Wessex.

3
Landscape with Figures
The Return of the Native (1878)

♣ I ♣

There are not many things which can be said with safety about *The Return of the Native*, but one which can is that the novel which Hardy began in the early part of 1877 was very different from the novel which we now know under that title. With the public success of *Far From the Madding Crowd* in mind Hardy decided, after the dubious experiment in social satire represented by *The Hand of Ethelberta*, to return to Wessex and write a novel similar in substance if not in mood to *Far From the Madding Crowd*. With some fifteen chapters completed he followed his previous practice and sent the new novel off to Leslie Stephen for publication in the *Cornhill*.

Stephen, however, had his misgivings, feeling 'the story might develop into something dangerous for a family magazine', and he refused to commit himself to publication until he could see the completed novel.[1] It would seem that at this point Hardy subjected his manuscript to basic revision, though he felt no inclination to resubmit the result to Stephen. Beginning his revision in the shadow of Bowdler, Hardy became so caught up in the process that, not only did the whole story emerge radically revised, but the revision enabled Hardy to discover, for the first time, the extent and depth of his imagined world.

In the original manuscript version of the first fifteen chapters the material was very close to *Far From the Madding Crowd* – Thomasin replaced Fanny Robin, Venn replaced Oak, Wildeve replaced Troy, and a more darkly passionate Eustacia replaced Bathsheba. Eustacia was made to have affinities with the demonic version of 'la belle dame sans merci' in contrast to the innocent heroine, represented by Thomasin. Clym, at this stage of the composition, had just

---

[1] Maitland, *Life and Letters of Leslie Stephen*, pp. 276–7, quoted in John Paterson, *The Making of* The Return of the Native, Berkeley (1960) p. 4. I am indebted to Paterson's excellent monograph for an account of the genesis of *The Return of the Native*.

79

arrived on the scene and so far as his background is sketched out it is cast in provincial rather than cosmopolitan mood, his success being achieved as a shopkeeper in Budmouth, rather than as a would-be diamond merchant in Paris. At this point Hardy began to revise his manuscript.

It is not difficult to guess the catalyst which began to transform the material. In the fifteenth chapter of the novel Clym's arrival is announced, and it was surely the possibilities which Hardy began to envisage here that made him shift his interest in the earlier material. With all the major characters, except Clym and his mother, Hardy was drawing on versions already created in *Far From the Madding Crowd*. It was simply a question of getting a new 'mix'. But Clym gave Hardy an opportunity to bring into Wessex not the sophisticated life of *The Hand of Ethelberta* but, much more important for his purposes, a sophisticated consciousness; and with that, his theme – the return of the native – began to shape itself as his central concern. By giving Clym a more travelled, more cosmopolitan background, Hardy can provide himself with the kind of consciousness which, if not authorial, can admit into Wessex a world beyond its boundaries, and, in so doing, can inoculate it against the quaint. Clym comes therefore to take up the central interest; and it is not difficult to see that the demonic element in Eustacia, provoked by her contrast in Thomasin, would have very much more interesting implications if set in contrast to Clym. She would give an added resonance to the notion of 'native'.

Once a central relationship became established between Clym and Eustacia, the whole novel was likely to be restructured in feeling. The 'demonic' side of Eustacia could still exist, but was available for much less literal treatment, and could release more understanding of her nature than could her practices. It was left to people like Susan Nunsuch to respond to the latter and use the needle and make the wax doll. The 'representativeness' of Clym begins to have, inevitably, an enlarging significance for the role of Eustacia.

With Clym and Eustacia established as centres of dramatic interest, the other characters begin to be regrouped. Thomasin remains the traduced heroine, but reveals a resilience and toughness not usually associated with that role. Wildeve too is a little altered from a middle-aged philanderer to a younger, sentimental and wayward lover – a much more credible and more sympathetic figure for Eustacia's lover. In some ways it is the successive transformations of Venn – reddleman, 'mephistophelean visitant', dairy farmer – that indicate most sharply the variety of imaginative pressures at work in the evolution of the novel. Paterson summarises his account of this evolution by remarking: 'The process exemplifies . . . the gradual and painful emergence of consciousness out of unconsciousness: the novel turns out to have been quite as much the product of revision as the product of vision. Up to a certain point, the work of a powerful imagination not fully aware of its own nature, it comes increasingly to be the work of an imagination awake to, and in control of, the possibilities it itself has created.'[1] In the chapter that follows I would like to argue that Paterson is describing not just 'the process of revision' but the novel's very subject matter. In the actual form of *The Return of the Native* we find, in Arnold's phrase, 'the dialogue of the mind with itself'.[2]

♣ II ♣

When the reader comes to reflect upon his experience of reading *The Return of the Native* he is left, I think, with the distinct impression that the dramatic life of the novel is most vividly present in the first book, which is dominated by Egdon Heath, and in the fourth book, which brings to a crisis the relationship between Clym and his mother. I think that the relationship between these two books tells us a good deal about the success, and the limitations, of the novel as a whole, and to look at each in turn is to obtain an insight into the peculiar nature of this novel.

It is a routine gesture by now to refer to that 'vast tract of unenclosed wild known as Egdon Heath' as 'the chief character in the novel'. If the claim is made as a way of registering the significance of the Heath as a presence throughout the novel, then it is difficult to dispute its justice. But it is a formulation which raises in a direct way the difficulty inherent in any discussion of the Heath – the

[1] Paterson, op. cit., p. 125.
[2] '. . . the dialogue of the mind with itself has commenced; modern problems have presented themselves.' Matthew Arnold, Preface to *Poems* (1853).

difficulty present in that transition from 'land' to 'character'. We have continuously to keep in mind that whatever metaphysical airs blow across the Heath, whatever interest there may be in Hardy's speculation that it may be the Heath of that traditionary King of Wessex – Lear,[1] Egdon is very much a tract of land, upon which people constantly walk, and have their houses, little more than pin-points of light in an enveloping darkness. 'Blooms-End', 'Mistover-Knap', 'The Quiet Woman', these are the elegaic and sardonic addresses where much of the drama, however epic in scope and intention, is to be located; they are isolated habitations, precariously managing to distinguish themselves from the surrounding Heath. But, in fact, they do succeed, and however much we are aware of the attenuated sense of community in this novel – we seem in a different world from the Wessex of Weatherbury, Casterbridge, Little Hintock – we feel the individual standing out starkly and stubbornly against the soft obliterations of the Heath. It is this tension between 'land' and 'character' which Hardy takes up at the outset of the novel, and he takes it up not in a metaphysical or psychological way – though those implications are present – but rather as something physically seen and felt. It is through the primal contrast of light and darkness that the novel begins to take shape.

The contrast is present throughout the opening chapters, but its significance can be seen if we look at a sequence of paragraphs in Chapter 3, 'The Custom of the Country'. The first one begins:

> Moreover to light a fire is the instinctive and resistant act of man when, at the winter ingress, the curfew is sounded throughout Nature. It indicates a spontaneous, Promethean rebelliousness against the fiat that this recurrent season shall bring foul times, cold darkness, misery and death. Black chaos comes, and the fettered gods of the earth say, Let there be light.

The tone is epic – we are recalled to the primal opposition between 'black chaos' and 'Promethean rebelliousness' – and in the first assertion the epic tone becomes biblical. It is a paragraph which leaves me in no doubt that Hardy conceived these opening chapters on the grandest scale; the conflict he intimated could recall the

Promethean quest itself, when fire was stolen from the gods to be given to men. It is the myth of man becoming conscious of his own nature and, despite odds, endeavouring to obey what he feels to be his destiny. The movement from 'lighting a fire' to 'Let there be light' is the proclamation of that destiny, and the paragraph pays its tribute to 'the instinctive and resistant act of man'.

It is however a paragraph which is succeeded by two others which radically alter the tone. The shift in the second paragraph is from the act of man, man as the bearer and stealer of fire, to man as acted upon, an object upon which the flames are reflected:

> All was unstable; quivering as leaves, evanescent as lightning. Shadowy eye-sockets, deep as those of a death's head, suddenly turned into pits of lustre: a lantern-jaw was cavernous, then it was shining; wrinkles were emphasised to ravines, or obliterated entirely by a changed ray.

This is man as appearance, a grotesque, existing and then being 'obliterated' by the play of light and shadow. 'Pits', 'caverns', 'ravines', the human face becomes one with the inanimate world. But such generalised sight begins to focus itself, and out of the darkness comes the face of an old man who was not 'really the mere nose and chin that it appeared to be, but an appreciable quantity of human countenance'. This is man no longer as pure will, or pure object, but someone 'sunning himself in the heat':

> The beaming sight, and the penetrating warmth, seemed to breed in him a cumulative cheerfulness, which soon amounted to delight. With his stick in his hand he began to jig a private minuet . . . he also began to sing . . .

The fire is now both inside *and* outside the man, it has warmed him into consciousness of himself and he seeks expression in dance and song. But for Hardy, that song can only be personal, and he is not just 'man', but a particular old man:

> A fair stave, Grandfer Cantle; but I am afeard 'tis too much for the mouldy weasand of such a old man as you. . . . Dostn't wish wast young again, I say? There's a hole in thy poor bellows nowadays seemingly.

83

'A hole in thy poor bellows' wryly, almost wittily, catches man's relationship with the fire as Hardy sees it, and in so doing goes back to
include all the perspectives which the sequence of paragraphs has
suggested. Its gentle note of affectionate humour establishes the encompassing tone of compassion for human frailty, and reminds us
not just of the character but of the author.

In the unfolding action of the novel, the episode is a marginal one,
but in its own way it reveals a stance and expresses the sense of
shifting perspective central to the working of Hardy's imagination.
When we think of Egdon it is as 'a Titanic form . . . unmoved, during
so many centuries', 'it had a lonely face, suggesting tragic possibilities', it can give 'ballast to the mind adrift on change', but it is also
where man has written his distinctive signature across its entire
length in the shape of 'the white surface of the road'. And it is life on
the road which also belongs to these opening chapters.

It is on the road, as so often in Hardy, that the human drama
begins. Thomasin, distressed by Wildeve's carelessness about the
details of their marriage certificate, has run away from him and has
been picked up by Venn and taken home in his van. On the way they
meet Thomasin's aunt, Mrs. Yeobright, who, although relieved at
finding Thomasin safe, nevertheless awaits the explanation of her
behaviour with extreme annoyance. Though it is the presence of
Egdon which broods over these opening chapters, it is important to
remember that this domestic drama also has its impression to make as
we begin to read the novel. On the heath great time-honoured rituals
take place with the lighting of the bonfires; on the road there is a
precise domestic drama involving the validity of a marriage certificate's being made correctly in terms of time and place. The fire and
the certificate initiate the plot of the novel, a plot which men partly
make themselves, and partly belong to.

In these opening chapters, however, it is the presence of Egdon
which dominates, and geographically and dramatically it finds its
centre on Rainbarrow, 'the pole and axis of this heathery world'.
From the road a figure can be seen on the summit:

Such a perfect, delicate, and necessary finish did the figure give to
the dark pile of hills that it seemed to be the only obvious justification of their outline. . . . The scene was strangely homogeneous,

84

in that the vale, the upland, the barrow, and the figure above it amounted only to unity.

It is another way, again in sharply visual terms, of expressing the shifting perspectives I described earlier in relation to the fire. Up to this point in the novel the emphasis has been on the time-lessness and the emptiness of the Heath, of the way in which it ignores or transcends the individual life But with this first impression of Rainbarrow we see the human form giving 'perfect, delicate, and necessary finish' to 'the pole and axis of this heathery world'. But then, as soon as we think that form is inseparable from the 'motionless structure', it moves and disappears 'with the glide of a water-drop down a bud'. Its place is taken by the locals who have to prepare and light their bonfire.

For 'the observer', however – that ubiquitous presence in Hardy – the imagination 'clung by preference to that vanished, solitary figure, as to something more interesting, more important, more likely to have a history worth knowing than these new-comers . . .'. It is an introduction, as prophetic as it is dramatic, to the still-unnamed Eustacia. What it establishes from the start is that our sense of Eustacia is to be intimately bound up with our sense of the Heath. Her drama will not be of a kind where an invalid marriage licence will have an important part to play. As Eustacia is standing motionless on the top of Rainbarrow, Thomasin is lying asleep in Venn's van on the road below, and the vignette is emblematic of the difference between them. For the observer, Thomasin asleep reveals 'An ingenuous, transparent life . . . as if the flow of her existence could be seen passing within her'. From the start Eustacia is associated with opacity, with night; and from the start too, appearance is not what it seems. 'The necessary finish to the hill' only exists in the eye of the observer; for Eustacia, the top of the hill has been chosen to catch the last glimmer of daylight, and her gaze strains to the horizon – if it falls upon Egdon, she feels it falls upon her gaol. The ambiguities which surround Eustacia are made explicit in the reader's formal introduction to her in a chapter significantly titled 'Queen of Night'.

This chapter once used to furnish extracts for anthologies of English prose, nowadays is more likely to furnish extracts for discussions about Hardy's delusions about 'fine writing'. Both sets of critics would agree it was highly wrought. For me it is precisely this, the manner of the writing, which constitutes its matter. In another writer, like Flaubert in his descriptions of Emma Bovary, this use of style is readily seen, and it is readily seen because we have come to associate this stylistic irony with impersonal narration. When it occurs in a novel in which the author is vividly present and where the manner of narration is always varying in tone, we are taken by surprise and fail to see the way in which the author has altered his distance from his character. The note of irony struck in the opening sentences is hardly aiming at subtlety of effect:

> Eustacia Vye was the raw material of a divinity. On Olympus she would have done well with a little preparation. She had the passions and instincts which make a model goddess, that is, those which make not quite a model woman. Had it been possible for the earth and mankind to be entirely in her grasp for a while, had she handled the distaff, the spindle, and the shears at her own free will, few in the world would have noticed the change of government.

With that passage in mind we can see why the presentation of Eustacia is more justly thought of as 'mock-heroic', than heroic, and a persuasive argument can be advanced along those lines.[1] But that description is rather too sharp, it fails to take into account the shift in tone which takes place in the very next paragraph: 'To see her hair was to fancy that a whole winter did not contain darkness enough to form its shadow: it closed over her forehead like nightfall extinguishing the western glow.' Here, in a rhythm reminiscent of *Antony and Cleopatra*, Hardy is striking an unequivocally romantic tone. The effect of these different tones is not to create any sense of moral complexity about Eustacia – Hardy is not interested in her in that way – but more simply to assert that there is something about her and the life she leads that makes us think of her as a tragic and beautiful woman, and yet at the same time as a woman whose mind and aspirations are those of a romantic schoolgirl. 'There was no middle distance in her perspective', that remark comes close to the

[1] As David Eggenschwiller does in his interesting article 'Eustacia Vye, Queen of Night, and Courtly Pretender', *Nineteenth-Century Fiction* (1971), pp. 444–54.

centre of Hardy's interest in her, as she wanders the Heath, tele-
scope in one hand, hour-glass in the other. Sometimes a single
sentence gives us the double tone:

> To be loved to madness – such was her great desire. Love was to
> her the one cordial which could drive away the eating loneliness
> of her days. And she seemed to long for the abstraction called
> passionate love more than for any particular lover.

From one point of view this reads as a judicial description of adoles-
cent fervour, a diagnosis of the source of Eustacia's weakness and
one that can only move the author to reproof if not to irony. But
from another point of view, it is the 'eating loneliness' of Eustacia's
days which commands attention, and the absence of 'love', whose
language alone can help her to an understanding of herself. In one
way it is right to think that her 'love' is not bound up with a particular person, it is invoked to overcome some deep-seated 'malaise'
within her about her own identity. 'Her appearance accorded well
with [her] rebelliousness, and the shady splendour of her beauty was
the real surface of the sad and stifled warmth within her.' In that
remark, untouched by irony, we feel what it is in Eustacia which
prompts Hardy's sympathy – a consciousness of the way in which
her intensities of feeling, her capacity for response, are never to find
satisfactory expression. That such a consciousness can accompany
behaviour which is self-deceiving and foolish is not something
which Hardy is concerned to deny or to excuse; but equally it is not
something which can conceal or dispel the genuine tragedy which is
involved.

Hardy's double-visioned view of Eustacia is not there to make her
a more complex psychological figure. It is there to render an individual in imaginative terms so that we can see her, simultaneously,
as Captain Vye's granddaughter, recklessly summoning her old
lover to meet her on the Heath, and also as that anonymous form
standing on the top of Rainbarrow, having her days 'eaten away' in
loneliness. It is a duality of view which is to persist to her death
itself, so that we do not know, when she drowns in the weir, whether
she accidentally mistook her path on her way to elope with Wildeve,
or whether, overcome by weariness and despair, she gave up her life

for lost. At one point she exclaims passionately to Wildeve: 'But do I desire unreasonably much in wanting what is called life – music, poetry, passion, war, and all the beating and pulsing that is going on in the great arteries of the world?' A question to which there can be no simple answer for Eustacia. Her desire is eminently reasonable in that it reveals her appetite for life; eminently mistaken, in that such an appetite can never be satisfied in terms of the images of romance provided in *The Lady's History* she read at school. The importance of this question to Wildeve goes, however, behind the details of its formulation; it is the existence of such a question which takes us back to the Promethean concern of the opening chapters, and it is in that unformulated drive that Eustacia claims epic status, not in 'the dark splendour' of her beauty, and certainly not in the details of her behaviour.

To say all this is not to say that Hardy was entirely successful in his aim, but it suggests ways in which Hardy thought of 'character'. In the last analysis, it seems to me that to use a term like 'mock-heroic' as descriptive of the presentation of Eustacia as the 'Queen of Night', while it might enable laudatory or disparaging estimates of Eustacia to be by-passed, nevertheless suggests a reconciliation of the conflicting impulses in terms which belong too exclusively to a moral plane. Hardy's interest in Eustacia is more existential than that, and can be brought out only when she is seen in conjunction with Clym. It is his consciousness which predicates hers, as almost certainly Hardy saw it would do, when he began his revision of the first fifteen chapters. Before we go on to a consideration of this relationship, however, something remains to be said about Hardy's 'fine writing' in this episode.

For those critics who find Hardy's writing less than fine in this chapter, there has been one sentence in particular which they have felt eloquently illustrative. Describing Eustacia's face Hardy says: 'Viewed sideways, the closing-line of her lips formed, with almost geometric precision, the curve so well known in the arts of design as the cima-recta, or ogee'. Admittedly, it is not a sentence remarkable for its felicity, but before wishing it away, it is worth pausing and asking what Hardy is trying to do here. It is perhaps the most extreme example in the chapter of those ostentatious references to the fine arts which characterise so many of Hardy's pages. It is usually considered that this is Hardy simply trying to win golden opinions, either for Eustacia, or for himself as 'a man of culture' – and not merely as someone 'who was a good hand at a serial', but as 'a man of culture'. With regard to the first, we have seen that Hardy is not really concerned with Eustacia in the way that would give meaning to 'opinions', golden or otherwise. With regard to the second, Hardy's personal relationship with his fiction is so oblique, that to use it for cultural self-advertisement would only have provoked his irony. Hardy's references to artists – and the same applies to all his 'cultural' allusions – have a dramatic function rather than a descriptive one. They are employed as means of altering the reader's response, so that he is kept moving, in the way that the novel itself is constantly moving, from a dramatic to a contemplative mood, and then back again. The allusions are one of the means through which Hardy keeps us alert to the mediating consciousness of the author, which is always integral to his meaning. In 'Queen of Night', however, the allusions have a more precise function to perform. The novel has begun with Egdon, finding in Eustacia its apparent queen, 'standing silently on its highest point'. As the novel has unfolded we find that, far from being 'queen of the solitude', Eustacia is in fact its prisoner. In this chapter Hardy dramatises the paradox. The Queen of Night is, in imagination, a Queen of the Salon, her desired setting is not the Heath, but Bourbon roses, rubies, the march in 'Athalie'; and if there has to be a moon behind her head, then it had better be the kind that passes muster on 'many respected canvases'.

The effect is analagous to that which I have been looking at throughout the chapter. At one level the baroque frame which Hardy put round his picture is a wry comment on the particular aspirations of *his* Queen of Night, but at the same time it is expressive of a consciousness trying to wrest a meaning out of a world where 'the clothing of the earth is primitive' and where 'swarthy monotony' predominates. For Hardy's 'Queen of Night', the Promethean quest is not to be found in fire, but in works of artifice. She herself would like to be thought of as one – 'viewed sideways, the closing-line of lips formed, with almost geometric precision . . .'. Hardy does not, of course, succeed here, the strengths of his imagination lay in other directions; but he was attempting something integral to his whole plot, and to see the change of style in this chapter as incidental, an indulgence in 'fine writing', is to miss the point as completely as if we were to identify Eustacia's viewpoint with that of her creator, and confuse her 'high gods' with his.

At the beginning of this chapter, I suggested there were two areas of the novel which lingered in the mind as possessing distinctive dramatic life. The first is Egdon Heath and Eustacia's relationship with it. The second, is the relationship between Clym and his mother, particularly as it approaches its crisis, where Eustacia has her own vital role to play. Where the first episode moves, as we have seen by resonance and fluent transition, the second is a fine instance not so much of sequence as of consequence. It is in the precise trajectory of plot that we find the significance of the episode as it gathers around impressions, not of a timeless region and hopeless aspiration, but in the history of the individual heart.

There is a particular point in this second episode where the difference in feeling from the opening chapters becomes immediately apparent. Clym and Eustacia have just got married, and the July sun is shining over their small cottage on Egdon: 'The heath and changes of weather were quite blotted out from their eyes for the present. They were enclosed in a sort of luminous mist, which hid from them surroundings of any inharmonious colour, and gave to all things the character of light.' The 'luminous mist' is a natural consequence of their new-found happiness, but it indicates a self-absorption which we are quickly told has the danger of 'consuming their mutual affection at a fearfully prodigal rate' It is this absorption, mutual though it is, which leads them on increasingly to emphasise their own wishes, careless of the fact that these are not also the wishes, or at least the consents, of the other. Clym becomes ever more intransigent about devoting himself to life on the Heath; Eustacia, no less intransigent about escaping from it. From desire to assertion; we find Clym singing to himself in defiant contentment as he works on as a furze-cutter; we find Eustacia bored to distraction, seeking relief at a near-by dance and finding Wildeve there:

> The enchantment of the dance surprised her. A clear line of
> difference divided like a tangible fence her experience within this

maze of motion from her experience without it. Her beginning to dance had been like a change of atmosphere; outside, she had been steeped in arctic frigidity by comparison with the tropical sensations here. She had entered the dance from the troubled hours of her late life as one might enter a brilliant chamber after a night walk in a wood.

That inner dislocation of experience is to be fatal for Eustacia, as she retreats ever further from what she feels to be 'the arctic frigidity' of her marriage into 'the brilliant chamber' of her own reveries. Widening the dislocation between Clym and Eustacia and giving it a language in which to express itself, there is Mrs. Yeobright's attitude to the marriage of her son.

For several months Mrs. Yeobright had been bitterly opposed to Eustacia, offering first one reason and then another to Clym as justification for her attitudes. We are made to feel, however, that the reasons simply act as a cover for an innate antagonism towards anyone who competes for Clym's love. Clym feels profoundly for his mother and, in a passage strangely prophetic of moments in *Sons and Lovers*, Hardy describes their relationship:

> The love between the young man and his mother was strangely invisible now. Of love it may be said, the less earthly the less demonstrative. In its absolutely indestructible form it reaches a profundity in which all exhibition of itself is painful. It was so with these. Had conversations between them been overheard, people would have said, 'How cold they are to each other!'
>
> His theory and his wishes about devoting his future to teaching had made an impression on Mrs. Yeobright. Indeed, how could it be otherwise when he was a part of her – when their discourses were as if carried on between the right and the left hands of the same body? . . . From every provident point of view his mother was so undoubtedly right, *that he was not without a sickness of heart in finding he could shake her*. (My italics.)

It is not difficult to see, with a passage like this in mind, that Clym, in going against his mother and marrying Eustacia, is almost willing his own self-destruction, driving a splinter between 'the right and the left hands of the same body'. It is a passage which casts light on Clym's relationship with Eustacia, a relationship significantly only rarely described from his point of view until it reaches its full development; and then, as so often in Hardy, it is already beginning to decline, finding expression only in the accents of bitterness and regret. The nature of the rent that parting from his mother makes in Clym's nature finds immediate expression on the night he leaves her. It is described obliquely in terms of an enclosure of fir and beech trees, which Clym passes on his way to his new cottage, an enclosure planted in the year of Clym's birth:

> The wet young beeches were undergoing amputations, bruises, cripplings, and harsh lacerations, from which the wasting sap would bleed for many a day to come, and which would leave scars visible till the day of their burning. Each stem was wrenched at the root, where it moved like a bone in its socket, and at every onset of the gale convulsive sounds came from the branches, as if pain were felt.

Clym's grief is for him the grief of the world; but we see that, in his case, the enlargement is working in the opposite direction from the way in which Egdon enlarged – and defined – the aspirations and needs of Eustacia. The mood there was to take the fire out into the darkness, to summon Wildeve out of the night, and to move away from the toils of the enclosed self to an undiscovered country beyond. But for Clym, the convulsive sob of the trees is the weeping within his own heart. In marrying Eustacia, Clym severs himself not only from his mother, but from his own being: 'He kissed her cheek, and departed in great misery. . . . The position had been such that nothing more could be said without, in the first place, breaking down a barrier; and that was not to be done.' The division between them has passed beyond articulation, speech can no longer carry, and when Mrs. Yeobright comes to knock unavailingly at the closed door of Clym's house, she is at a barrier long since constructed between them. The knock sounds only in the turmoil of his dream.

If we are tempted into thinking of that knock as 'a knock of fate', it is worth looking back and seeing how many of the incidents that have led to Mrs. Yeobright's starting out on that fatal walk to Clym's cottage have been characterised by the folly of the participants. Mrs. Yeobright's sustained hostility to Eustacia, though expressed in terms of reason, is founded on baseless suspicion. Her charge that she is indebted to Wildeve for money since her marriage to Clym is the kind of insult impossible to overlook. When she thinks of sending the money to Thomasin she entrusts it to the unreliable Christian Cantle, and is indifferent as to whether Thomasin's husband knows about the arrangement or not. Clym's behaviour to Eustacia since his marriage becomes increasingly self-absorbed and boorish, and however much she knew of his desire to remain on Egdon, she can never have anticipated his total obsession with it, matched by total indifference to her own wishes. He can only begin to communicate with her in terms of moral rebuke: 'Has your love for me all died, then, because my appearance is no longer that of a fine gentleman?' Eustacia herself, though more sinned against than sinning in these later stages, nevertheless makes no attempt to do anything except reiterate her constant desire to escape from Egdon; but given the circumstances of an implacably hostile mother-in-law, and a husband who spends sixteen hours a day cutting furze, and sleeps largely for the remainder, it is not difficult to sympathise with her wish. It may be argued by way of defence that the reason for Clym's absorption in his work on the Heath is his failing eyesight, but although this is certainly presented as a fact, the impression it makes, dramatically, is oddly perfunctory. It comes to seem more of an expression of Clym's inner failings than a fact in its own right, existing much in the way Mrs. Yeobright intends when she remarks about Eustacia, 'You are blinded, Clym. . . . It was a bad day for you when you first set eyes on her.'

Given that it is possible to offer such an account of personal folly, we must go on to ask why it is that when we come to the climactic episode – the walk across the Heath, the closed door, the fatal return – we forget this to such a degree that we begin to think in terms of Tragic Fate and a Malevolent Universe. Hardy manages an extraordinarily skilful change of mood, so that it is not too much to say that when Mrs. Yeobright starts out on that walk she is, in our imagination, an elderly, embittered woman, often the victim of her own folly. When, later in the day, the Heath-dwellers gather round her, as she lies exhausted and dying, we feel in the presence of a tragedy, which is much more than an individual one.

It might be said that the transforming factor lies simply in the suffering that the episode involves, but while this is certainly true, it can only be a partial truth. If we assent to that suffering, and feel moved by it, it is only because it is psychologically and dramatically coherent with what has gone before. Hardy has been able to reveal in this episode a new dimension in the previous catalogue of individual folly, and give it the status of genuine tragedy.

The central moment in the scene occurs below the level of wakeful consciousness – when Clym, dimly roused by the knock on the door, stirs in his sleep and murmurs, 'mother'. Eustacia hears his murmur, concludes he is awake and will answer the knock on the door. It is from her misinterpretation and her failure to check on her impression that the tragedy arises.

The episode exposes with startling clarity that element in Hardy which Virginia Woolf described as 'the margin of the unexpressed'. Below the pettiness, the egotism and the sheer folly of the quarrels between the Yeobrights, there are great surges of feeling which escape this kind of naming. It is these feelings which the scene on the Heath brings into view, and reveals, not in the language of metaphor and allusion, but in the detail of the unfolding narrative. Indeed it is the very 'factuality' of the scene which contributes to its almost hallucinatory intensity. The mood is set in the opening sentence:

> Thursday, the thirty-first of August, was one of a series of days during which snug houses were stifling, and when cool draughts were treats; when cracks appeared in clayey gardens, and were called 'earthquakes' by apprehensive children; when loose spokes were discovered in the wheels of carts and carriages and when stinging insects haunted the air, the earth and every drop of water that was to be found.

Aridity within and without – the parched throat and the cracks in the earth – this is the mood of foreboding in which the episode is to take place. In this light the eye observes, with extraordinary intentness, the surfaces of things, so that 'seeing' becomes a way of 'seeing through'. When Mrs. Yeobright observes Clym on the Heath, 'not more distinguishable from the scene around him than the green caterpillar from the leaf it feeds on', she sees not so much a figure at work on the Heath as the Heath at work upon him: 'He appeared as a mere parasite of the heath, fretting its surface in his daily labour as a moth frets a garment, entirely engrossed with its products, having no knowledge of anything in the world but fern, furze, heath, lichens, and moss.' This is not the intensity of awareness, but drugged absorption, seeking to forget the wound his mother's absence has caused. Even his sleep is torpid, and as with the fir trees Hardy expresses the inner landscape in terms of the outer one:

> There lay the cat asleep on the bare gravel of the path, as if beds, rugs, and carpets were unendurable. . . . A small apple tree, of the sort called Ratheripe, grew just inside the gate, the only one which throve in the garden, by reason of the lightness of the soil; and among the fallen apples on the ground beneath were wasps rolling drunk with the juice, or creeping about the little caves in each fruit which they had eaten out before stupefied by its sweetness.

The cat's sleep, Clym's sleep, a common feeling encloses them – a feeling here expressed in terms of fecundity and decay, 'the smooth surface' and 'the little caves . . . eaten out'. And so it is with the cottage itself which slumbers in the sunlight, but nurses a turmoil of destructive feeling within. When Mrs. Yeobright's knock comes it dramatically 'freezes' the scene, and for an instant the emotional complex of the Yeobrights and Wildeve is laid bare. There is Clym self-absorbed, but inwardly disturbed by his mother's knock; Mrs. Yeobright vainly trying to claim his conscious attention; Eustacia torn between her attentions to Clym and her attentions to Wildeve, fatally indecisive, a pale face at a window, at once custodian and prisoner; Wildeve, impetuous in his arrival, prudent and submissive in his willingness to depart. In a shuttered house on the Heath, far removed in mood from the cosmic sweep of Rainbarrow, the private history of the novel reaches its crisis. Outside, the scene is indistinguishable from what it was before Mrs. Yeobright knocked, 'by the scraper, lay Clym's hook and the handful of faggot-bonds he had brought home; in front . . . the empty path, the garden gate standing slightly ajar; and, beyond, the great valley of purple heath thrilling silently in the sun'. The only distinction from the earlier scene is that the observing eyes are those now of Eustacia. It is the only distinction that matters.

'Mrs. Yeobright was gone' – rejected by a 'pale face at a window' and by the silence of her son. That indeed would be Mrs. Yeobright's account of the incident, but throughout this whole episode Hardy is giving access to a consciousness in the Yeobrights which they themselves only dimly apprehend, if at all. The people involved in the situation begin to feel an odd self-estrangement, expressed lightly in Johnny Nunsuch's remark to Mrs. Yeobright as she walks back from the cottage, that he once, looking at a pond, 'seed myself looking up at myself and I was frightened'. And it is in that state of suspended consciousness that Mrs. Yeobright, lying back on the bank, sees a colony of ants 'never-ending and heavy-laden'. Their movement reminds us of the way she once saw communities 'from a distance . . . vast masses of beings, jostling, zigzagging, and processioning in definite directions, but whose features are indistinguishable' in the 'very comprehensiveness of the view'. They remain to her anonymous, oppressive, she can live only at the nerve's end of the individual history, and that nerve would seem to have been severed. She longs to escape the world,

> While she looked a heron arose . . . and flew on with his face to the sun. He had come dripping wet from some pool in the valleys, and as he flew the edges and lining of his wings, his thighs, and his breast were so caught by the bright sunbeams that he appeared as if formed of burnished silver. Up in the zenith where he was seemed a free and happy place, away from all contact with the earthly ball to which she was pinioned; and she wished that she could arise uncrushed from its surface and fly as he flew then.

In this response to the pain her son's seeming desertion has given her, she reacts in the opposite way to Clym. Where he finds in Heath 'a soothing self-absorption', she can only feel herself 'pinioned', where he loses himself in torpor, she seeks the self-extinction of activity. In both cases, however, they have lost that tension between 'character' and 'land' which the novel poses as a necessary condition for human equilibrium. These concluding images open perspectives very different from those seemingly announced in that opening sentence, 'Thursday, the thirty-first of August, was one of [those] days . . .'; but the overall movement of this episode has made it possible, and by filling in 'the margin of the unexpressed', Hardy has added an insight into human folly, and stature to people who are otherwise perversely self-willed, without in any way mitigating those failures.

We have an opportunity to judge how far Hardy has been success-ful in this when, soon after Mrs. Yeobright's departure, Eustacia comes to reflect on her role in these proceedings.

She had certainly believed that Clym was awake, and the excuse would be an honest one as far as it went; but nothing could save her from censure in refusing to answer at the first knock. Yet, instead of blaming herself for the issue she laid the fault upon the shoulders of some indistinct, colossal Prince of the World, who had framed her situation and ruled her lot.

The interesting thing about this authorial intervention is our reaction to it. Earlier in this episode, we would have been moved simply to agree, but now we can feel that, while Eustacia's rhetoric has its own romanticism, the crisp authorial alternative, 'instead of blaming herself', will not do either. The effect of the journey on the Heath has not been to alter our view about the folly of the characters and their self-engrossment, but to have softened outlines, to have established 'a blur of indistinctness', so that we can see 'our will' not operating certainly at the command of a Prince of the World, but not operating either in the lucidities of its own devising. It is a supreme irony that any sentence in Hardy should provoke us into arguing for a more guarded view of the autonomy of the individual will; that one should do so, should alert us to the too easy inter-vention of the authorial voice.

With the death of Mrs. Yeobright the episode closes, and it is sig-nificant that though Hardy seeks an emotional intensity in Clym's denunciation of Eustacia, it disintegrates largely into rant. It comes to that because there has never been any intensity of feeling between them in the first place; its absence has been masked by the vehe-mence of Mrs. Yeobright's opposition, which has helped to create in the reader's mind a feeling between Clym and Eustacia which has never really been there. With his mother dead, all Clym's feelings are directed towards her, for Eustacia he has only condemnation, and a recanting letter which, almost perfunctorily, goes astray. There is however one moment – significantly it is the moment of Eustacia's departure from Clym – where genuine feeling breaks through and finely reveals Hardy's feeling *for* his characters as well as with them:

> She hastily dressed herself, Yeobright moodily walking up and down the room the whole of the time. At last all her things were on. Her little hands quivered so violently as she held them to her chin to fasten her bonnet that she could not tie the strings, and after a few moments she relinquished the attempt. Seeing this he moved forward and said, 'Let me tie them.'

It recalls another moment when Eustacia's hands were very much under her control, and when it was a favour to be allowed even to touch them. Charley has claimed his 'payment' for getting her into the mummer's play; he takes her hand in both of his:

> . . . with a tenderness beyond description, unless it was like that of a child holding a captured sparrow.
> 'Why! there's a glove on it!' he said in a deprecating way.
> 'I have been walking,' she observed.
> 'But, miss!'
> 'Well – it is hardly fair.' She pulled off the glove, and gave him her bare hand.
> They stood together minute after minute, without further speech, each looking at the blackening scene, and each thinking his and her own thoughts.
> 'I think I won't use it all up tonight,' said Charley devotedly . . .

I instance these two moments because they would not usually get into any formal account of the novel, and yet they seem to me to release a feeling, uniquely Hardy's, and one essential to our experience of his power as a novelist. Though the mood of the two is very different, they both have a mute appeal of one person to another, a tenderness quite free from mawkishness. The scenes have a point beyond their immediate setting in that they serve as a reminder of how much Hardy is concerned with the individual response, and it is this which underlies the historical sweep of his imagination and gives it poignancy.

If then *The Return of the Native* draws its strength from the cosmic perspective seen from Egdon, we have also to say that it draws its strength from the individual histories of the Yeobrights, reaching their climax in a shuttered room. But the overall structure of the novel demands that we go on to ask what relationship exists between these contrary perspectives. We come back to a question I proposed at the outset about the relationship of 'land' to 'character', or to put it in the more precise terms encouraged by this novel, what kind of a man is the native, and what does he return for?

At the beginning of this chapter I suggested that one of the features that distinguished *The Return of the Native* from *Far From the Madding Crowd* was its concern with forms of consciousness. In the two extended episodes I have looked at, consciousness has been present in terms of place and in terms of individual relationships, but of all Hardy's novels, with the exception of *Jude*, *The Return of the Native* is the most preoccupied with a social consciousness. Clym we might go on to say is a forerunner of Jude, but as soon as the matter is put like that, we begin to have certain hesitations about the kind of consciousness he embodies and, as a consequence, the consciousness of the novel also.

Clym's decision to remain in Egdon and not return to Paris is announced in a conversation he is having with the locals:

> 'I was endeavouring to put off one sort of life for another sort of life, which was not better than the life I had known before. It was simply different.'
> 'True; a sight different,' said Fairway.
> 'Yes, Paris must be a taking place,' said Humphrey. 'Grand shop-winders, trumpets, and drums; and here be we out of doors in all winds and weathers————'
> 'But you mistake me,' pleaded Clym. 'All this was very depressing. But not so depressing as something I next perceived – that my business was the idlest, vainest, most effeminate business that ever a man could be put to. That decided me: I would give it up and try to follow some rational occupation among the people I knew best, and to whom I could be of most use. I have come home . . . I shall keep a school. . . .'
> ' 'Tis good-hearted of the young man,' said another. 'But, for my part, I think he had better mind his business.'

Clym's 'business' is not something which is easy to respond to, and this passage indicates the difficulty. It is clear why Clym should find his work in Paris – 'making' as Fairway puts it 'a world-wide name for yourself in the nick-nack trade' – an idleness and an affront to his notion of what is fitting for a man of education. And it is not difficult to see that coming home to extend the awareness of 'the Egdon eremites' in the way the world is going is 'fitting' in a way that his work in Paris can never be. Nevertheless, we feel that Fairway has a sharper perception of the gulf that separates Clym from them than he has; in their bluff but general replies to him, there is a firmer grasp of social realities than any exhibited by their teacher, in the sense that they feel his aim, 'I shall keep a school', less potent in effecting change than he does. But by the time we come to the end of the passage, we feel that their dismissal of Clym, simply in terms of good-heartedness and their too easy conviction that he should mind his own business, is too patronising, too complacent. The effect on the reader of the passage as a whole is a switchback of sympathies, not because of some complexity within Clym, but because there seems to be some hesitation within the author himself as to just what to make of that decision to 'come home'. We recall an early moment in the introduction of Clym to the reader:

> In Clym Yeobright's face could be dimly seen the typical countenance of the future. Should there be a classic period to art hereafter, its Pheidias may produce such faces. The view of life as a thing to be put up with, replacing that zest for existence which was so intense in early civilizations, must ultimately enter so thoroughly into the constitution of the advanced races that its facial expression will become accepted as a new artistic departure.

This description directs our attention to the gap between nature and nurture, seen here in the difference between this face and 'the face on which time makes no impression'; the contrast is striking, and Hardy is at some pains to make it so. Clym registers in his face the cost of self-awareness, and for Hardy, this is an inescapable part of the evolution of human consciousness, as much a fact as 'the vast tract of unenclosed land'. And he seems to be saying further that it is the artists who have helped to make us aware of this: each age needs its own Pheidias. But Clym's face is not a passive register recording endurance of 'life as a thing to be put up with', it seeks to shape life, to give it meaning and, 'As is usual with bright natures, the deity that lies ignominiously chained within an ephemeral human carcase shone out of him like a ray.' The Promethean urge may be 'chained', but it is defiantly present, and it commands Hardy's admiration. This aspect of Clym Hardy presents fully and sympathetically, and, trying to characterise it, we could say that it is his recognition of the needs and the power of the human mind. But within the recognition lies a more uncompromising assertion, an assertion expressed in the quotation which provides a chapter with its title, 'my mind to me a kingdom is', and it is this which constitutes, for Hardy, Clym's real limitation. Basically, it is the imperial claims of 'mind' that give the defence of his decision to stay in Egdon its sense of unreality and strain; Clym makes a fatal identification of contemporary consciousness with contemporary 'mind'. And it is this exclusive emphasis on 'mind' that makes him conceive of 'coming home' – the return of the native – in terms simply of finding 'some rational occupation among the people I knew best'.

The consequence of this attitude emerges in two ways. The first lies in his notion that what Egdon needs, above all, is knowledge. The authorial comment is sharp:

> We can hardly imagine bucolic placidity quickening to intellectual aims without imagining social aims as the transitional phase. . . . A man who advocates aesthetic effort and deprecates social effort is only likely to be understood by a class to which social effort has become a stale matter.

The force of 'social' is not simply in its conjunction with 'effort'; it suggests that knowledge, 'aesthetic effort', is not something that can ever be aimed at in isolation, but is itself part of the total consciousness of the age. The second way in which Clym's attitude towards 'mind' reveals itself is, significantly enough, in his response to Egdon, which had been 'inwoven' with his life. He contemplates it and sees the various attempts which have been made to cultivate it but, 'when he looked from the heights . . . he could not help in indulging in *a barbarous satisfaction* (my italics) at observing that, in some of the attempts at reclamation from the waste, tillage, after holding on for a year or two, had receded again in despair, the ferns and furze-tufts stubbornly reasserting themselves'. Intellectuality is partnered by primitivism, a heady brew for the sophisticated, and stirred up in Clym's case because, between 'the kingdom of the mind, and 'the vast tract of unenclosed land', there is nothing that can lay claim to his imagination. He is trapped between two versions of experience, 'I shall keep a school' and 'barbarous satisfaction' at the domination of the Heath over man's attempts at cultivation. For him 'character' and 'land' remain disjunct, and when he is made to feel the conflict between them, then he becomes radically self-estranged.

The first intimation of this conflict comes when he makes his successful proposal to Eustacia:

> This was the end of their talk, and Eustacia left him. Clym watched her as she retired towards the sun. The luminous rays wrapped her up with her increasing distance, and the rustle of her dress over the sprouting sedge and grass died away. As he watched, the dead flat of the scenery overpowered him, though he was fully alive to the beauty of that untarnished early summer green which was worn for the nonce by the poorest blade. There was something in its oppressive horizontality which too much reminded him of the arena of life; it gave him a sense of bare equality with, and no superiority to, a single living thing under the sun.

It is a strange, almost hallucinatory, passage in which Clym is made to feel a disorientation in his decision to marry Eustacia. He is made to feel in 'the bare equality' of the Heath a force which has laid siege to the 'kingdom of the mind'. It is a force which he feels drains him of individuality, and leaves him vulnerable to his mindless absorption in the land. He can no longer 'look down from the heights . . . in barbarous satisfaction', the land in its 'oppressive horizontality' overpowers him and he gives his body over to the Heath – and to Eustacia. After the threat to his sight, he retreats into himself, so that he becomes virtually inseparable from the Heath:

> He was a brown spot in the midst of an expanse of olive-green gorse, and nothing more. . . . His daily life was of a curious

microscopic sort, his whole world being limited to a circuit of a
few feet from his person. His familiars were creeping and winged
things, and they seemed to enroll him in their band.

As he becomes one with 'the creeping and winged things', the proud
isolation of 'mind' fades, and there is an accompanying estrangement,
first from his mother and then from his wife.

It has been argued that this collapse of Clym's is only a stage in
his progress and that, after the tragic deaths of his mother and
Eustacia, he recovers. To some extent this is, of course, true. He does
emerge from the life of the furze-cutter and he overcomes that consciousness of vast impassivity that the Heath induces in him, so that
by the end he can climb Rainbarrow Hill, as Eustacia had done, and
once again 'look down from the heights'. There is a resolution here,
but it is difficult to see a vindication. For one thing his behaviour
prior to his new career as an itinerant preacher has not been of a
kind to win much sympathy: he remains morose, morbidly self-
righteous and self-pitying. The fruit of his reading would seem to
have left him with the fear that his life may be invaded by a proposal
of marriage from Thomasin. When he discovers that Thomasin
wishes to marry Venn, who has just saved his life, he can only remark
that she might have made a better match. These are hardly the attitudes which an author, anxious to show the ennoblement of his hero
through suffering, would put on display. On the other hand, there is
no suggestion of hypocrisy or humbug about Clym's adoption of the
life of an itinerant preacher, and Clym, as he stands 'a motionless
figure' on the top of Rainbarrow, is meant to command something
of the sympathy, certainly the seriousness, which Eustacia commanded in a similar position at the beginning of the novel.

The cause of the uncertainty in these final stages of Clym's career
seems to me that he has become, for Hardy, less and less a character
and more and more the embodiment of a dilemma; for his problems
are those of his creator. Dramatically, he has been kept alive by his
relationship with his mother and Eustacia: they are now dead.
Conceptually, he has been kept in control because he embodied a
contemporary consciousness which, however, really existed only at
the level of statement. This is revealed in the concluding authorial
comment, where we feel a fatigue about the first sentence in striking

contrast to the bracing analysis with which Clym was first introduced:

> Some believed him, and some believed not; some said that
> his words were commonplace, others complained of his want of
> theological doctrine; while others again remarked that it was well
> enough for a man to take to preaching who could not see to do
> anything else. But everywhere he was kindly received, for the
> story of his life had become generally known.

But behind this official invitation to make what you like of Clym's
life at the end, there is an important point for Hardy. That is, quite
simply, that Clym should 'go on', he is part of the evolving consciousness of the age, and in his presence at the end, there is the tacit
belief that a truth about life cannot be adequately expressed by the
deaths on the Heath and in Shadwater Weir. That presence is an
integral part of Hardy's belief in the future, and though, for Hardy,
Clym individually no longer seems able to provide a dramatic en-
dorsement of that, 'his story' nevertheless can.

It may well be argued however that, whatever dubieties attend the
affirmation present in Clym's life, surely the real affirmation of the
novel is to be found in the marriage of Thomasin and Venn. It was
a marriage which provoked Hardy into being his own editor. At the
end of the penultimate chapter there appears the following footnote:

> The writer may state here that the original conception of the
> story did not design a marriage between Thomasin and Venn. He
> was to have retained his isolated and weird character to the last,
> and to have disappeared mysteriously from the heath, nobody
> knowing whither – Thomasin remaining a widow. But certain
> circumstances of serial publication led to a change of intent.
>
> Readers can therefore choose between the endings, and those
> with an austere artistic code can assume the more consistent con-
> clusion to be the true one.

It is a remarkable note for an author to make, virtually disavowing
his final chapter, and yet nevertheless continuing to retain it in
successive editions, long after the 'circumstances of serial publication' had been forgotten. It could be argued that once Hardy had
given his novel this particular ending it was hard for him to change

it, however much he was inclined in that direction; I think however that, if we see the problem in the context of the novel as a whole, it becomes another instance of Hardy's genuine uncertainty about what does constitute the appropriate ending. And we can read the footnote as part of the text, dramatising that uncertainty.

The title of the first chapter of the last book – 'The Inevitable Movement Onward' – announces the difficulty. For readers who have what Hardy describes sympathetically as 'an austere artistic code' that title can only be a matter for regret, there being no movement 'onward' in the disappearance of Venn and in Thomasin's widowhood. But for Hardy such a movement is central to his imaginative undertaking. To have left Thomasin as a widow, when throughout the book she has provided a centre of gravity from which other, more notable characters, have continually departed, would be to give the deaths on the weir and on the Heath a cosmic inevitability which much of the book is concerned to deny. We are continually made to feel that there is a life which extends beyond that of the central characters, and it is Thomasin who helps to give that central drama an important frame. Alone of her family she will not be deceived by false lights on Egdon:

> The drops which lashed her face were not scorpions, but prosy rain; Egdon in the mass was no monster whatsoever, but impersonal open ground. Her fears of the place were rational, her dislikes of its worst moods reasonable.

For someone whose face can reveal 'an ingenuous, transparent life . . . as if the flow of her existence could be seen passing within her', Egdon is neither a gaol nor an arcady. To make such a figure finally isolated would be alien to important authorial concerns in the novel, the kind of concerns which, in a much more calculated way, Elizabeth-Jane expresses in *The Mayor of Casterbridge*. Thomasin's final accommodation within the social structure enables Hardy to offer us a perspective on the tragic deaths in the novel which her isolation would deny him, a perspective which reveals an element of folly in their tragedy.

That Venn should be Thomasin's partner in marriage is inevitable if she is to marry at all. She owes her survival largely to his help, and their particular coming together strikes that note which Hardy was so anxious to strike at the end of another relationship of waiting and caring. We could say of Thomasin and Venn, as Hardy said of Bathsheba and Oak, that their romance had grown up 'in the interstices of a mass of hard prosaic reality'. It is that note which has to be sounded, because it conveys so distinctly the endurance that for Hardy is the dynamic behind 'the inevitable movement onward', an endurance which is not a passive resistance but a shrewd responsiveness to the way things are. Venn 'endures' in that he waits with unflagging patience for Thomasin, but it is a patience continuously sustained by energy and enterprise.

Having said these things, however, it is not difficult to see what it is in the marriage between Thomasin and Venn which makes Hardy so uneasy about its serving as a conclusion to the novel. It is too simply emblematic, and even conceding that it is related to Hardy's purpose in the way I have suggested, it is a way which is only marginally connected to the dramatic life of the novel. It belongs much more happily to the simpler fictional world of *Far From the Madding Crowd*, where to acquire, within a few pages, money, fifty cows and a farm would not be too closely inquired into. But Venn's transformation from reddleman to dairy-farmer is not really a question of unsatisfactorily bridging a credibility gap. Venn's role in the novel is directly related to the fact that he is a figure of the past, a reddleman 'filling . . . in the rural world the place . . . the dodo occupied in the world of animals'. So far as the reader's response to the novel is concerned Venn remains dyed to the end. Significantly, his wooing of Thomasin begins with a maypole dance at a place where 'the instincts of merry England lingered on . . . with exceptional vitality'. We must take the author's word for it, it is all he has on offer. The trouble is this. If we find difficulty in accepting the marriage between Thomasin and Venn, and, in consequence, difficulty in seeing it as a resolution to the novel, this is not because it offends our sense of credibility or, more grandly, our 'austere artistic code', but that the dramatic life which Hardy has been able to give such a marriage is too frail to provide an effective sense of 'the inevitable movement onward' in a novel which contains Egdon Heath and the tragedy of the Yeobrights.

♣ III ♣

There the form stood, motionless as the hill beneath. Above the plain rose the hill, above the hill rose the barrow, and above the barrow rose the figure. Above the figure was nothing that could be mapped elsewhere than on a celestial globe.

Such a perfect, delicate, and necessary finish did the figure give to the dark pile of hills that it seemed to be the only obvious justification of their outline.

From a distance there simply appeared to be a motionless figure standing on the top of the tumulus. . . . But now it was fine warm weather, with only a summer breeze blowing, and early afternoon instead of dull twilight. . . . Round him upon the slopes of the Barrow a number of heathmen and women were reclining or sitting at their ease. They listened to the words of the man in their midst, who was preaching . . .

The two scenes, calculatedly recalling one another, pin-point the conflict that has operated throughout *The Return of the Native* and which, in various ways, I have tried to illustrate. In the first scene the figure, Eustacia, is imaged as an integral part of the universe she inhabits – at one with the body of the Heath, 'whose dark soil', Lawrence wrote, 'was strong and crude and organic as the body of a beast'.[1] In Eustacia's case, of course, it is a partial irony in that her heart, wherever her body may be, is over the hills and far away. Nevertheless, in her sensuous understanding, she is at one with the Heath. For Clym, the characteristic stance on Rainbarrow is not a tensed silhouette giving 'necessary finish . . . to the dark pile of hills' but 'a convenient signal to those stragglers who wished to draw near'. The Heath is now an arena for discourse, a place where his audience 'abstractedly pulled heather, stripped ferns, or tossed pebbles down the slope'. It is the daylight world. It is difficult not to feel that, in the logic of the novel, the distinction between the two scenes lies in the evolution of consciousness, and that, for Hardy, the second has come to replace the first. If we feel that Hardy fails to present all this convincingly, however, it is because the dramatic

[1] D. H. Lawrence, 'Study of Thomas Hardy', *Phoenix*, I, p. 415.

tensions of the novel run in other directions than between time past and time present. They lie, as I have attempted to suggest, between the vast impersonality of the heath and the claustrophobic intensity of the individual relationships of the Yeobrights. This leads to that bifocal view of character, so distinctive a feature of the novel; Eustacia as Queen of Night and as romantic day-dreamer; Clym as Prometheus and as a slower-moving scholar gypsy; Mrs. Yeobright as having 'singular insight into life', and also 'a curate's daughter, who had once dreamt of doing better things'. If these contrasting perspectives eventually become unsatisfactory, this is not because of a failure on Hardy's part to give psychological credibility to his characters, but because the underlying dialectic between the cosmic and the personal loses tension and becomes simply flaccid.

About the characters we feel that they become either too self-consciously representative or too self-consciously individual. Of the unfolding narrative, we can say that there is no line of communication between the drama of the Heath and the drama of Clym's cottage. What is missing from both these aspects is that fluent assimilation whereby individual lives can be taken up into a history wider than themselves, and the way in which, in its turn, that wider history can be seen to return them to the sharp particulars of living in this time and that place. At one point in the novel Hardy is very much aware of this and in the long description of Clym he makes it explicit. But it is an awareness which exists only at the level of meditation. By the end of the novel Clym's character has been bifurcated – the morose self-centred widower fearing that Thomasin may make unwelcome demands upon him, the unconvincing cut-out of a contemporary sage being 'sometimes secular, and sometimes religious, but never dogmatic'. The ironies which attend Clym's presence in the last chapters of the book are Hardy's distress signals about a character who has outstayed his welcome. Clym, who at the beginning of the novel had provided Hardy with an opportunity for dramatising a much more sophisticated consciousness than he had every attempted before, has by the end come uncomfortably close to simply representing his author's dilemma about the gains and losses inherent in evolving consciousness.

Part of the difficulty for the characters in *The Return of the*

Native is not their self-awareness, but a passivity, a passivity which acts in defence of deep self-absorption. The characters tend to perceive that they are acting in two plots, one of their own devising, one of vast impersonal forces, but in this novel they see no relationship between the two. It is precisely this perception which gives Henchard, Tess and Jude their tragic stature and comes to constitute, for Hardy, their 'character'. These are characters who are prepared to live between two worlds, and though they never achieve a resolution, they become genuinely aware of the tension and in that awareness find wisdom. They find it at least partly because they belong to a world which has a precise *social* history, as well as an individual and a cosmic one. Nowhere is this more sharply revealed than in the crucial role assigned to work in these later novels, work which for Hardy is always a form of learning. When we look at *The Return of the Native* we find that work is either perfunctory or emblematic: Clym as furze-gatherer or preacher; Venn as reddleman or dairy-farmer; Wildeve as engineer or inn-keeper; even the locals act really as commentators or messengers and have no independent life of their own such as they had in *Far From the Madding Crowd*. The consequence of this for the characters in *The Return of the Native* is that there is no form of learning which is available to them in public and social terms; they live at extremes where a man can become 'a mere parasite of the Heath', or where a woman can observe herself as 'a disinterested spectator' and think herself 'a sport for heaven', or where both can become screened by 'a luminous mist' of mutual regard. The effect of this on the reader is that he takes the tragedy of the novel persistently at one remove from his own situation. When Wildeve and Venn gamble on the Heath for instance, there are considerable issues at stake, but we feel that these are rooted only in the exigencies of the story. Memorable as the episode is, it is self-enclosed, taking place in a never-never land. In the novels to come Hardy will make sure that risks of fortune will be illuminated not by the light of glow worms, but by those of the market place. The tragedy of *The Mayor of Casterbridge* may, like the present novel, conclude on Egdon Heath, but it will begin with a stranger unfolding 'five crisp pieces of paper' and throwing down on the tablecloth, 'Bank of England notes for five pounds'.

If, however, *The Mayor of Casterbridge* is to provide Hardy with fresh possibilities for his art, it would be unjust to *The Return of the Native* to conclude on a note which did not emphasise its own positive achievement. It is a novel which has behind it that moment of imaginative growth revealed in the storm-scene in *Far From the Madding Crowd* – and by giving a new dimension of understanding to region, and human feeling, Hardy has effectively explored the relationship of 'the infuriated universe' and that 'feeling' which the earlier novel had brought him to ponder. When we compare that storm with the use to which Egdon is put, or compare the treatment of obsessive feeling in Boldwood with that of Mrs. Yeobright, we can see the fresh insight that the later novel has afforded. *Far From the Madding Crowd* has its own particular assurance – there seems nothing as comprehensively sustained in the later novel as the sheep washing and celebratory supper – but in introducing Clym, Hardy has introduced a contemporary consciousness into Wessex, and it is this which takes *The Return of the Native* beyond the range of anything in *Far From the Madding Crowd*. It provides him with a theme as well as a method, and enables him to realise that he can find in fiction expression for questions which not only trouble his characters, but trouble himself; if the resolution he aimed at in the novel fails, in the end, to carry conviction, it was because of its very closeness to irresolutions deep within his own thinking. But the drama on Egdon has shown him that these irresolutions cannot be resolved simply by 'taking thought'; it has searched out and tested his dramatic imagination, engaged it at full stretch. In other words, we could say that in *The Return of the Native* Hardy reveals himself as a major novelist; he sees for the first time his fictional world – and sees it whole. He will go on to explore it more deeply, but not more extensively.

4

A Man and his History
The Mayor of Casterbridge (1886)

While his eyes were bent on the water beneath there slowly became visible a something floating in the circular pool formed by the wash of centuries; the pool he was intending to make his death-bed. At first it was indistinct by reason of the shadow from the bank; but it emerged thence and took shape, which was that of a human body, lying stiff and stark upon the surface of the stream.

In the circular current imparted by the central flow the form was brought forward, till it passed under his eyes; and then he perceived with a sense of horror that it was *himself*. Not a man somewhat resembling him, but one in all respects his counterpart, his actual double, was floating as if dead in Ten Hatches Hole.

In that memorable moment we find revealed an essential perspective for *The Mayor of Casterbridge*. No longer, as in *The Return of the Native*, is there 'a dialogue of the mind with itself' expressed in diverse ways – the Heath, the acts of human desire, the self-conscious meditation on what the age demands – but rather a mute self-recognition, taking place within an individual consciousness fatally divided against itself. It was a shift which Hardy recognised in his Preface to the novel: 'The story', he writes, 'is more particularly of one man's deeds and character than, perhaps, any other of those included in my Exhibition of Wessex life.' 'One man's deeds' is a phrase which describes the great achievement – and the limitations – of the novel.

For Hardy, with *The Return of the Native* behind him, to be able to find in one man his governing interest suggests how richly he felt himself able to register a notion of 'character', capable of containing within it all the essential interests so lavishly dispersed in the earlier novel. That is to say, we do not feel, as we move from one novel to the other, any narrowing of scope, any diminution in tragic scale. The title page defines the arena of dramatic interest – *The Life and Death of The Mayor of Casterbridge: A Story of a Man of Character.* In that tension between the public circumstances and the individual response, we have the dynamic of the novel. Continually, we are made aware of both elements operating throughout the novel, so that we cannot think of Henchard apart from his work, his work apart from the town, the town apart from the age, whether it is the age which 'bespoke the art of Rome, concealed dead men of Rome', or the age which finds the town still just beyond the outstretched arm of the railway. But no more can we think of Henchard without hearing 'a laugh not encouraging to strangers', without seeing a man 'reckon his sacks by chalk strokes . . . measure his ricks by stretching with his arms', without feeling 'the blazing regard' he gave to those who won his feelings. If we were to try to characterise the distinctiveness of this 'one man' we might echo Kent's remark to Lear:

> 'You have in your countenance that which I would fain cal master.'
> 'What's that?'
> 'Authority.'[1]

In describing Henchard in these terms I am thinking more of the decisive imaginative impact he makes on the reader, than of the detail of his own personality. When we reflect on the latter, we are faced with sustained ambivalence. The adjectives crowd in to make their rival claims – egotistic, rash, jealous, generous, self-critical, honourable. And these claims are pressed home with force and precision – there are no half-measures, no truce between them.

If, however, we ponder the force that is 'Henchard', we cannot really say that it arises from the interplay, however vigorous, of these various elements. We cannot, in other words, feel that he inhabits Hardy's imagination, and in turn ours, as a complex psychological figure. For Hardy, the imaginative pressure at work in the creation of Henchard is not expressed in individual analysis, but in terms of a series of actions whose effects can be neither determined nor confined. 'One man's deeds' in this novel can contain the exploration of a community, not in the sense of its detail, but in the contrast be-

---

[1] *King Lear*, I, iv.

tween the solidity of its present and the haunting power of its past.

It is Hardy's ability to find within Henchard a multidimensional perspective which prompts the word 'epic' as an appropriate descriptive term. The force that he exerts, the authority with which he speaks, these belong to someone who can be titled, with propriety, 'The Mayor of Casterbridge', and in that role he can add a footnote to history, and play a part in a tragedy. But within the Mayor is the hay-trusser, the man who sold his wife at a fair in a drunken stupor, who later deceived a father about the existence of his child so that 'scarcely believing the evidence of his senses, (he) rose from his seat amazed at what he had done'. For Hardy, then, to explore 'the volcanic stuff beneath the rind' in Henchard, is to explore the whole area of conflict which so preoccupied him in *The Return of the Native*: the divisiveness of consciousness within man himself whereby his very energies become directed towards his self-destruction, and the relation of that consciousness to inevitable processes of change, whether these are seen in terms of society or in terms of nature. If we isolate any of these elements, so that we see Henchard as a psychological case study, or a tragic hero, or as the last representative in a changing agrarian order, we fail to do justice to Hardy's conception of character, to the fact that 'one man's deeds' can serve as an 'Exhibition of Wessex life'. 'Egdon', 'Clym', 'Eustacia' – all these elements are present in that confrontation Henchard has with 'himself' in Ten Hatches Hole.

That Henchard should permit Hardy this inclusiveness of vision is certainly one of the triumphs of this novel; it is also its limitation. If we say that Henchard drains life out of the other characters, this is not to say that he is the only convincing character in the novel. Elizabeth-Jane, and certainly Farfrae, can be thought of as genuine presences. The way he affects the life of the other characters is in making us feel they are never allowed to live and breathe apart from him. At the level of plot, he systematically dismisses them from his life: Susan, Farfrae, Lucetta, Elizabeth – all are cut off from him as severely as he aims to cut himself off from the human community in the prescriptions of his Will.

In both Elizabeth and Farfrae we sense an intended elaboration of character which we can only observe through a glass darkly.

Elizabeth's pursuit of learning is perfunctorily presented, her books become stage properties, her reunion with her father is hurriedly dismissed. Farfrae in his relationship with Henchard is skilfully presented; in his relationship with Lucetta and Elizabeth, he hardly exists. If it comes as a shock to read his reflection on Lucetta's death, 'it was hard to believe that life with her would have been productive of further happiness', it is not so much because of its crude insensitivity, as because we realise that Farfrae's relationship with her has hardly been created for us at all. Newson only lives as a simple device of the plot, because for Henchard that is all he is. Susan's case is a particularly revealing one, as R. B. Heilman has pointed out in a shrewd essay on the novel.[1] Heilman traces out her 'career', that of one continuously presented as meek and barely competent; he concludes: 'Hardy might well have told us about Susan's energy, spirit, inventiveness, native shrewdness amounting at times to foxiness, strategic sense and managerial skill little short of brilliant, and pointed out that she was one of the few women who get what they want.'[2] If Susan does not quite strike us in that way, Heilman's account makes us sharply aware how much we have become influenced by Henchard's reaction to her and how, indeed, he seems to have persuaded Hardy to connive in his account too. What all these incidents have in common is that all these characters draw their dramatic life directly from Henchard, and that once they become involved in scenes which do not concern him in any direct way, then they would seem to forfeit not only Henchard's interest but Hardy's also. It is wryly amusing to see that Henchard's power is such that it appears to cut the author off too, so that his occasional *obiter dicta* seem to italicise themselves awkwardly, and remain rather sour asides having little to do with the actual drama that is taking place.

It is, of course, the dominance of Henchard that causes Hardy to get into a great deal of trouble with his plotting in this novel; in order to keep it moving, he has to have recourse to letters which are not properly sealed, parcels which are badly packed, and conversations which are overheard. These always remain devices and have none of the resonance that so often accompanies Hardy's plotting.

[1] Introduction to *The Mayor of Casterbridge* (Riverside Edition), 1962.
[2] Introduction, p. xxiii.

Hardy himself was very conscious of this defect in *The Mayor* and remarked that 'it was a story which he had damaged more recklessly as an artistic whole . . . than perhaps any of his other novels'.[1] He attributes the damage to serial pressures, which had led him into over-plotting. This may have been the effect upon him, but the cause lay in the conception of a novel centred on 'one man's deeds', which required leisurely development, careful distribution of interest, and a plot stripped of superfluous incident.

In beginning this chapter in this way I have tried to describe the dominant impression which I think *The Mayor of Casterbridge* could make on the reader, and I have set it out in this rather stark way at the outset because I think it can exert a misleading influence on our reading of the novel as a whole. The impression I have described centres on the force of Henchard's character and, as a corollary, the relative weakness of the other characters and the inadequacies of the plot. What makes that impression misleading is that it is too static; 'character' for Hardy can never be seen in a tightly inclusive way, and plot is not to be identified with that sense of irresistible movement which is so powerful an element in this novel.

I shall try to illustrate this, first by examining the initial impression made by the novel in the opening two chapters, then by looking at a chapter where a significant development does take place, apart from Henchard, and finally, by looking at the closing two chapters where the novel finds its resolution.

♣ II ♣

The function of the opening two chapters is to initiate the action and to serve as an overture to the novel as a whole. Their subject matter is the arrival of Henchard with his wife at the Fair in Weydon-Priors; the selling of Susan to the sailor in a mood of drunken frustration; Henchard's recognition, the following day, of the terrible deed he has done; his solemn vow never to touch alcohol for twenty-one years, 'being a year for every year I have lived'; and his setting off alone to Casterbridge to look for work and to begin a new life.

[1] *Life*, p. 179.

One evening of late summer, before the nineteenth century had reached one-third of its span, a young man and woman, the latter carrying a child, were approaching the large village of Weydon-Priors, in Upper Wessex, on foot. They were plainly but not ill clad, though the thick hoar of dust which had accumulated on their shoes and garments from an obviously long journey lent a disadvantageous shabbiness to their appearance just now.

The novel opens in these classical cadences of 'once upon a time'. At the centre, taking the attention, is Henchard, at first sour and indifferent, then made quarrelsome and pugnacious by drink, then bewildered but finally determined in his remorse. It is a kaleidoscope of moods all being lived out at the nerve's end, and fuelling them all, there is a deep and diffused sense of self-estrangement. Self-enclosed, his wife appears 'to walk the highway alone, save for the child she bore'. About the family there is an 'atmosphere of stale familiarity', and in Nature too, life has faded, the leaves are 'doomed' and 'blackened green', the 'grassy margins of the bank' are 'powdered by dust'. The mood is suggestive of that described by Donne in 'The Nocturnall upon St. Lucie's Day':

> The world's whole sap is sunke:
> The generall balm the hydroptique earth hath drunk,
> Whither, as to the bed's-feet, life is shrunke.

That is the general mood of these opening pages; Henchard's particular mood is more difficult to define. We feel in it bafflement, frustration, a sense that life has possibilities which have been denied him. It is interesting that the very first words which are spoken in the novel, the first gesture towards self-fulfilment, takes the form of the question 'Any trade doing here?' It is the sense of the centrality of work in finding fulfilment that is such a major preoccupation of this novel.

As soon as we put it that way we can see what a rare novel *The Mayor of Casterbridge* is in the history of English fiction, where the model of self-fulfilment is found, invariably, in personal relationships. If we think of Lawrence, a novelist who comes very close to Hardy in many ways, and think of the self-estrangement of Tom Brangwen and the self-estrangement of Henchard, the rarity of

Hardy's position becomes plain. *The Mayor* is an intensely public novel in its drive; how public can be gauged from the fact that it must be one of the very few major novels – or for that matter, very few novels – where sexual relationships are not, in one way or another, the dominant element. That Hardy can write a novel which engages his full imaginative range without making us feel the relative absence of such relationships, suggests that it is not the individual human heart which beats at the centre of his fictional world.

The marriage that is broken at Weydon-Priors is not, so far as Hardy is concerned, an individual affair. In these opening chapters we move steadily away from the individual – we are never, at any point, taken 'inside' Henchard – to the world in which he is finding it difficult to make a living, the world of houses being pulled down and people having nowhere to go. There is the voice of the auctioneer selling off the last of the horses and gradually insinuating into Henchard's mind a wish to start again, to shake himself free from all encumbrance, to sell his wife. Susan is sold at a strange dream-like auction in which there are no bidders, but the price goes up and up. I think it is possible to make too much of the particulars of this vivid and bizarre scene, so that the whole emphasis falls on the act of selling itself, the reduction of a person to a commodity. But Hardy's interests are not those, say, of James in *The Spoils of Poynton*. His eye is not so much on money, as on the notion of 'freedom' it appears to offer, and which Henchard is so intent on grasping, 'if I were a free man again I'd be worth a thousand pound before I'd done o't'. That is the sentence which catches the undercurrent of meditation that runs persistently through the chapter, the keenly felt 'if I were'. It is that sentiment which is present in the visitation of the late swallow finding its way into the tent, like the men who watch it, 'absently', a migrant, but unlike them free in a way they can never be. This meditative note is struck most firmly at the end of the chapter when we are taken outside the tent, and the sight of the horses 'crossing their necks and rubbing each other lovingly' is set in contrast to the harsh act of humanity we have just witnessed. But, immediately, that note is played in a different key: we are asked to reflect on the occasions when humanity sleeps innocently while inanimate nature rages round him. And there at the end of the paragraph we find an unobtrusive phrase which gives us bearings on the whole scene – 'all terrestrial conditions were intermittent'. In other words those who seek to impress themselves on the universe, to lay violent hands on time, to forget that man is the slave of limit – such men can only succeed in destroying themselves. They will be extinguished as surely as the last candle is, when the furmity seller goes out to leave Henchard alone in the tent sunk in a drunken sleep.

But for Hardy flux is always followed by reflux, an essential element in his narrative compulsion, no less than in his metaphysical outlook. Chapter 1 then tells for Hardy precisely half of the human story; Chapter 2 reverses the emphasis and, in so doing, tells the other half.

Henchard is again at the centre, Henchard now waking to find 'the morning sun' streaming through the crevices. Outside, 'the freshness of the September morning inspired and braced him as he stood.' He can see far across the valleys 'dotted with barrows, and trenched with . . . prehistoric forts'. *This* is a world upon which man has impressed himself, so that 'The whole scene lay under the rays of a newly risen sun, which had not as yet dried a single blade of the heavily dewed grass.' The voice of the weak bird of the previous night singing 'a trite old evening song' gives way to 'the yellow-hammers which flitted about the hedges with straws in their bills'. This vitality and purposiveness encompasses Henchard too.

The previous night he sought to set aside time, to disown his past; now he will bind himself to time, more, he will mortgage his future. He gave himself away in a drunken stupor in a furmity tent, now in re-collecting himself he swears his great vow on the clamped book which lies on the Communion table in a nearby village church. Instinctively, he seeks a ritual gesture, 'a fit place and imagery', which will release him from the thraldom of the moment. 'He shouldered his basket and moved on' – that is the driving sentiment of this second chapter. Purposeful and resilient, Henchard has now a full consciousness of his position. He tries, without success, to find his wife and family and then, learning of their emigration, 'he said he would search no longer. . . . Next day he started, journeying southwestward, and did not pause, except for nights' lodgings, till he reached the town of Casterbridge, in a far distant part of Wessex.' In that closing sentence of the chapter we hear the classical cadences of the archetypal story, present in the opening paragraph, announce themselves again. And it is to be there, in Casterbridge, that the complementary tensions so explicitly set up in these two opening chapters will be developed and pursued.

'A series of seemings' – the opening of *The Mayor of Casterbridge* reveals, in a remarkably pure way, the characteristic Hardy stance towards experience. Within each chapter a set of reverberations is released from a single violent act – the sale of the wife, Henchard's vow. A perspective on the human deed is established. The act of an individual person cannot be contained by that individual life; it leads persistently outwards to the whole social context, a context both personal and social, as the full title of the novel we are considering makes plain: *The Life and Death of the Mayor of Casterbridge*. The 'seemings' are here, but in themselves they don't constitute the shape of a life. They are true to consciousness heightened in moments of vision; they fail to do justice to consciousness as continually present, continually altering. It is here that 'series' has its part to play, with its emphasis on process and continuity.

In the aesthetic structure of a Hardy novel the tension between the terms is expressed in the dynamic interplay between plot and image, and encompassing both is the compassionate presence of the narrator, whose mediating consciousness is an integral part of the drama he is concerned to reveal. In the very elements which go to make up his fiction – the narrative trajectory, the sudden moment of symbolic concentration, the oscillations between story and commentary – in all of these elements, Hardy is acting out his own impression of life as a series of seemings, and the novelist's art is here not simply to reveal but to enact it. In particular terms, this is communicated most frequently in that air of ambivalence which hangs over so many incidents in the novel) an ambivalence which creates in the reader not so much an awareness of complexity as a desire to suspend judgement and to sense a more inclusive view.

It is an air which is strongly present in the presentation of Casterbridge itself. Our first glimpse of the town is in lamplight 'through the engirdling trees, conveying a sense of great snugness and comfort inside'. But to the eyes of the travelled, if inexperienced, Elizabeth-Jane it already seems 'an old-fashioned place'. Hardy holds a delicate balance in his initial presentation of Casterbridge between the warm nostalgia prompted by his boyhood memories of Dorchester in the 1840s and the reflections of an adult already aware of its remoteness, its inability to adapt itself to a changing world. 'Country and town met at a mathematical line' – it is like a child's drawing, and like such a drawing exhibits its own charm, its own falsity. The town's band may be shaking the windows with 'The Roast Beef of Old England', Henchard may be re-introduced to us through his laughter, but outside in the streets, the newly arrived wayfarers hear that he has over-reached himself: he has sold 'blown wheat', and there has never been such 'unprincipled bread in Casterbridge before'. The adjective does more than catch the vivacity of dialect, it casts a sardonic eye on one aspect at least of the Mayor's rise to prosperity. To the wayfarers, Casterbridge offers 'a sense of great snugness and comfort', but to Buzzford, the local dealer, it is 'a old hoary place o' wickedness'.

From the outset of the novel the reader is made quietly aware of ambivalence, and aware of it as arising from 'the way things are' rather than through the artifice of the novelist. Consider the relatively unobtrusive, but significant, play which is made of Farfrae's songs of home. The tone is lightly ironical at the expense of a man who looks back fondly on a country he has certainly no wish to return to; but at the same time, his sentiments are expressed in song, indicative of his resilience, his desire to travel, the ease he feels in company, and the unfeigned pleasure he gives to others. As the rivalry between Farfrae and Henchard builds up, we feel the same duality of feeling present, so that when Abel Whittle is reprimanded for his lateness at work, we feel Henchard's treatment is concerned, but humiliating, Farfrae's impersonal but just. In the rival entertainments they set up for the town, Henchard is bountiful but patronising, Farfrae cannily prudent, but infectiously ingenious.

The oscillation of sympathy is not confined to the main action. It is present in that fine town-pump chat which followed the death of Susan Henchard. 'She was as white as marble-stone,' says Mrs.

Cuxom with evident relish, as she proceeds to relay the details of Susan's preparations for her burial. 'Ah, poor heart!' – and a general sigh goes up. Then suddenly the tone changes from elegy to indignation. Christopher Coney has removed the pennies from the dead woman's eyes and spent them at The Three Mariners. ' "Faith," he said, "why should death rob life o' fourpence . . . money is scarce and throats get dry." ' Beneath the humour a genuine point is being made. Just as suddenly the tone shifts back again, not to the gossipy note of concern with which the conversation began, but to an impersonal note of elegy, which both pays tribute to Susan and also recognises the substance in Coney's remark, though without approving his action:

> 'Well, poor soul; she's helpless to hinder that or anything now,' answered Mother Cuxom. 'And all her shining keys will be took from her, and her cupboards opened; and little things a' didn't wish seen, anybody will see; and her wishes and ways will all be as nothing.'

It is a small incident, existing in the margin of the main action, but like Abel Whittle's speech about the death of Henchard in the last chapter, making the grain of the novel suddenly glow – the cadence may point to the inevitable obliterations of time, but there, in the centre, taking the eye, hard and personal, are Susan's 'shining keys'.

All this indicates something of the distinctive rhythm of the novel; but before looking at the resolutions towards which it moves, I would like to examine a chapter which exists almost at the very centre of the novel. I emphasise the word 'chapter' here because it is the rhythm established by that aesthetic unit that I wish to draw attention to. It is Chapter 24 and the subject matter is simply told.

Lucetta, now a lady of means, and Elizabeth-Jane are regarding the affairs of the Casterbridge market-place. From Lucetta's window they can observe the varied activity, and one day they see the arrival of a new seed-drill. Going out into the market-place to satisfy their curiosity, they find its arrival due to Farfrae, who is busy examining and displaying it. Hesitantly, the two women meet Henchard, who is also looking at the machine, and there is a sardonic

exchange about the latest innovation. Both women are made increasingly conscious of their emotional involvements. Elizabeth,
isolated from her father, has a growing sense of Lucetta's fascination
with Farfrae. Lucetta admits as much, and the episode closes with
an oblique attempt on her part to seek Elizabeth's advice.

Even from such a summary as this it is clear that Hardy, in a sure
and economical way, is securing the interpenetration of the public
and private themes of the novel and bringing them into sharp focus,
almost wittily, in Farfrae's singing his romantic song of exile from
inside the new agricultural machine. As he sings about Kitty 'wi' a
braw new gown', we remember that Lucetta is also wearing a new
gown which alone rivalled the machine in colour. New machines,
new London fashions: the complementary development is made.
Lucetta looking at her gown spread out on the bed chooses 'to be
the cherry-coloured person at all hazards' as surely as Mixen Lane
will choose that particular gown to identify her in the skimmity-ride.
These are ironies of a now familiar kind, but what ought to take our
attention in this chapter is not the oscillation of feeling, but a point
of growth, a decisive move forward in the articulation of the novel.

The chapter opens with the phrase 'Poor Elizabeth-Jane', and it
closes with the sentence 'For by the "she" of Lucetta's story
Elizabeth had not been beguiled.' The decisive move in this chapter
lies not in the scene contemplated from the window or in the market-
place, sharp and vivacious as it is, but in Hardy's creation of 'a
contemplative eye' for Elizabeth. He is in the delicate process in this
chapter of merging the authorial consciousness of the veiled narrator
with that of Elizabeth. Hinted parallels between the artist's eye and
Elizabeth's begin to be made. We are told that the market-place
offers itself to the House like a stage for a drama, and when Elizabeth reacts to the new seed-drill it is in a very literary manner. Responding to Farfrae's enthusiasm about its efficiency she says, 'Then
the romance of the sower is gone . . .' and then, more characteristically, 'How things change!' It is worth observing the reactions of
Farfrae and Lucetta to this. Farfrae says, 'But the machines are
already very common in the East and North of England.' And
Lucetta, whose acquaintance with Scripture is, as Hardy says,
'somewhat limited', remarks admiringly and practically, 'Is the

machine yours?' It is a small exchange, but it neatly conveys a new authorial relationship to 'poor Elizabeth-Jane'. This, of course, is given a decisive orientation at the end of the chapter when Elizabeth is asked to respond to Lucetta's carefully contrived story of her past. She has no difficulty in interpreting its true meaning. Interpreting, but not condemning, this provides her initiation into sympathetic detachment, beginning paradoxically with her own increasing emotional involvement with Lucetta and with Farfrae. And in that paradox Elizabeth is revealing herself not simply as a companion for Lucetta, but as a companion for Hardy too. In Chapter 24 we have a decisive step in her education: she is to learn the distinction between the fictive world and the real one, Newson's daughter, not Henchard's.

The full importance of Elizabeth's role, which begins to appear in this chapter, becomes quite clear in the final chapters of the novel. Hardy is going to need her 'quiet eye' less in the dramatic unfolding of the tale – though she has her small part to play here too – than as a way of enabling us to understand its resolution. It is a resolution which will involve the most dramatic nuancing of 'the series of seemings', and which will incorporate the developed consciousness of Elizabeth-Jane as part of its meaning.

The last two chapters stand in the same dramatic relationship to the novel as the first two. The main action is completed and the centre of our attention is Henchard – once more a wayfarer and a hay-trusser. 'He could not help thinking of Elizabeth' – that is the dominant mood of the penultimate chapter, everything else takes its bearings from that. But first Henchard must encounter his past again. He returns to the hill at Weydon-Priors where the furmity tent had stood twenty-five years previously, 'Here we went in, and here we sat down'. With absorbed intentness he recreates the scene of his crime and the authorial voice lends him support: 'And thus Henchard found himself again on the precise standing which he had occupied a quarter of a century earlier. Externally there was nothing to hinder his making another start on the upward slope. . . .' But it is too late in the day for that. Haunted by thoughts of Elizabeth in Casterbridge, he hears that arrangements have been made for her wedding to Farfrae, and he resolves to return for the occasion.

Delaying his arrival until the festivities are well under way, he makes himself known at the house, after unobtrusively leaving his gift in the garden – a caged goldfinch. It is the first time he has met Elizabeth since she discovered that Henchard had delayed Newson's return to her. Face to face now, he seeks forgiveness, but she rejects him, and without any further defence of his conduct he bids her a final farewell and goes out into the night.

It is interesting to recall that it was this chapter which Hardy decided to omit from the first edition of the novel, fearing that Henchard's return to Elizabeth would weaken the final effect of the tragedy. Hardy was prevailed upon to restore the chapter, and this was done for the 1895 edition. And rightly, because its inclusion gives the emphasis to two essential elements in the conclusion of the novel. The first is the force given to Henchard's isolation from the community, not simply by a kind of muted withdrawal, but by rejection. The second is the creation of a reverse effect. Elizabeth's life with Farfrae is, we must feel assured, to be one of happiness. Whatever happens to Henchard that relationship will prosper in its own quiet way. And so we find the chapter reaching out towards that balance of contraries so characteristic of the novel as a whole. And reaching out in a way that quite naturally will employ the rhetoric which conveys a classical ending to an archetypal story – the marriage and wedding feast on the one hand, the exclusion of the disruptive force on the other.

But Hardy distrusts this kind of finality, this confident distribution of sympathy. And so in his final chapter Hardy is concerned to de-individualise his novel, to distance its themes. There is a moment in the penultimate chapter where we can see the kind of temptation which hovered over the ending, a temptation to go for emotional 'bravura'. Henchard's wedding gift to Elizabeth, the caged goldfinch, remains an unfocused poignancy – the size of the gesture concealing its imprecision, so that if it is meant as some kind of symbolic expression about Henchard's fate, we remain uneasy as to whether the expression is Henchard's or Hardy's. I draw attention to the goldfinch only to show how sure Hardy's touch is in the remainder of the last chapter, where there is no forced symbolism of any kind, nothing mawkish in a situation where that tone is difficult to resist. And, when we consider that the chapter is written from the vantage point of a worried and remorseful daughter, the achievement becomes all the more remarkable.

It is the discovery of the bird-cage which sets Elizabeth and Farfrae off to look for Henchard. If it is Casterbridge and the wedding feast which set the mood for the preceding chapter, so now, in the last chapter, it is the heath and an isolated hut which 'of humble dwellings was surely the humblest'. Henchard has returned to a tract of land 'whose surface never had been stirred to a finger's depth, save by the scratching of rabbits, since brushed by the feet of the earliest tribes.' In this sense everything is to be stripped to essentials, the world which is to be seen by the travellers is a moral landscape as well as a natural one, and we are moved to see, in Wordsworth's phrase, into 'the life of things'. Characteristically, on this bedrock of human experience, Hardy continues his contraries.

The perspective the Heath offers is one of timeless change, the endless ebb and flow of human existence, stretching back to a limitless past, forward to a limitless future. At the centre, two wayfarers pursue a difficult search. The scene offers itself irresistibly as an image of our terrestrial condition. Then, suddenly, casually, a figure appears, Abel Whittle, whose only role in the novel so far has been to provide the first occasion when Henchard and Farfrae clashed. And now – like Mother Cuxom on the death of Susan – it is this marginal figure who is chosen to express, in one of the most moving passages of the novel, the contrary perspective to that proffered by the Heath. Comparison has sometimes been made between Whittle's role here and that of the Fool in *King Lear*. Like the larger comparison, the smaller is wide of the mark. The Fool proffers 'wisdom', a self-conscious commentary on Lear's plight. Whittle offers the purest form of human gesture, the instinctual made sublime by its disinterestedness, 'ye wer kind-like to mother if ye were rough to me, and I would fain be kind-like to you.' It is 'love thy neighbour as thyself', presented with total dramatic simplicity and conviction. It is the felicity of 'kind-like' with all its overtures of kinship and kindred, that demands, in Hardy's eyes, no less recognition as part of our terrestrial condition than the humbling perspectives suggested by the Heath. In Henchard's Will we find the confluence of these views.

There is the wish for annihilation in death, 'that no man remember me'; there is also the unshakable belief in the personal rightness of the testimony, 'To this I put my name – Michael Henchard', just as twenty-five years before, 'Dropping his head upon the clamped book which lay on the Communion-table, he said aloud – "I, Michael Henchard, . . ." '. It is a perspective which resists challenge and remains untouched by irony, Hardy's sense of 'a man of character'.

For Henchard life has been tragic, but never at any time has it lost dignity and it is this which Elizabeth responds to when she comes finally to mediate this experience for us. The Heath, Abel Whittle – the contraries caught here are too intense for the ebb and flow of ordinary lives. It is 'the ordinary' Elizabeth offers. When she responds to Henchard's Will it is not to the prescriptions, but to the knowledge that 'the man who wrote them meant what he said . . . (they) were not to be tampered with to give herself a mournful pleasure, or her husband credit for large-heartedness.' She disclaims 'mournful pleasures', and with Henchard's life now behind her she is given full liberty to reflect. It is a reflection which attempts to render continual justice to the contraries of existence, to the series of seemings, as these make themselves felt in the last, and much misunderstood, sentence of the novel:

> And in being forced to class herself among the fortunate she did not cease to wonder at the persistence of the unforeseen, when the one to whom such unbroken tranquillity had been accorded in the adult stage was she whose youth had seemed to teach that happiness was but the occasional episode in a general drama of pain.

How often the final phrase has been wrenched from its context and made to do duty for a view not only of this novel, but of the general tenor of Hardy's fiction. 'The persistence of the unforeseen', it is this phrase which mobilises the paragraph, keeps the contraries open, and is as resistant to a view of life as 'a general drama of pain' as it is to one of 'unbroken tranquillity'. Elizabeth's eye – and Hardy's too – is on the wonder of change here, on flux and reflux, putting her youth beside her 'adult stage', not intent on finding in those phases prescriptions for life in general. It is not simply the unseen that keeps us alert to such change, but its *persistence*: it is this which becomes part of the fabric of everyday living. At times, Henchard had tried to separate out the unseen from that fabric and to live by it, and the past and the future devoured his present; at times, Farfrae was so totally absorbed by the fabric that being out on the heath was being 'reduced', and staying overnight there a matter of making 'a hole in a sovereign'. Elizabeth, like Thomasin in *The Return of the Native*, accepts the Heath, and the drama it has witnessed, calmly, and for what it is, neither an implacable force nor a backdrop to man's desires.

♣ III ♣

If at the end of *The Mayor of Casterbridge* Elizabeth leaves us thinking about the relation of past to present, we are taken back to consider an issue which I considered at the beginning of this chapter, Hardy's sense of man-in-history, and the way in which this is present in *The Mayor of Casterbridge*.

The Preface which Hardy wrote for the 1895 edition reminds us directly of this:

> The incidents narrated arise mainly out of three events, which chanced to range themselves in the order and at or about the intervals of time here given, in the real history of the town called Casterbridge. . . . They were the sale of a wife by her husband, the uncertain harvests which immediately preceded the repeal of the Corn Laws, and the visit of a Royal Personage to the aforesaid part of England.

Of these, the first and third have little literary-critical interest, though as always it is interesting to watch Hardy, particularly in the case of the wife-sale, feel the necessity of validating its inclusion by reference to factual circumstances. He would appear to have come across several instances in the pages of the *Dorset County Chronicle*, which he began to read in 1884 in preparation for his novel.[1] Beginning with the issues of January 1826, he read through the files in a systematic way as far as late 1829 or early 1830. In the course of this reading he discovered no less than three instances of wife-selling, one of the most relevant of which reads:

[1] See Michael Millgate, *Thomas Hardy: His Career as a Novelist*, pp. 237–43.

Selling Wife: At Buckland, nr. Frome, a labring (sic) man named
   Charles Pearce sold wife to shoemaker named Elton for £5 and
   delivered her in a halter in the public street. She seemed very
   willing. Bells rang.

It is an incident which Hardy's love of the factually bizarre would find
highly congenial, but it was a remarkable sense of confidence that
allowed him to open the novel with this incident, and give it the
tragic, as distinct from the merely bizarre, resonance which he
needed.

   The appearance of the Royal Personage sits very lightly to
Hardy's main interests in the novel. It would seem almost certain
that the reference was to Prince Albert who passed through Dorchester in July 1849 on his way to Weymouth to lay the foundation
stone of Portland Breakwater. The incident obviously provided
Hardy with an opportunity for parodying pomp and circumstance,
and, more to his interest, for showing the blight that ran throughout Casterbridge, so that the preparations being made in the Council
Chamber for the Royal visit occur simultaneously with the preparations being made in Mixen Lane for the skimmity-ride. But this
kind of social satire engages Hardy's attention only lightly, and it is
difficult not to regard the whole episode as one of those which he felt
had been forced upon him by the constant demand made by the
serial form for continuous plotting.

   The third factor which Hardy draws attention to in his Preface,
the repeal of the Corn Laws, is very different in importance. Indeed,
it has an importance which has influenced the way the novel, as a
whole, has been read. It shapes, for instance, the kind of reading
which Douglas Brown offers in his perceptive study of Hardy:[1]

The Mayor of Casterbridge, then, is the tale of the struggle between the native countryman and the alien invader; of the defeat
of dull courage and traditional attitudes by insight, craft and the
vicissitudes of nature; and of the persistence through that defeat
of some deep layer of vitality in the country protagonist. . . . *The
Mayor of Casterbridge* turns on the situation that led to the repeal
of the Corn Laws. The consequences of that repeal to Victorian

[1] Brown, *Thomas Hardy*, pp. 65–6, 70.

agricultural life are the centre of this book, provide the impulse that makes it what it is.

'The native countryman', 'the alien invader' – this is the kind of polarity that a concentration on the phrase 'the repeal of the Corn Laws' can lead to, so that Brown can go on to say that the consequences of the repeal are 'the centre of the book'. But, as Hardy's Preface makes clear, he is not talking about the repeal of the Corn Laws as such; his emphasis is on 'the uncertain harvests which immediately preceded their repeal', and his emphasis will not really encourage a reading of the novel which sees it in terms of a polarising conflict between 'the native countryman' and 'the alien invader'.

If we look at 'the native countryman' we find a good deal that is less flattering than 'dull courage'; he is tetchy, grasping, superstitious, and indifferent to any consequences beyond the immediate present. If we look at 'the alien invader' we find that, so far from invading the community, he actually joins it (a point which Brown concedes in a later account of the novel without, however, feeling that this calls for an overall revision of his general reading),[1] and indeed Farfrae goes on to give it whatever prosperity it can obtain. If we are concerned with the Corn Laws at all directly in this novel then, as J. C. Maxwell has pointed out, Hardy is going out of his way, in his remark about 'the uncertain harvests', to indicate that he is choosing 'the *latest* period at which the uncushioned dominance of price fluctuations depending on the home harvest ... still persisted'.[2] In other words, far from presenting an innocent agrarian economy undermined by new grasping business methods, Hardy shows in Henchard (if we really want to talk in these terms) the last of the old profiteers, existing by courtesy of a closed system of economic protection. With the repeal of the Corn Laws, the local weather ceased to exert its tyranny on the market, and Farfrae certainly began to prosper by 'canny moderation'; but as Maxwell remarks, it is really Henchard's colleagues who are 'the lineal descendents of Shakespeare's farmer who hanged himself on the expectation of plenty'.[3]

[1] Brown, *The Mayor of Casterbridge*, p. 31.
[2] 'The Sociological Approach to *The Mayor of Casterbridge*' in *Imagined Worlds: Essays in Honour of John Butt*, ed. Maynard Mack and Ian Gregor, p. 232.   [3] Maxwell, p. 231.

Clearly, it would be absurd to read the novel in such a way as to make it an indictment of Henchard and a vindication of Farfrae. I have put the counter-case simply to show that when concentration is made too directly on the historical implications of the novel, so that we see a precise agricultural crisis constituting its 'centre', then the move takes us further and further away from its imaginative life.

The sense in which history is deeply meaningful in *The Mayor of Casterbridge* can be suggested, I think, by looking at a passage which captures with some of the intensity of his lyric poetry a basic apprehension about the passage of time. Elizabeth has been sitting up through the night looking after her mother who is dying:

> the silence in Casterbridge – barring the rare sound of the watchman – was broken in Elizabeth's ear only by the time-piece in the bedroom ticking frantically against the clock on the stairs; ticking harder and harder till it seemed to clang like a gong; and all this while the subtle-souled girl asking herself why she was born, why sitting in a room, and blinking at the candle; why things around her had taken the shape they wore in preference to every other possible shape. Why they stared at her so helplessly, as if waiting for the touch of some wand that should release them from terrestrial constraint; what that chaos called consciousness, which spun in her at this moment like a top, tended to, and began in. Her eyes fell together; she was awake, yet she was asleep.

That is a moment of imaginative distillation in the novel. 'The subtle-souled girl' has little reality for us; it is rather the author caught reflecting on the nature of the imagination itself. Elizabeth is caught suspended between two levels of reality, so that she becomes the subject and object of her own perceptions. Withdrawing from the particularities of the scene about her, the girl knows a moment of heightened consciousness, but the intensity brings with it its own chaos, and then it subsides into the forgetfulness of sleep. The paragraph links time with consciousness, and that link is built into the very shape the novel takes.

'What is your history?', the question Lucetta puts to Elizabeth, is a question which Hardy puts to the reader, puts to himself, and puts to his characters. The way in which it is put to the reader is to be found in the opening paragraph of the Preface:

Readers of the following story who have not yet arrived at middle age are asked to bear in mind that, in the days recalled by the tale, the home Corn Trade, on which so much of the action turns, had an importance that can hardly be realized by those accustomed to the sixpenny loaf of the present date, and to the present indifference of the public to harvest weather.

'The days recalled . . . the present date', the whole novel was coloured by that interplay for Hardy's readers and it gave depth to its meaning. With time's lengthening perspective *The Mayor of Casterbridge* takes its place as a Hardy novel of the mid 1880s, but we should remember that for Hardy and his readers this was 'a historical novel' about the 1840s, and more briefly, about the 1820s. We get something of the effect if we imagine ourselves reading in the 1970s a story set in the 1930s, whose opening lies in the years immediately preceding the First World War. It is the layering of time, the years between, that help to create the perspective within which we read, and extend the novelist's meaning. By the 1880s readers really *are* aware of the consequences of the repeal of the Corn Laws, the agricultural depression created by the importation of wheat from across the Atlantic really has affected the domestic market, and Farfrae's career for good or for ill can already be thought of as completed. But this is not a perspective which is sardonic. Hardy's eye, like Elizabeth's at the end of the novel, is on change, on flux and reflux; it is that idea that the dates are there to suggest, rather than any particular events with which they might be associated. Thus, the question 'What is your history?' has a personal significance, as well as a public one. The author, in recalling the Dorchester of the 1840s, is recalling the period of his own boyhood, and the novel is as much concerned with recapturing the feeling of that period, as it is with charting social and economic change. Hence – we might go on to say – the deliberate blur that Hardy creates over a precise chronological scheme.

Implicit in memory for Hardy is tension, the inevitable tension between past and present; and this applies not only to the reader's experience of the novel and to the author's experience of writing it but also to the characters within it – most noticeably of course, to Henchard. Here again we have a history which is both public and private. It is public in the clash of interests between Henchard and Farfrae, a clash suitably described by the townspeople when they say of Henchard that 'His accounts were like a bramblewood when Mr. Farfrae came. He used to reckon his sacks by chalk strokes all in a row like garden-palings, measure his ricks by stretching with his arms, weigh his trusses by a lift, judge his hay by a chaw, and settle the price with a curse. But now this accomplished young man does it all by ciphering and mensuration.' That is the notion of change which belongs to the public history of the nineteenth century.

But the notion of history has for Henchard another, more urgent aspect. Henchard is looking at his daughter asleep: 'He steadfastly regarded her features. . . . In sleep there come to the surface buried genealogical facts, ancestral curves, dead men's traits, which the mobility of daytime animation screens and overwhelms. . . . He could not endure the sight of her and hastened away.' It is the hunger of a father for a child which he wants to claim as his own. Henchard's feeling for Elizabeth moves from that moment of anger when Susan takes her away, 'She'd no business to take the maid – 'tis my maid,' to that moment of renunciation when he leaves her to Farfrae and goes to make his Will. That is a moment which could find suitable expression in lines from Eliot's 'Marina', even though the mood which prompts them is very different:

> This form, this face, this life
> Living to live in a world of time beyond me; let me
> Resign my life for this life . . .

This is a longing inseparable from the needs of the human heart and such a coming to terms with change constitutes, for Hardy, a profound wisdom.

As we ponder this sense of a public and a private history we become aware that the particular tension which this novel describes works to keep them distinct from one another. On the one side, there is the element of 'work', on the other, the element of 'love'. What is absent is that sense of interrelatedness presented most clearly in sexual relationships. There is passion in *The Mayor of Casterbridge*, but it is the passion of individual assertion, a passion which finds an appropriate epigraph in the phrase 'A Man and his

History'. It is precisely this element of human relatedness which is to preoccupy Hardy in the remainder of the Wessex novels, and from *The Woodlanders* onwards sexual and economic possession will be seen as different aspects of a common process, so that in *Tess of the D'Urbervilles*, Hardy will find a history which is neither public nor private, but both, in the human body itself.

5
The Great Web
The Woodlanders (1887)

No matter on what terms we leave *The Mayor of Casterbridge*, it is difficult not to feel a reasonableness in the claim that the novel has an epic quality about it. We may, in using that description, intend a variety of things – the authority with which Henchard dominates the reader's imagination, the scope and implications of his conflict with Farfrae, the compelling bleakness of his death – but whatever reason we offer, we would find it hard to dissent from the proposition that the novel makes a claim to deal with tragedy on the grand scale, and whether or not it succeeds in making good that claim, we are not puzzled as to why it should have been made. When, however, we find a similar claim being made by Hardy's next novel, *The Woodlanders*, then I think we must feel much less sure.

The claim is made early in the first chapter, when the narrator moves outside his tale and offers a description of its scope. It is to be a novel which is set in one of those 'sequestered spots outside the gates of the world', but where, nevertheless, 'dramas of a grandeur and unity truly Sophoclean are enacted in the real, by virtue of the concentrated passions and closely-knit interdependence of the lives therein'. Even if we consent not to lean too hard upon the word 'Sophoclean', 'dramas of grandeur and unity' seems overpitched for the novel which follows. Reference to Greek tragedy inevitably makes us think of a central figure grandly conceived with a theme to match, but in *The Woodlanders*, most strikingly of all Hardy's major novels, we find such a figure quite absent. The mood of the novel seems elegaic, rather than heroic, and though we may be moved by its low-keyed pathos, we would seem far away from the mood which produced *Oedipus* and *Antigone*.

If I raise the matter in this way it is not in a pedantic spirit, trying to keep the record of literary lineage clear, but rather as a way of indicating a crucial difference between *The Mayor* and *The Woodlanders*. It is a difference which marks out a new phase in Hardy's development as a novelist, but it is a development which, at first sight, looks like a loss of power, and it is not hard to see how that loss might be described.

Starting from the absence of a central and dominating figure, an unsympathetic account of the novel would go on to argue that Hardy barely justifies such a dangerous dispersal of his interest. Grace and Melbury come through as static and idealised creations, Grace as frivolous and petty in her interests, Melbury as a well-meaning but naïvely snobbish father, Mrs. Charmond and Fitzpiers as the stereotypes of rakish and self-regarding outsiders who first destroy others only to go on and destroy themselves. It is only in Melbury's case, the account might continue, that we have any sense of a deeply felt personal conflict which makes us feel that the character is 'alive' – alive to the author and to his readers. The setting of the novel, as both woodland and orchard, has an undeniable presence, but it is hardly a dramatic presence like Egdon or like Casterbridge, an inseparable part of the action of the novel; it is there as a mood, and it reminds us more that Hardy was a poet than that he was a novelist. Presumably, such an unsympathetic account would go on to indicate certain failures in plotting, such as the lightning exits and entrances of the 'South Carolina gentleman of very passionate nature', and what might be thought of as the near-farce of Giles lying fatally ill outside his own hut for days on end for fear of offending Grace's sense of propriety. Of course, even such an account of the novel would not feel prevented from conceding a measurement of achievement, and this would almost certainly include, in addition to the rather ambiguous praise of 'the setting', the striking reality that is given to work – as always in Hardy – and the impressive incarnation of that sense in the stoical figure of Marty South. But these, the critic would probably argue, are moments in a novel which, in terms of its total movement and structure, fails to convince, the more so if we have just finished reading *The Mayor*, which immediately preceded it.

If I begin my discussion of *The Woodlanders* by sketching in an unfavourable reaction to the novel, this is not because I see my own account in terms of a counter-case. Indeed in the assumptions which my putative account makes – that the characters should have a strongly defined inner life and a plot to articulate that life – the case is persuasive. What I want to argue is that if *The Woodlanders* strikes us as a better novel than my 'sketch' suggests, this is because it is a different kind of novel to *The Mayor*, aiming at a different kind of unity, even if we freely concede it is not Sophoclean. It emerges from a significantly different set of interests, interests which have been in Hardy's mind for some years, but are now related to a shift in his views about the nature of fiction. To talk of Hardy 'shifting his views' is always hazardous, because the expression of these views as they occur in the *Life* is invariably random, and the chronology dubious. But to say the least, we can indicate from the entries in the *Life* for the years 1885–7, during the time he was at work on *The Woodlanders*, an unusual degree of self-awareness about the relationship between fiction and reality, and this casts light on what he was attempting to do in that novel.

It would seem that the idea for a novel, at least resembling *The Woodlanders*, came to Hardy in the mid 1870s, and came to him presumably very much in the pastoral terms of *Under the Greenwood Tree*. For various reasons the project was shelved, or, more accurately, allowed to remain dormant in his mind. During the next ten years Hardy's attention was absorbed in writing two major novels, *The Return of the Native*, and *The Mayor of Casterbridge*. In the first of these, I have tried to show, he became concerned with self-estrangement, as it expressed itself in a dialectic between the impersonality and timelessness of the Heath and the individual history of the Yeobrights. In the second, *The Mayor of Casterbridge*, the perspective was significantly altered. A single character dominated the novel, a character who already belonged to history, and this released in the novel a dialectic, not between the timeless opposites of man and nature, but within a precise crisis in the history of south-west England in the 1840s. In that crisis Hardy found an archetypal dimension. When Hardy returned to *The Woodlanders* in the mid 1880s he had then behind him *The Return of the Native*, and *The Mayor*, and though the 'issues' with which those novels deal exist more as tendencies, pre-occupations, they are nevertheless distinctly present, and when they become operative within the simple pastoral framework of the early version of 'my woodland novel', we get the distinctive character of *The Woodlanders* as we now know it. 'Looking back' – that is a phrase which summons up the mood of the novel – and Hardy is encouraged to take that stance both from the point of view of the pastoral form itself, with its built-in distinction between the sophistication of the narrator and the simplicity of the material, and also from the point of view of his own development as a novelist, at work on a novel conceived at a much earlier stage in his career. Recollection, the remembrance of things past, a concern to render a consciousness increasingly susceptible to the tensions of the present, these elements give the peculiar colour to *The Woodlanders*. The role of 'place' in *The Return of the Native*, of 'character' in *The Mayor*, is now occupied by 'time', and it is this which enables us to get rather different bearings on the novel from those suggested in my preliminary sketch. All Hardy's novels are concerned in one way or another with 'time', but *The Woodlanders* is marked out from the others by the detachment of its narration, and in that detachment we find implied a dimension of time which is peculiar to that novel, enabling us to see the particular details I singled out earlier for unsympathetic attention, but to see them now at one remove.

On 17 November 1885 we find Hardy recording in his diary, 'Have gone back to my original plot for *The Woodlanders* after all', and from then, until 4 February 1887, he is at work on the novel. To read through the entries in the *Life* for that period is to find a remarkable consistency in his remarks on art and reality; I begin with an entry which contains a less abstract reflection:

> *2 January 1886*: Cold weather brings out upon the faces of people the written marks of their habits, vices, passions, and memories, as warmth brings out on paper a writing in sympathetic ink.[1]
> *3 January*: My art is to intensify the expression of things . . . so that the heart and inner meaning is made vividly visible.[2]
> *4 March*: Novel-writing as an art cannot go backward. Having reached the analytic stage it must transcend it by going still further in the same direction.[3]
> The human race to be shown as one great network or tissue which quivers in every part when one point is shaken, like a spider's web if touched.[4]

[1-4] *Life*, p. 177.

In December he records with approval a visit to an Impressionist Exhibition in London. The diary continues:

> *January 1887*: I don't want to see landscapes, i.e., scenic paintings of them, because I don't want to see the original realities – as optical effects, that is. I want to see the deeper reality under-lying the scenic, the expression of what are sometimes called abstract imaginings.
>
> The 'simply natural' is interesting no longer. The much decried, mad, late-Turner rendering is now necessary to create my interest. The exact truth as to material fact ceases to be of importance in art . . . when it does not bring anything to the object that coalesces with and translates the qualities that are already there, – half-hidden, it may be – and the two united are depicted as the All.[1]
>
> *4 February, 8.20 p.m.*: 'Finished *The Woodlanders*. Thought I should feel glad, but I do not particularly, – though relieved.' In after years he often said that in some respects *The Wood-landers* was his best novel.[2]

'The deeper reality underlying the scenic' for the painter, 'the transcending of the analytic' for the novelist, the language may be vague and awkward, but the drift is clear, the rendering of a con-sciousness which both observes the natural world and is itself an in-escapable part of all that it contemplates. This going beyond the analytic is for Hardy a fresh awareness of the recording conscious-ness, a consciousness interlocked with the different levels of con-sciousness in nature itself. This is the kind of 'grandeur and unity' he is now seeking. As J. Hillis Miller puts it, 'The landscape, the past, language, art; facts old and new, men and women in their living together – these for [Hardy] form a complicated structure of interpenetrating realities, a dynamic field of tensions and interactions both spatial and temporal.'[3] This, of course, has always been present in his work, but what gives it special prominence in *The Wood-landers* is that it moves from being an implication of his fictional world constituting its subject. It is a movement initiated by a

---

[1] *Life*, p. 185.
[2] *Life*, p. 185.
[3] J. Hillis Miller, *Thomas Hardy: Distance and Desire*, p. 110.

heightened sense of the narrator's presence, so that at the beginning of the tale, it is *his* consciousness we are taken into.

Dramatised as a rambler pursuing a deserted coach-road, 'for old association's sake', the narrator ponders the distinction between the empty highway and the empty woodlands which border it:

> The physiognomy of a deserted highway expresses solitude to a degree that is not reached by mere dales or downs, and bespeaks a tomb-like stillness more emphatic than that of glades and pools. The contrast of what is with what might be, probably accounts for this. To step, for instance, at the place under notice, from the edge of the plantation into the adjoining thoroughfare, and pause amid its emptiness for a moment, was to exchange by the act of a single stride the simple absence of human companionship for an incubus of the forlorn.

That distinction between solitude and loneliness is one that is to play a considerable part in the novel. It is a distinction which turns on memory: the wood lives because of 'old associations', the highway only when it is being actively used, somewhere to go to, not merely come from. We can see that distinction at work both in the lives of the characters and in the narrator who reveals those lives. There is the community of Little Hintock sustained by memory and its routine of work, but it is a community which can no longer cohere; in the sense that it is vulnerable to forces beyond its control, it is devoured by its isolation. The narrator too, is able to weave his tale out of old association, summon up memory, but it is a tale which derives its pathos and power from the dissolution of those memories, the growing necessity of recognising a world elsewhere. At one point Marty and Giles are seen in terms which reveal a continuity of related perspectives; we see the characters in relation to each other, the narrator in relation to his characters, the reader in relation to the narrator. It is a moment which distils the mood of the novel and suggests why, in this novel, the individual character and the individual plot are there to serve a wider purpose:

> Hardly anything could be more isolated or more self-contained than the lives of these two walking here in the lonely hour before day, when grey shades, material and mental, are so very grey.

And yet their lonely courses formed no detached design at all, but were part of the pattern in the great web of human doings then weaving in both hemispheres from the White Sea to Cape Horn.

'The great web', the phrase describes the manner and the matter of the novel which follows it, and initiates a pondered meditation on that barely veiled antithesis, 'Hardly anything could be more isolated or more self-contained . . .'.

If this account of the mood and structure of *The Woodlanders* be allowed, then it will follow that such a mood and structure can only be apprehended obliquely, when indeed the whole pattern of human doings is complete. To sense the web, we have to forget it – at least for a time. We might, in fact, begin outside the novel altogether with that singularly graceless sentence with which Hardy opens his Preface:

In the present novel, as in one or two others of this series which involve the question of matrimonial divergence, the immortal puzzle – given the man and woman, how to find a basis for their sexual relation – is left where it stood . . .

It is an odd sentence, odd in tone as well as substance, as if Hardy wished to draw attention to an issue which might escape the reader's notice and then felt absolved from pursuing it. Finding a basis for sexual relationships is more likely to bring twentieth-century writers to mind than Hardy's contemporaries, and indeed there is one major work of the twentieth century which does, I think, cast considerable light on Hardy's concerns in *The Woodlanders*, and that is Eliot's *The Waste Land*. Like that poem, Hardy's novel is concerned with sterility, a sterility which can be imaged in terms which are at once personal, communal, and located within nature itself; it is to preoccupy itself with calculatedly juxtaposing past and present; it creates a context in which incidents suggestive of mythic ritual can be accommodated with those of daily living; above all, it allows a voice to be heard from time to time of one who, like Tiresias, has foresuffered all.

There is in *The Woodlanders* the sterility of self-abnegation – an abnegation which can never be confined to the self but is common

145

to the whole way of life. This finds its clearest expression in the characters of Marty and Giles. It is however a sterility of a very particular kind, and to get the sense of it, we can turn to that famous passage, celebrating their work in the woods:

> Marty South alone, of all the women in Hintock and the world, had approximated to Winterborne's level of intelligent inter-course with Nature. In that respect she had formed his true complement in the other sex, had lived as his counterpart, had subjoined her thoughts to his as a corollary.
>
> The casual glimpses which the ordinary population bestowed upon that wondrous world of sap and leaves called the Hintock woods had been with these two, Giles and Marty, a clear gaze. They had been possessed of its finer mysteries as of common-place knowledge; had been able to read its hieroglyphs as ordinary writing. . . . They had planted together, and together they had felled; together they had, with the run of the years, mentally collected those remoter signs and symbols which seen in few were of runic obscurity, but all together made an alphabet.

The eloquence of the writing, the plangency of its rhythms, pays simple testimony to the value being accorded to such 'intelligent intercourse' with nature. The adjective can be pondered, the sexual intimacy finding its complement in a rational acknowledgement, which appropriately seeks its expression in language. Marty and Gildes find in their 'reading' of Nature a bond which defies their own relationship, a relationship expressed in the rhythms of work that is shared: 'They had planted together, and together they had felled.' That sense of mutuality, so removed from the area of 'personal re-lationships', is splendidly evoked and gives memorable extension to the significance of 'work' for Hardy, so that it becomes not only, as in *The Mayor*, a process of learning, but a process of feeling too. But there is a price to be paid for such a feeling too exclusively pur-sued and Hardy does not hesitate in naming it:

> 'He ought to have married *you*, Marty, and nobody else in the world!' said Grace with conviction. . . . Marty shook her head. 'In all our outdoor days and years together ma'am,' she replied, 'the one thing he never spoke of to me was love; nor I to him.'
>
> 'Yet you and he could speak in a tongue that nobody else could

know – not even my father, though he came nearest knowing – the tongue of the trees and fruits and flowers themselves.'

'The tongue of the trees and fruits and flowers', Grace's sentimental translation of Nature's 'alphabet', does not conceal Hardy's sharp point within it, that 'intercourse' with Nature, however intelligent, is not to be equated with the intelligent intercourse of man with man, or man with woman, if such discourse is to include love. If there is shared feeling between Marty and Giles, it is a feeling which can blanket out the individuals, so that Marty becomes mute in the presence of someone she can only feel her superior, and Giles can become oblivious of her womanhood. The clarity of gaze they extend upon Nature is a blur when they gaze upon each other. Language deserts Marty when she tries to communicate with Giles, and gesture becomes her only expression.

Her most memorable gestures are her refusal of the barber's offer to cut her hair, and then, on finding Giles's interest lies elsewhere her acceptance of it. Like the woman in *The Waste Land*:

> Under the firelight, under the brush, her hair
> Spread out in fiery points
> Glowed into words, then would be savagely still.

The fierce assertion of her sexuality in Marty's refusal, 'My hair's my own and I'm going to keep it', is followed by the ruthless self-mutilation, her plundering of her self-hood, as surely as Alec is to plunder Tess's. The hair lies 'savagely still' 'upon the pale scrubbed deal of the coffin-stool table . . . stretched like waving and ropy weeds . . .'. The gesture for Marty is to be a final one, so that after Giles's death, she looked 'almost like a being who had rejected with indifference the attribute of sex'. 'The wondrous world of sap and leaves' which Marty and Giles share as their common element will not hide the private desert between them.

'Why, Marty – whatever has happened to your head?' . . .
  Her heart swelled, and she could not speak. At length she managed to groan, looking on the ground, 'I've made myself ugly – and hateful – that's what I've done!'
  'No, no,' he answered. 'You've only cut your hair – I see now.'

'I see now', the irony quivers throughout the novel.

If despairing gesture is the only language that seems available for Marty as she seeks to communicate with Giles, so he, in his turn, is forced into such a gesture in his communications with Grace, and like Marty, he seeks an extinction in work. The first of these gestures is quite literal. Grace has come to tell Giles that her father feels that they should no longer marry and that she concurs in his decision. She finds Giles at work one misty day chopping down the branches of John South's tree:

> While she stood out of observation Giles seemed to recognize her meaning; with a sudden start he worked on, climbing higher into the sky, and cutting himself off more and more from all inter-course with the sublunary world.

Eventually, he disappears from view, and Grace calls out the news to him from below. At the top of the tree Giles sat 'motionless and silent in that gloomy Niflheim or fogland which involved him, and she proceeded on her way'. It is the companion portrait to Marty's contemplating Giles's grave. The self-enclosure is complete and the only communication between Grace and Giles is that of her disembodied voice coming out of the mist and the sound of his axe in reply. It is a poignant demonstration of the void between them.

It is a void which is not filled by the removal of Fitzpiers from Grace's life, even though there is a renewed sense of hope. The difference between Grace and Giles is not as Hardy sees it a simple matter which could have been overcome by a more generous interpretation of the divorce laws. What separates them is a difference of consciousness, that 'magic web', which Walter Pater describes, 'woven through and through us . . . penetrating us with a network, subtler than our subtlest nerves, yet bearing in it the central forces of the world'.[1] Theirs is the crisis of a community as much as the crisis of individuals. The mist that screens Giles from Grace is always present, as surely as the mist that screens Marty from Giles. He sees her as an ethereal being, an alien to Little Hintock, and her remoteness sustains his fascination. He feeds on her inaccessibility. For Grace, too, Giles has no human solidity; he is seen

[1] Walter Pater, 'Winckelmann', *The Renaissance*, p. 231.

148

either simply in terms of his work, or as a human distillation of nature, 'autumn's brother'.

It is considerations like these which lie behind that strange scene in the woods when Giles, already ill, sleeps outside his own cottage for several days rather than compromise Grace by sharing it. In the account of *The Woodlanders* which I sketched in at the beginning of this chapter, I referred to the scene as 'near-farce', and if that was felt too hostile, we could alter the tone, but retain the point, by saying that it strains our credulity. And we can find even an acute and sympathetic critic like Irving Howe saying in some exasperation, 'no one, neither man nor dog, should have to be that loyal.'[1]

It is not difficult to see why the scene should provoke these re-actions, but I think it is important to see that the irritant is not really 'the scene', but the handling of the scene. There is a precise techni-cal failure here, in that the imaginative purpose is defeated by obdurate detail. We find a similar failure in one of Lawrence's scenes in *Lady Chatterley's Lover*, where Connie, about to go out into the woods for a rhapsodic nude encounter with Mellors, pauses to collect her rubber shoes. Like Lawrence, Hardy is in need of a greater stylisation at this point, the kind of effect he obtains so effortlessly in the scene of Marty's hair, which was 'depicted with intensity and distinctness, while her face, shoulders, hands, and figure in general were a blurred mass'. If Hardy had been able similarly to blur his later scene, we would see more closely that, in fact, the whole episode is an effective expression of the structure of feeling which he has established between Grace and Giles throughout the novel. It is a moral convention, not moral decorum, that Hardy is anxious to put to work in this scene, and a convention which by definition extends beyond the individuals in-volved. From Giles's point of view, such a convention is operative and mandatory, because what has separated Grace from him is a whole area of consciousness, which again and again has found expression in social behaviour, in manners; and if this is a frustra-tion it is also a fascination. Grace lives most intensely for him 'at a distance'. From her point of view, it is convention which has enabled her to feel most sharply her differences from Little Hintock,

---

[1] Irving Howe, *Thomas Hardy*, p. 104.

and those 'differences' have become a part of her being. More radically, with Giles in mind, they have enabled her to draw on his companionship without committing her as a lover, a relationship which instinctually she withdraws from, as his sharing of the hut would have disconcertingly revealed. Added to the proprieties of this is the fact of Giles's illness. This, too, cuts deeply back into the novel, being the result of his indifference to self now that he has lost his house and his girl. That Grace should never think of Giles's being 'ill' is because she never considered him in such physical and individual terms. He is simply there as a fond presence, a wise counsellor, a family friend. Taken as a whole, the scene reveals the blankness that has always existed in the relationship between Giles and Grace – a blankness perpetuated, if not brought about, by social and economic pressures on his side, by psychological pressures on hers. If we feel that something has gone wrong with the scene, the fault lies not in the employment of the moral convention itself – a convention which indeed, as so often in Victorian fiction, enables the novelist a rich registration of elusive truths – but in the rigidity of its handling. The result is that complex shades of feeling are lost beneath a hard veneer of moral scruple, feelings, in particular, which are intimately related to the whole presentation of Grace, as I will try to show a little later in this chapter.

♣ II ♣

If the words that come to us about Marty and Giles have a kindred feeling about them – control, self-effacement, denial, frustration, resignation – those which attach themselves to Mrs. Charmond and Fitzpiers have a similar kinship, though from a rival family. In both cases the characters share a common sense of isolation. The isolation which is present to Marty and Giles finds expression in their absorption in their work; the isolation of Mrs. Charmond and Fitzpiers is in their enclosure within their own fantasies. This receives its most extreme expression in Fitzpiers's analysis of 'love' to Giles, for whom it is the mute worship of 'the other'.

> . . . people living insulated, as I do by the solitude of this place, get charged with emotive fluid like a Leyden jar with electric, for

want of some conductor at hand to disperse it. Human love is a subjective thing . . . I am in love with something in my own head, and no thing-in-itself outside it at all.

The Proust of Little Hintock, Fitzpiers is doomed at the outset, doomed not because of his philandering – though clearly he would have felt at home with Troy and Wildeve – but because he is incapable of feeling the reality of any world outside himself, whether it is the woods or the people who live there. In common with Mrs. Charmond he sees that world as composed of discrete objects, existing for his own purposes, and where he puts down money for Grammer Oliver's brain, she puts it down for Marty's hair. Fitzpiers lives within his own Leyden jar, passively awaiting 'a conductor' to activate him.

Fitzpiers's jar finds its complementary setting within the drawn curtains of Mrs. Charmond's drawing-room, where she sits at midday, with a large fire burning in the grate, 'though it was not cold'. They are obviously kindred spirits, but there are significant differences between them. In our first encounter with Mrs. Charmond we recognise a familiar Hardy character – the wealthy lady of mysterious origin who has surrendered to boredom in her search for life's purpose, 'I think sometimes I was born to live and do nothing, nothing, nothing but float about, as we fancy we do sometimes in dreams.' Idiom, tone, movement, all add up to a description of Mrs. Charmond as 'theatrical' in a way in which Fitzpiers is not, or at the least, apparently not. Where she is indolent, he is restlessly energetic, bored where he is curious, arch where he is passionate. But with both of them we are aware of 'a style', and in this sense Fitzpiers is as 'theatrical' as Mrs. Charmond. Fitzpiers playing the part of the romantic seducer, Mrs. Charmond assuming the disdain of the lady of the manor, the roles are consciously adopted and they complement each other. There is, however, a desperation about the playing of these roles which suggests the fundamental instability of their inner selves. If they both communicate extravagantly, we feel this is because it is the only way they *can* communicate; they are the victims of a devouring restlessness, whether it takes the 'analytic' form of Fitzpiers – 'In the course of a year his mind was accustomed to pass in a grand solar sweep throughout the zodiac of the intellectual heaven' – or the emotional form of Mrs. Charmond, – 'she was losing judgement and dignity . . . becoming an animated impulse only, a passion incarnate'.

Despite her weakness and extravagance, Hardy has a sympathy for Mrs. Charmond which is not present in his treatment of Fitzpiers. Perhaps this is precisely because she feels so much more keenly, and is a natural victim in the way that Lucetta was a victim in *The Mayor of Casterbridge*. Men after all have much more scope in arranging their downfall. Mrs. Charmond feels for Melbury, in her interview with him, in a way quite alien to Fitzpiers, and when she bursts out, 'O! why were we given hungry hearts and wild desires if we have to live in a world like this?' we sense the genuine pang, for all the theatrical bravura of its expression. *A Sentimental Journey* may indeed be the ideal book to accompany Mrs. Charmond on her European travels, but they are travels of keenly felt isolation.

Perhaps the relationship between the two is given its most complete expression in that moment when, following a bitter quarrel, they meet on the roadside, unaware that they are watched by Melbury. Melodrama, sexuality, indifference, fatality, all come together and reveal the opposite pole to Marty and Giles's 'intelligent intercourse with nature':

> They looked in each other's faces without uttering a word, an arch yet gloomy smile wreathing her lips. Fitzpiers clasped her hanging hand, and, while she still remained in the same listless attitude, looking volumes into his eyes, he stealthily unbuttoned her glove, and stripped her hand of it by rolling back the gauntlet over the fingers, so that it came off inside out. He then raised her hand to his mouth, she still reclining passively, watching him as she might have watched a fly upon her dress.

It is a passage symptomatic of a certain aspect of Hardy's prose style, awkward and cliché-ridden for much of its length, but giving none the less a quite startling sense of sexual feeling, none the less vivid for all Fitzpiers's stagey gestures and Mrs. Charmond's indifference. It is a striking passage in that the acuteness of feeling, which is almost palpably present, is not in the least compromised by 'the acting' of the protagonists. Indeed, it only serves to enforce the sense of sexual feeling, so purely expressed that it does nothing to disturb the barren isolation of the people involved. This is a moment which italicises the nature of the relationship between Fitzpiers and Mrs. Charmond in the way that Marty cutting off her hair, Giles lying out in the rain, italicises theirs. All four relationships, so radically different in nature, have in common an acute sense of self-estrangement seeking expression in terms of 'theatrical' gesture. The sterile abnegation of Marty and Giles, the sterile fulfilment of Fitzpiers and Mrs. Charmond – all four characters have complementary roles to play in the novel, so that if we think of them as isolated 'characters', rather than as versions of consciousness taking their substance from a total design, they will offer little to arrest attention. With the two remaining characters, Grace and George Melbury, the situation is very different.

It is useful to approach a consideration of Melbury and Grace with other Hardy characters in mind. To consider Melbury first. We can think of him as an epilogue to Hardy's interest in Henchard, for like him, 'he was of the sort called self-made'. He has risen to prosperity, but he is haunted by a foolish act in his youth and feels that his own future, and that of his family, are bound up with honouring a vow. Unlike Henchard, Melbury has learnt the lesson Farfrae had to teach. He has learnt the nature of social change, the importance of adaptation, and that what was good enough for him is no longer good enough for his daughter. The conflict between Melbury's obligation to the past, in which Grace was promised to the son of his old friend, and his awareness of the future, for which he has sought to provide her with an education which takes her out of the world of Little Hintock, constitutes his dilemma. In Melbury, Henchard and Farfrae resume their debate, with Grace as an Elizabeth-Jane – a prize possession testifying to the work of her father, but also a human being with a destiny of her own.

The point of making these comparisons between Melbury and Henchard is not just that they show the persistence of that character in Hardy's imagination, but that in the difference between the two men we can sense the increasing movement in that imagination towards the embodiment of contemporary consciousness in terms of social institutions. In Clym, this consciousness of change took the form of abstract reflection, in Farfrae of economic awareness. But with Melbury such a consciousness is aware, however dimly, of multiple implications. He can say, in a way that Farfrae might have done, 'learning is better than houses or lands', but it is also already clear to him that learning is the passport to freedom of movement within the class structure, and that a suitable marriage will guarantee it. In this respect, *The Woodlanders* takes us into a much more modern world than anything in the earlier novels. Melbury himself, of course, is only fitfully aware of the implication of his perceptions, and what gives the latter half of his tale its poignancy is that the 'the modern world' invades his life in ways that he could hardly have calculated. Fitzpiers deserts Grace and Melbury has to resort to simple, face-to-face encounters, whether it is appealing to Mrs. Charmond to release Fitzpiers, or going to London in the belief that he can facilitate the working of the new divorce laws. He sees the institutionalising of contemporary consciousness in terms of an educational system, but he sees the process simply as an individual ascent up the rungs of the social ladder. He fails to see that the process has altered the entire social structure. The individual becomes impotent. And so we find Melbury in retreat from that world back into himself, a self which has been severely fractured in a way that Henchard's never is:

> He had entirely lost faith in his own judgement. That judgement on which he had relied for so many years seemed recently, like a false companion unmasked, to have disclosed unexpected depths of hypocrisy and speciousness where all had seemed solidity.

The collapse of his judgement, which had arranged the world for him and made him declare that 'learning is better than houses or lands', has now made even houses and land remote phenomena to him.

> Melbury sat with his hands resting on the familiar knobbed thorn walking-stick, whose growing he had seen before he enjoyed its use. The scene to him was not the material environment of his person, but a tragic vision that travelled with him like an envelope. Through this vision the incidents of the moment but gleamed confusedly here and there, as an outer landscape through the high-coloured scenes of a stained window.

That strange interior numbness, 'when we are frozen up within, and quite the phantom of ourselves',[1] brings Melbury, in his turn, to that self-alienation which all the other characters, in their various ways, come to know. Unlike them, however, he is able to retreat back into the company of the woodlanders, and consign Grace, his pride and hope, to Fitzpiers, with the observation, 'It's a forlorn hope for her; and God knows how it will end'. If Melbury's retreat into the woods seems more of a total extinction than Henchard's return to the Heath, for all the self-laceration implied by the terms of his Will, this is not primarily because of a difference in their individual characters, but because the world in which Melbury has lived has a complexity about it which Henchard's never had, not just a complexity of institutions but a complexity of character shaped by those institutions, with which 'the self-made man', the man of simple vows to the past and judgement about the future, is ill-equipped to deal.

The embodiment of that complexity for Melbury is not in Fitzpiers, but in his own daughter, Grace. Perhaps the importance of the role of no other character in Hardy's major fiction has been so underestimated as Grace's, and it is difficult not to feel that this proceeds from the reader's chagrin, in that he expects a heroine and gets somebody disconcertingly less. Failure to see her significance has been the result of irritation with her character. This is a pity, because she is by far the most important character in the novel.

In saying that, we are not making a claim that she is a more sympathetic character, and Hardy himself confessed that 'he was provoked with her all along. If she could have done a really self-abandoned, impassioned thing . . . he would have made a fine tragic ending to the book, but she was too commonplace and straight-laced and he could not maker her.'[2] Commonplace and straight-laced Grace may be, but the obduracy with which she resists her creator's wish to turn her into a tragic heroine is testimony to the solidity of her imaginative presence; she has made the terms on which she will conduct her life, and she will drive a hard bargain with her creator. Just how hard is suggested by the despairing aside made by

[1] Matthew Arnold, 'Growing Old'.
[2] Quoted in Weber, *Hardy and the Lady from Madison Square*, p. 89.

the narrator when he is driven, in a way unusual in Hardy, to reflect on the problem of doing justice to his character:

> It would have been difficult to describe Grace Melbury with precision, either then or at any time. Nay, from the highest point of view, to precisely describe a human being, the focus of a universe, how impossible!

Her little snobberies, her docile submission to her father, her school-girl 'crush' on Fitzpiers, her relative indifference to his desertion of her, her coy resumption of a relationship with Giles, her primly fierce adherence to moral proprieties when he is dying, her indulgent grief over his death and the arch and tentative resumption of her relationship with Fitzpiers – it is 'a biography' which can with some justice be summed up in the hollow-turner's words when he observes her renewed relationship with Fitzpiers, 'the way she queened it, and fenced, and kept that poor feller at a distance was enough to freeze yer blood. I should never have supposed it of such a girl'. It is not necessary to think of Fitzpiers as a 'poor feller' to feel a truth in this and that the marriage of Dr. and Mrs. Fitzpiers, whatever else it might be, will be a marriage of equals. If then I make a claim that the creation of Grace is of striking significance in Hardy's development as a novelist, it is not based on her intrinsic worth, but rather on the fact that she is a creation who has released in him a new complexity of insight into aspects of the contemporary consciousness.

To give my claim direction, I see the significance of Grace to lie in the fact that she provides Hardy with an opportunity to do a first sketch for Sue Bridehead. Sue, of course, is the full-length portrait, with every detail pondered and heightened; she is a genuinely intellectual woman whereas Grace has little more than educational gentility; she is an epicure of emotions, whereas Grace is only timid and vacillating; and in every way Sue is the more interesting and profound creation. If I bring them together it is not to suggest a comparable interest, but to show where the importance of Grace lies: that she gives Hardy a new feeling for 'modern nerves' in relation to 'primitive feelings', which he is to explore so thoroughly in his last novel. Grace is the point of growth in the novel, the difficult element, and perhaps it was this, rather than any traits of character, that was really responsible for Hardy's being 'provoked with her all along'.

Earlier I suggested the *The Woodlanders* might usefully be compared to Eliot's *The Waste Land*, and in citing the poem I was thinking not only of a pervasive theme like sterility and its multi-dimensional treatment, but of the way in which the characters reveal themselves *characteristically*, rather than as individual studies. In doing this, they help to make transparent the inter-penetrating realities between man and man, man and nature, man and the cosmos, the great web, which make Hardy's world so distinctively his own. But in the case of Grace, practically alone in the novel, this way of regarding 'character' applies less. Her peculiar timbre derives very much from the fact that she *is* an individual – however much she frustrates our sympathies – and, moreover, it is her curiously wrought individuality which constitutes her particular fate.

This becomes explicit at a moment when Melbury is reflecting on her desertion by Fitzpiers:

> Besides, this case was not, he argued, like ordinary cases. Leaving out the question of Grace being anything but an ordinary woman, her peculiar situation, as it were in mid-air between two storeys of society . . .

This is to put 'her peculiar situation' abstractly. The dramatic effect of that situation we see in a very sympathetic passage, close in feeling to that moment in Sue's life when she takes refuge in Phillotson's cupboard:

> In the darkness of the apartment to which she flew nothing could have been seen during the next half hour; but from the corner a quick breathing was audible from this impressionable creature, who combined modern nerves and primitive feelings, and was doomed by such coexistence to be numbered among the distressed, and to take her scourging to their exquisite extremity.

That is the perspective from which Sue's story is to be written, and it is not difficult to see that it is in the sexual life that the drama between 'nerves' and 'primitive feelings' will find its most intense expression. The conflict between 'man' and 'nature' can take place here; it is no longer in need of an Egdon Heath. In his later novels Hardy finds a grammar of modern consciousness in the sexual life, and it is this rather than any concern for 'candour' that makes that life of increasing concern to him. It was, of course, Lawrence who perceived this most clearly, and in the long study he wrote on Hardy he took this as the substance of his argument, an issue I will return to at the end of this book.

Though Lawrence is preoccupied in that essay with Sue, he would have understood Grace well. He would have understood that nullity at the centre which makes it so difficult for her to respond either to Fitzpiers or to Giles. And this is a nullity written into her consciousness, a part of her situation as much of as her temperament. The fact that we have no sense of Grace being married to Fitzpiers is not due to any lack of candour on Hardy's part, or to deference to his reading-public, but because the marriage has no existence in any real sense, an impression which is made plain when we see Grace's indifference to Fitzpiers's departure with Mrs. Charmond. At first sight, this may look like a repetition of that familiar fate which Hardy's women suffer immediately upon a certain kind of marriage – we recall Bathsheba's 'listlessness' with Troy, Eustacia's with Clym. But although Fitzpiers acts upon Grace 'like a dream', the effect on Grace is of an intensely vital kind in a way that it isn't for either Eustacia or Bathsheba. Grace's 'love' is 'the quality of awe towards a superior being' and once that being is shown to be the slave of his own passion, then he ceases to exist for Grace, 'She was but little excited, and her jealousy was languid even to death'. This is something that could never have been said about Bathsheba and Eustacia, and certainly part of the reason is that they were not involved in the hazard of self-conscious-ness which living 'between two storeys of society' has produced in Grace.

The effect of this is seen lightly, but firmly, in the part played in this novel by 'manners', which Hardy, revealing an unusual element in his work, uses as an index marking the precarious sense that Grace has of her own identity. There occurs a moment when Giles, having resumed his relationship with Grace, arranges for her to have a meal in an unobtrusive inn at Sherton:

She was in a mood of the greatest depression. On arriving and seeing what the tavern was like she had been taken by surprise; but having gone too far to retreat she had heroically entered and sat down on the well-scrubbed settle, opposite the narrow table with its knives and steel forks, tin pepper-boxes, blue salt-cellars, posters advertising the sale of bullocks against the wall.

What that scene releases in Grace is an acute awareness of herself, merely as an object among other objects, but an awareness also that sees in objects, 'knives and steel forks', 'tin pepper-boxes', 'a style of living'. She is no longer at ease with that style, and the effect is not so much the rejection of it, as the sense of self-diminution. Her instincts are at war with each other: 'While craving to be a country girl again . . . her first attempt had been beaten by the unexpected vitality of that fastidiousness.' Hardy has managed here a subtle registration of complex feelings which are inextricably personal and social, and managed it the more surely for leaving it quite free from authorial irony, giving unfeigned seriousness to the overall effect that her 'education', together with her association with Fitzpiers, has had upon her.

'While craving to be a country girl again . . .', that is the other side of the story, and Hardy takes the measure of that impulse exactly. It finds clearest expression in one of the most quoted paragraphs in the novel, a paragraph invariably quoted out of context, so that it is made an authorial description of Giles, rather than Grace's reflections on Giles at the crucial moment in her relationship with Fitzpiers. Grace has seen him riding away to Mrs. Charmond, when suddenly Giles appears on the scene:

He looked and smelt like Autumn's very brother, his face being sunburnt to wheat-colour, his eyes blue as corn-flowers, his sleeves and leggings dyed with fruit-stains, his hands clammy with the sweet juice of apples, his hat sprinkled with pips, and every-where about him that atmosphere of cider which at its first return each season has such an indescribable fascination for those who have been born and bred among the orchards. Her heart rose from its late sadness like a released bough; her senses revelled in the sudden lapse back to Nature unadorned.

This idealised version of Giles emerges directly from Grace's abandonment by Fitzpiers, and the form it takes is to emphasise everything that Fitzpiers ignored. Hungry for sensuous experience, Grace finds in Giles a rich embodiment of her mood, and though she names her feeling as a seeking for Nature unadorned, it is very much Nature adorned by the person who gives her the stability and the caring she craves. The 'sudden lapse back' reminds us that, even here, Grace is aware of her feelings being given leave, that she is in need of a version of pastoral, and Giles is there to provide it. It is a version which soon speaks to her in classical accents: 'Honesty, goodness, manliness, tenderness, devotion, for her only existed in their purity now in the breasts of unvarnished men.' No tree of Evil is allowed to grow in these orchards, and Little Hintock becomes, like that 'outer landscape' of her father's, a high-coloured scene of 'a stained window'. When Grace, claiming a kinship with the wood-landers, observes that her blood is no better than theirs, Fitzpiers's reply becomes self-evidently true: 'Ah, *you* – you are refined and educated into something quite different.'

Grace lives to learn the truth of that remark, and her divided consciousness finally assumes a visible form. Like Fitzpiers, en-grossed with 'something in my own head', and like Mrs. Charmond in her curtained room, Grace too will anticipate the tones of that voice in *The Waste Land*:

> I have heard the key
> Turn in the door once and turn once only
> We think of the key, each in his prison
> Thinking of the key . . .

'Propriety', 'the unexpected vitality of the fastidious', 'primitive feelings', 'modern nerves', all these elements come together when Grace accepts Giles's offer that she live alone in the hut.

> Without so much as crossing the threshold himself he closed the door upon her, and turned the key in the lock. Tapping at the window he signified that she should open the casement, and when she had done this he handed in the key to her. 'You are locked in', he said, 'and your own mistress.'

Unlike the closing of the door in *The Return of the Native* this is not the separation of one person from another; it is a separation *within*

the self. 'You are your own mistress', the phrase takes on increasing
ironies, as her will becomes assailed by all that it has excluded and
'the primitive feelings' take over and exact their toll:

> No sooner had she retired to rest that night than the wind began
> to rise, and after a few prefatory blasts to be accompanied by rain.
> The wind grew more violent, as the storm went on it was difficult
> to believe that no opaque body, but only an invisible colourless
> thing, was trampling and climbing over the roof, making branches
> creak, springing out of the trees upon the chimney, popping its
> head into the flue, and shrieking and blaspheming at every
> corner of the walls. As in the grisly story, the assailant was a
> spectre which could be felt but not seen. She had never before
> been so struck with the devilry of a gusty night in a wood, because
> she had never been so entirely alone in spirit as she was now. She
> seemed almost to be apart from herself – a vacuous duplicate only.
> The recent self of physical animation and clear intentions was not
> there.

The outer landscape becomes inner, and Grace reaches that terrible
dissociation of self which Bathsheba and Eustacia undergo; but
whereas for them, the conflict can be objectified and contained,
Grace is the prey of an assailant who could only be felt, not seen:

> Taking no further interest in herself as a splendid woman,
> [Bathsheba] acquired the indifferent feelings of an outsider in
> contemplating her probable fate as a singular wretch.

> Eustacia could now, like other people at such a stage, take a
> standing-point outside herself, observe herself as a disinterested
> spectator, and think what a sport for Heaven this woman Eustacia
> was.

For Grace no such standpoint is available, she is driven from within
by forces she cannot name – so that she sees her consciousness
seemingly separated out from her body, 'a vacuous duplicate only'.
Her experience is an intimation of Hardy's next creation:

> Tess had spiritually ceased to recognize the body before him as
> hers – allowing it to drift, like a corpse upon the current, in a
> direction dissociated from its living will.

These passages serve to make plain not only Hardy's intense pre-occupation with the divided self, but the way in which that pre-occupation is increasingly apprehended as something rooted within the individual, and much less in 'the probable fate', 'the sport for Heaven'.

If Grace 'recovers', it is a recovery in which the division within her is allowed to shape her behaviour. She becomes increasingly like Mrs. Charmond, submissive, demanding, impulsive, calculating, learning to live by the adoption of roles. She assumes the first of these roles unwittingly, and out of an instinctual loyalty to Giles, when she declares to Fitzpiers that she has, in fact, been his lover. If it is a deception which eventually worries her, it also gives her pleasure, re-establishing her in the eyes of Fitzpiers, who feels 'he had never known her dangerously full compass if she were capable of such a reprisal'. The deception encourages him to resume his relationship, and Grace allows it to develop on terms and in a manner which Mrs. Charmond would have approved. What Melbury once called their 'freemasonry of education' begins, ironically, to reveal itself in an unsuspected way. For Fitzpiers, the scenario Grace arranges for their second courtship has its fascination – the carefully arranged meetings, the strict intervals between, the decorous exchanges, punctuated at times by quotations from *Measure for Measure*, and *Julius Caesar* – we can see Fitzpiers earning his description, 'a subtlist in emotions, he cultivated as under glasses strange and mournful pleasures that he would not willingly let die just at present'. And appropriately, when the time is right, the courtship finds its conclusion in a fine *coup de théatre*.

Timothy Tangs, jealous of his new wife's former liaison with Fitzpiers, and seeing the resumed relationship with Grace, resolves to punish him by setting a man-trap at the place where the couple are accustomed to meet. The plan goes awry and Grace gets trapped instead, or more accurately her dress does. Fitzpiers, hearing her scream, fears the worst. In their common relief, however, at finding one another unharmed, they declare their love and life together can begin again. It is melodramatic, and the whole point of the episode is that it should be seen to be so.

Tangs's gesture takes its place, with Marty's charcoal scrawl and

Melbury's visit to his lawyer in London, as an ineffectual single action belonging to an older, simpler community which persists uncomfortably in a world where cause and effect have become increasingly difficult to locate. The man-trap, once a means of dispensing rough justice and enforcing the social and economic *status quo*, has now become 'a cobwebbed object'. The traps for sexual offenders lie within the interpretation of the law itself. There is a sense in which Fitzpiers and Grace are 'made' for each other, and when the man-trap is thrown by Grace, and Fitzpiers takes her into his arms, 'the cobwebbed object' reveals itself as a man-trap indeed.

This romantic reunion is played deliberately off-key, as it has been throughout their renewed relationship, though its resolution has been nicely taken out of the control of the two individuals involved. 'A probable fate' has entered. Grace appears to Fitzpiers's startled gaze 'lacking the portion of her dress which the gin retained', but 'By their united efforts . . . it was then possible to extract the silk mouthful from the monster's bite, creased and pierced with small holes, but not torn. Fitzpiers assisted her to put it on again; and when her customary contours were thus restored they walked on together . . .' The restoration of Grace's 'customary contours' suggests, lightly but effectively, the nature of her reunion with Fitzpiers. She has drawn on her 'fastidiousness' and found in it a sustaining role, the 'spectre which could be felt but not seen' has been put to rest. How far this process has gone with Grace is neatly – and sardonically – suggested in her exchange with Fitzpiers, when he proposes that they leave Little Hintock straightaway and spend the night at the Earl of Wessex Hotel:

> 'But that newly done-up place – the Earl of Wessex!'
> 'If you are so very particular about the publicity I will stay at a little quiet one.'
> 'O no – it is not that I am particular – but I haven't a brush or comb or anything!'

'Appearances' are not a matter now of reputation, but of a brush and comb. Giles's hut is forgotten, Grace prepares a face to meet the world and intends to enjoy it – at least for a while.

This conversation, and indeed the whole treatment of Grace's and

Fitzpiers's renewed courtship is remarkably assured, in that Hardy manages a detachment sufficient to release the comedy, but not so distant that it becomes censorious. The result is that he is able to catch, in a way unusual for him, a subtle interplay of emotion, in protagonists for whom he feels little sympathy. That Hardy was very conscious of his attempt at *comédie noire* is suggested by Grace's remark on finding herself and Fitzpiers unscathed by the man-trap: 'O, Edred, there has been an Eye watching over us tonight, and we should be thankful indeed!' The measure of the pious platitude is taken in the fact that Grace is right, there has indeed been an Eye watching over them, one belonging, however, not to the President of the Immortals, but to Timothy Tangs. It is the point, made now in terms of bizarre comedy – which is being made elsewhere with increasing insistence and elaboration – that if we are victims, then we are more likely to be the victims of men than of the gods.

♣ III ♣

With that thought in mind we might now turn away to that element in the novel which is not contained within any individual character or in the relationship between them, namely the woods themselves. It is tempting to regard them as playing a part similar to that of the Heath in *The Return of the Native* or Casterbridge in *The Mayor*, and while it is true that Hardy is using them as he does the heath and the town, to give substance and coherence to his theme, they have a quite distinctive significance. It is a significance caught in a passage like this:

> The leaves over Hintock unrolled their creased tissues, and the woodland seemed to change from an open filigree to a solid opaque body of infinitely larger shape and importance.

That moment, in which the woods move from being 'leaves' to a body 'of . . . larger shape and importance', is indicative of their multi-dimensional presence in the novel, a presence which is both outside man and within him too.

Whatever ramifications 'the woods' may have, we must start by registering the vivid actuality of their presence and the way that that presence shapes the lives of those who live there. We cannot think of Melbury without thinking of him as a successful timber merchant, or of Giles without thinking of him at work on the trees or taking his cider branch into Sherton. It is tempting to go on to think, especially in retrospect, of these activities as 'dying', but there is nothing to suggest this, except in one respect, and perhaps in the end it is the only respect which matters: namely, that if this work is presented as 'antique', it is only in the sense of its being self-enclosed, belonging to a sequestered world bisected by a now deserted highway. We can feel this increasing self-enclosure of the rural world if we take note of the diminishing role 'the locals' are called upon to play in the successive novels. The locals who gather in Melbury's timber-yard seem withdrawn and marginal to the life of the novel, in a way quite unthinkable of the company in The Buck's Head, or those who gathered round the bonfire on the Heath; and even those who met in Mixen Lane, disreputable as they were, seemed to occupy a place in Casterbridge life which Creedle and company are generally either unable or unwilling to. Of course, this declining role of the locals only reflects the shifts in Hardy's interests, but the fact that they no longer energise, or even engage, his imagination is symptomatic of the changes that have taken place in his fictional world.

It is a change which can be described in a variety of ways – the sharpened sense of the interpenetration of different levels of reality, the increasing emphasis on the human will, whether it is a will seen in terms of history or of social institutions. There is, however, one change which the woods emphasise in a quite distinctive way and one which is peculiar to this novel, and that is a sense of passive exhaustion and melancholy. This is a note which is not struck in either of the two major novels which are to come, and though *Tess* and *Jude* are tragic on a scale much greater than anything in *The Woodlanders*, there is a mood operative in that novel more deeply pessimistic than anything else in Hardy's fiction. I am anxious to emphasise the phrase, 'a mood operative', because throughout this study of Hardy I have tried to contend for the variety of mood within a Hardy novel, and in drawing attention to this pessimism, I don't think of it as enveloping the novel. In relating this dark mood to the presentation and influence of the woodland descriptions, I have in mind a passage like this:

> On older trees still than these huge lobes of fungi grew like lungs. Here, as everywhere, the Unfulfilled Intention, which makes life what it is, was as obvious as it could be among the depraved crowds of a city slum. The leaf was deformed, the curve was crippled, the taper was interrupted; the lichen ate the vigour of the stalk, and the ivy slowly strangled to death the promising sapling.

That stark reflection does, I think, work its way into the texture of the novel, and lodges there, unlike some of the reflections in *The Mayor*, for instance, which, as I remarked earlier, remain authorial *obiter dicta* and are less comfortably accommodated within the tale. It is at work in nearly all those passages directly descriptive of the trees: 'two overcrowded branches . . . which were rubbing each other into wounds'; 'a half-dead oak, hollow and disfigured with white tumours, its roots spread out like claws grasping the ground'; 'above stretched an old beech, with vast arm-pits, and pocket-holes in its side where branches had been removed in past times; a black slug was trying to climb it'; 'next were more trees close together, wrestling for existence, their branches disfigured with wounds resulting from their mutual rubbings and blows.' What is striking about this collection of passages – and it is a collection which could be extended – is not just the sense of passive suffering which the trees endure, but the violence and grossness of their disfigurement, as if Hardy's imagination here was stretched and oppressed by the burden of its gloom. Majestic things are diseased, life is thwarted and deformed, suffering prevails – it is difficult not to let phrases like these describe the mood these passages give rise to.

This is a mood which extends beyond the flora and fauna and invades the woodlanders themselves. We find George Melbury speaking to Giles rather ominously and remarking on their 'living here alone', and not noticing 'how the whitey-brown creeps out of the earth over us'. The impression is that of a living entombment. The most dramatic instance of this is the tall tree which grows outside John South's house and which he feels will fall and crush him. The tree grows in his mind; it does fall and, in effect, crushes not only him but his daughter and Giles. In an attempt to overcome South's obsession, Fitzpiers orders the tree to be felled. The result is that he dies of shock when he sees it is gone. On his death, the life-hold on his property expires, and both South's house and Giles's, whose lease lasted as long as South lived, revert to the owner of the estate, Mrs. Charmond. When Giles loses his house, his last hope that he might marry Grace vanishes, and the lines are drawn for the tragic drama to follow. South, Marty, Giles, Mrs. Charmond, the tall tree grows into all their lives, but it is a process which passes unnoticed, so that the tree which John South declares is 'killing him' is unknown to Mrs. Charmond.

In that interlocking drama, we catch a glimpse of the woods as 'a body of . . . larger shape and importance', giving a habitation, if not a name, to the inner conflicts of the characters. We find Fitzpiers, for instance, unhappy in his recent marriage with Grace, gazing across to Melbury's timber-yard:

> The early morning of this day had been dull, after a night of wind, and on looking out of the window in the grey grim dawn Fitzpiers had observed some of Melbury's men dragging away a large limb which had been snapped off a beech-tree. Everything was cold and colourless. 'My good God!' he said, as he stood in his dressing-gown, 'This is life!'

The broken tree crystallises Fitzpiers's mood, and his exclamation, 'This is life!' can be used indifferently of his own marital unhappiness and of the dull routine of the work in the timber-yard; and the general situation in which the line which can be drawn between place and person, the observer and the observed, blurs, and 'everything' becomes 'cold and colourless'.

The woods then establish an atmosphere, pervasive and persistent, of deep melancholy; they are capable of giving definition to the plot, they crystallise the fears of the characters – yet, extraordinary as it may seem, they do not in the last analysis darken our total impression of the novel. By that I mean when we come to ponder that total impression, an impression which cannot but be influenced by these passages of melancholy, we find, strangely enough, that the summarising word which comes most readily to us is not 'tragic' or 'pessimistic', but 'mellow'. How does this come about? For an answer I suggest we should go back to the account, which I gave at the outset of this chapter, of an unsympathetic reader's response to the novel, and which, up to now, I have attempted to outflank rather than counter directly.

Broadly speaking, the account which finds *The Woodlanders* an unsatisfactory novel is based on two main considerations: the faintness and fixity of the characterisation, a weakness emphasised further by the absence of a central governing presence, and a plot which, in its awkward marriage of romance and melodrama, seems unable to release a theme of substance. In my version, I have tried to offer an account of *The Woodlanders* which will make the elements of 'character' and 'plot' much less extractable, more elements in a total design, so that we think of 'character' more in terms of 'consciousness', 'plot' as created not simply by interaction of people, but by interpenetration of people with nature. From this point of view, I have tried to argue that, in human terms, the most vivid drama of the novel takes place within the consciousness of Grace Melbury, but we can get the sense of that drama, only if we see her as being defined in relation to other characters, to place, and to the narrator. Only by seeing these constant extensions can we take the drift of scenes like Giles lying outside of his hut, or Grace caught in the man-trap. As Hardy said in his diary entry, 'The human race to be shown as one great network or tissue which quivers in every part when one point is shaken, like a spider's web if touched.' And this, in its turn, involving a novel which like a late Turner painting will seek 'the reality underlying the scenic', whether in terms of landscape or of people, made me suggest that the organisation of *The Woodlanders* has more in common with a poem like *The Waste Land* than with a novel like *Adam Bede*. Such, in outline, has been my argument, but it does not, directly at least, enable us to say why the novel, so pessimistic in detail, offers us in total effect an impression of mellowness. To understand that, we have to consider the tone in which it is told.

I remarked earlier that it is one of the curious features of *The Woodlanders* that it lacks a central character, but it is precisely the absence of such a character that allows us to feel the pervasive presence of the author. By this I do not mean the author as a definable, obtrusive presence, but more negatively, as evenly distributing his sympathies among his characters, creating, in the detachment of his telling, a sense of story about a world already completed.

At the start of the novel, we are very deliberately placed in the past, the phrase 'for old association's sake' takes the eye, and as the details accumulate – the deserted road, the dark woods, the mysterious traveller from outside – we feel that we are at the beginning of an archetypal story, and 'once upon a time . . .' exerts its spell. Marty's temptation to cut off her hair is the distillation of every temptation story: the defenceless girl threatened by forces over which she has no control, the desperate attempt to keep her own sense of well-being, and then the framed image of her tragedy, in which the story-teller reminds us that she has taken her place with other victims:

> She would not turn again to the little looking-glass out of humanity to herself, knowing what a deflowered visage would look back at her and almost break her heart; she dreaded it as much as did her ancestral goddess the reflection in the pool after the rape of her locks by Loke the Malicious.

It is that encompassing sense of 'story' which is there as a murmur throughout *The Woodlanders*, memorialising the past, unobtrusively keeping a tension between it and the present, making us aware of the unfolding design. The sense of 'story' is created not so much by self-conscious insistence, as by the conventional furnishings – the ominous woods, the great house, the simple woodcutters, the possessive father, the dutiful daughter, the rakish seducer, the wealthy lady, the lover scorned and then redeemed by death – an index of primal experience, endlessly capable of adaptation and repetition. When Melbury at his most intense moment of feeling in the novel pleads with Mrs. Charmond to release Fitzpiers, he becomes a character in his own fiction, speaking in the timeless rhythms of story as if to assure himself of his identity:

> I am an old man . . . that, somewhat late in life, God thought fit to bless with one child, and she a daughter. Her mother was a very

dear wife to me; but she was taken away from us when the child was young; and the child became precious as the apple of my eye to me, for she was all I had left to love.

It is the accent of Zachary, of Pericles.

Story is, however, present in *The Woodlanders*, in rather less general terms than this: it is there as pastoral. Finding its introduction in that moment when Giles meets Grace under the apple-tree which he holds aloft in the market-place, the pastoral element is most fully treated in the scene when Fitzpiers sits reading in the woods, and sees the workers around him as 'a scene and actors': 'The thought that he might settle here and become welded in with this sylvan life by marrying Grace Melbury crossed his mind for a moment.' When later he goes to elope with Mrs. Charmond, 'the sylvan scene' becomes 'orchards lustrous with the reds of apple-crops, berries, and foliage, the whole intensified by the gilding of the declining sun. The earth this year had been prodigally bountiful, and now was the supreme moment of her bounty.' For Grace looking at him going, that scene has already become fixed into art, 'Her Tannhäuser still moved on, his plodding steed rendering him distinctly visible yet.'

Remembrance of things past, the pastoral mood, allusions to poetry and to music, all these help to create what we might think of as the gauze of 'story', enclosing the novel, softening its outlines, giving it unity: and turning tragedy into mellowness because that story brings with it an implicit assurance that this experience has been encompassed and assimilated by this narrator – or nearly so. The reminder of 'story' is maintained in the closing sections of the novel by the shift in tone, that serio-comic attitude that I looked at earlier in the resumption of relations between Grace and Fitzpiers. It is an attitude that is not confined to that relationship, but flickers in a whole series of little episodes which self-consciously play with romance or melodrama. Fitzpiers, drunk on horseback, meets Melbury and, failing to recognise him, abuses his daughter; Grace and Mrs. Charmond, irritated by meeting in the wood, depart firmly in opposite directions, only to go in a circle, meet again, and then like babes in the wood spend an uneasy night together clinging to each other for warmth and comfort. Suke and Mrs. Charmond, hearing that Fitzpiers has fallen off his horse, rush to Grace's house and insist upon seeing him:

> Indeed, you have a perfect right to go into his bedroom; who can have a better than either of you. . . . Wives all, let's enter together . . .

Scenes like these have a calculated effect, they keep us *looking at* the characters, as they spin their plots and then get caught up in the plot they spin; we are not drawn in, not involved, and consequently we keep alert to the whole design and the bounding frame.

If *The Woodlanders* creates a mood, of which 'once upon a time' helps to indicate the meaning, its conclusion is not quite 'and so they lived happily ever after'. As so often in Hardy's novels the ending, as we have seen before, is multi-dimensional. There is the departure of Grace and Fitzpiers from 'the newly-done-up' Earl of Wessex Hotel to that practice in the Midlands; the retreat of Melbury and the woodlanders in their 'much stained' aprons, first into the antique tavern and then back into the woods; and Marty, now quite alone, keeping her vigil with Giles, speaking her monologue to the dead. In each of these three elements there is a reminder of the 'story' Hardy has to tell. It is there, most obviously, in the antique tavern where the woodlanders, for the first time in the novel, are allowed, however briefly, to take the centre of the stage, and take it characteristically with anecdote and recollection. They have stories to tell, stories that will show that, in marriage, appearance can deceive, but though these obviously echo the substance of the novel, they are a comment not so much on the characters, as on the narrator, showing the endless fascination to be found in the story of man's idiosyncrasy. 'I know'd a man and wife – faith, I don't mind owning, as there's no strangers here, that the pair were my own relations . . .'; 'I knowed a woman; and the husband o' her went away for four-and-twenty year. And one night . . .' The delight of the woodlanders is in the tale they have to tell, as for the author, for whom 'A story must be exceptional enough to justify its telling. We tale-tellers are all Ancient Mariners, and none of us is warranted in stopping Wedding Guests . . . unless he has something more unusual to relate than the ordinary experience of every average man and woman.'[1]

With Marty the sense of 'story' takes on a more sombre tone. Giles's death has now left her free to arrange the scenario for his life, and in shaping and recalling that scenario, she finds her own strength to go on living: 'Whenever I plant . . . whenever I turn the cider wring' – the heart of the monologue is not Giles but her memory, 'If ever I forget your name let me forget. . . !' Her most intense life is to be lived as story, as filling the vacancy of the present with the heroism of the past. For Marty it is a past already serenely in her possession, and it is her serenity, rather than her desolation, that the book finally conveys.

'For old association's sake . . .' – the novel looks as if it might end in the manner in which it began, but in the kind of elements that make up the resolution of the novel, the relationship between Grace and Fitzpiers, there can be no sense of 'ever after'. With Marty 'the story' stops. Grace and Fitzpiers have to go forward to a world elsewhere, a world beyond the woodlands and the orchards, along the deserted highway and out into life – the author's life and our own. Faced with that, the story-teller falls silent and his tale is closed.

[1] *Life*, p. 252.

6

'Poor Wounded Name'
Tess of the D'Urbervilles (1891)

Let me begin with critical debate. Charles Darwin was once moved to reflect on what he considered to be a criterion for excellence in fiction. 'A novel,' he wrote, 'according to my taste, does not come into the first class, unless it contains some person whom one can thoroughly love, and if it be a pretty woman so much the better.'[1] In other, rather more judicial tones, we find Lionel Johnson in the first critical study written on Hardy, turning to his most celebrated novel, *Tess of the D'Urbervilles*, and remarking, 'I want definitions of *nature, law, society* and *justice*: the want is coarse, doubtless, and unimaginative, but I cannot suppress it.'[2]

I begin my account of *Tess* with these remarks because they express, in a very pure way, feelings which have characterised a whole debate about the novel – a debate which raises in an insistent form questions about the role of character in Hardy's fiction, about the presence of ideas in his novels, and about the relationship that might obtain between these elements.

To take the question of 'ideas' first. Lionel Johnson's remark anticipates that whole area in the discussion of Hardy's novel which has been concerned with his philosophical and metaphysical 'intrusions' – or with their incoherence ambiguity, or with both. A classical instance is customarily thought to be his treatment of nature, and though this is present everywhere in his work, *Tess* offers the most crucial example. The argument goes like this. At some stages of the novel 'nature' is treated as a matter of social custom. And so we find Tess 'ashamed of herself for her gloom of the night, based on nothing more tangible than a sense of condemnation under an arbitrary law of society, which had no foundation in Nature'. And later when the author comes to reflect on her

[1] *The Autobiography of Charles Darwin* (1958 edition), pp. 138–9.
[2] Lionel Johnson, *The Art of Thomas Hardy*, p. 246.

experiences with Alec, he remarks, 'But for the world's opinion those experiences would have been simply a liberal education'. 'An arbitrary law of society', 'a liberal education', the fault and the remedy would seem to lie within man's control, 'nature' is what man has made of man.

At other stages of the novel, however, 'nature' appears as something very different. There is Tess's famous description of the world as 'a blighted star'; there are the milkmaids, who in their hopeless love for Angel, 'writhed feverishly under the oppressiveness of an emotion thrust on them by cruel Nature's law – an emotion which they had neither expected nor desired'; there is the rather bitter interrogative of the narrator, 'some people would like to know whence the poet whose philosophy is in these days deemed as profound and trustworthy as his song is breezy and pure, gets his authority for speaking of "Nature's holy plan".' There is no doubt of the drift of these remarks, 'nature' is the name of all our woe; we are victims, not agents, of our misfortunes. The ambivalence present in the idea of nature could be said to extend, the critics argue, into neighbouring concepts such as those which Johnson cites, 'law, society and justice'. The question then arises as to what effect this has upon the novel as a whole. In other words, to what extent does the apparent philosophical incoherence of ambiguity damage the fictional achievement?

As might be expected, the answers to the question vary a good deal, but for those who admire the novel, as well as for those who do not, the issue looms large. The difference lies in the use to which the criticism is put. For those who dislike the novel it is built into the centre of the argument; for those who admire it, a concession of ground is made, and the exchange is removed to other, safer ground. That ground is, of course, the character of Tess herself, where the power of Hardy's achievement is thought to be unanswerably displayed. She dominates and shapes the novel, a palpable presence to the reader with 'her cheeks chill as the skin of mushrooms', 'the stopt-diapason which her voice acquired', 'warm as a sunned cat', she is loyal, courageous, passionate in her own feelings, acutely sensitive to the feeling of others. As Carl Weber puts it, she exhibits quite simply:

176

a fortitude in the face of adversity and self-sacrificing devotion to others that make her the finest woman in all the Wessex novels.[1]

The admiration she has provoked has been unstinted and widely shared: it is the creation of 'a woman whom one can thoroughly love' and whose tragedy one can thoroughly believe in, that will silence, even if cannot answer, the conceptual problems inherent in the novel. Such is the usual case of those who seek to defend the novel against the kind of criticism made by Lionel Johnson.

I would like to argue, in the account of the novel which follows, that this critical debate which, when all qualifications have been made, is polarised around 'character' on one side and 'ideas' on the other, relies, as a condition of its existence, on certain common assumptions about the nature of fiction, assumptions alien to the kind of fiction Hardy wrote. In the opening chapter of this study I have tried to enlarge on this. It is perhaps enough here simply to recall Henry James's famous sentence from 'The Art of Fiction', to indicate the nature of those assumptions:

> I cannot imagine composition existing in a series of blocks, nor conceive, in any novel worth discussing at all, of a passage of description that is not in its intention narrative, a passage of dialogue that is not in its intention descriptive, a touch of truth of any sort that does not partake of the nature of incident, or an incident that derives its interest from any other source than the general and only source of the success of a work of art – that of being illustrative. A novel is a living thing, all one and continuous, like any other organism, and in proportion as it lives will it be found, I think, that in each of the parts there is something of each of the other parts.

In this description interpenetration and harmony are seen as the criteria for a satisfactory unified whole. For a novel which seems to contain within itself diverse energies, energies at times in seeming conflict with each other, and which comes over to us more as a process than a stasis, the art of fiction will not be as James conceives it. My contention is that the debate about *Tess* is, more often than not, a debate not about a particular interpretation, a particular emphasis, but about an 'art of fiction'.

[1] C. Weber, *Hardy of Wessex*, p. 132.

By the time he comes to write *Tess of the D'Urbervilles* and *Jude the Obscure*, Hardy's fiction has begun to acquire a very distinctive form, and by trying to get a sharper sense of that form we will, I thing under the sky'. 'Everything' – the world of the author as well novels, to which, as a descriptive epigraph, a sentence from *Tess* might be applied with equal relevance to both manner and matter, 'so do flux and reflux – the rhythm of change – alternate in everything under the sky'. 'Everything' – the world of the author as well as the world of his creation, and in *Tess* we feel the two as transparently close to one another. In the account of the novel which follows I would like to accept James's phrase about the novel being 'all one and continuous', but to go on to argue that, so far as Hardy is concerned, the notions of unity and continuity will have to be seen rather differently.

❧ II ❧

In discussing the novels which preceded *Tess*, I have tried to show Hardy's continuous preoccupation with human consciousness, a consciousness which has found, in the conflict with itself and with its environment, the price of its development. As one novel followed another, Hardy's sense of a deep interrelationship between the individual, the social, and the metaphysical sharpened, so that by the time he came to write *The Woodlanders*, he was able to image the sexual and economic concerns of a society as part of a single process. In that novel, as I have tried to show, Hardy traces out the great web of man's doings; in the novel that follows, *Tess of the D'Urbervilles*, he returns to that web, but watches now more intently the strange process of its spinning. The novel finds a single person capable of revealing the conflict which, in the earlier novel, had been widely dispersed. The temptations of Sue, the endurance of Marty, the troubled consciousness of Grace, come together and find a fresh definition in Tess. In its continuous movement from 'a world' to 'a character', from 'a character' to 'a world', the novel finds its distinctive rhythm.

We can catch this rhythm if we look at two passages relating to Tess. In the first, the narrator describes her in her family home:

Mrs. Durbeyfield habitually spoke the dialect; her daughter, who had passed the Sixth Standard in the National school under a London-trained mistress, spoke two languages; the dialect at home, more or less; ordinary English abroad and to persons of quality. . . . Between the mother, and her fast-perishing lumber of superstitions, folk-lore, dialect, and orally transmitted ballads, and the daughter, with her trained National teachings and Standard knowledge under an infinitely Revised Code, there was a gap of two hundred years as ordinarily understood. When they were together the Jacobean and the Victorian ages were juxtaposed.

Some years later, Angel Clare hears 'a fluty voice' which he later learns is that of Tess Durbeyfield talking to Dairyman Crick:

'I don't know about ghosts,' she was saying; 'but I do know that our souls can be made to go outside our bodies when we are alive.'
. . . 'What – really now? And is it so, maidy?' he said. 'A very easy way to feel 'em go,' continued Tess, 'is to lie on the grass at night and look straight up at some big bright star; and, by fixing your mind upon it, you will soon find that you are hundreds and hundreds o' miles away from your body, which you don't seem to want at all.'

Both passages turn on a sense of divisiveness, both have Tess at their centre, but they move in opposite directions. The first takes us out into the public world, into the world of custom and communication, its crises belong to history. The second affects our own sense of what it is like simply to be, of knowing oneself apart from time and space, its crises are those of the individual psyche. The two are held in tension, and the novel is to explore the intimacy of relationship between them.

It is a commonplace by now to say that at every stage – or phase – of *Tess*, Hardy employed region and landscape as a means of communicating feeling and states of mind. A region of heaths and tracks, towns and alehouses, Wessex also indisputably provided Hardy with a psychological language. What has I think been less noticed is that the region as interior landscape is much more equivocal in implication than we might think.

In the first phase of the novel, titled 'The Maiden', the action is fairly evenly divided between Tess's life with her family at Marlott and her life at Trantridge with the Stoke-D'Urbervilles. The moment of transition occurs when Tess, accompanied by Alec in his cart, goes off to meet her new employer: 'Rising still, an immense landscape stretched around them on every side; behind, the green valley of her birth, before, a grey country of which she knew nothing. . . .' 'The green valley . . . a grey country', it is descriptions like this that we tend to seize on, and in so doing, simplify the significance of Tess's move from Marlott to Trantridge so that it becomes simply a journey from Innocence to Experience. It is that, of course, but the formulation is too brisk, too complacent, and we become deaf to the overtones which attend the journey.

If, in our first encounter, Marlott, in the Vale of Blackmoor, seems 'an engirdled and secluded region, for the most part untrodden as yet by tourist or landscape-painter', we are at the same time reminded that it is 'within a four hours' journey from London'. If this is Wessex, it is only with something of an effort that it is being kept far from the madding crowd. There may still be the old rites, such as the May-Day Dance, but it contains, among the young girls, 'elderly women . . . having almost a grotesque, certainly a pathetic, appearance in such a jaunty situation', and though the dancers may be 'a votive sisterhood' bearing a 'peeled willow wand', they are watched by young men who carry books with titles like *A Counterblast to Agnosticism*. In the cottages, however, the reading may still be the *Compleat Fortune Teller*, a book not allowed to be kept in the house overnight. Life for the Durbeyfield family is hard, but in The Pure Drop and Rolliver's it can be made to acquire 'a sort of halo, an occidental glow'. It is there in the inn that dreams can be indulged, and the Durbeyfields can believe that they are the true descendants of the D'Urberville family. But around them press the economic realities, and when the horse dies, their livelihood is jeopardised and Tess is encouraged to claim kin with their reputed family at Trantridge. When she falls into her sad reverie on the cart, she shows herself, in her 'dreaminess', a true daughter of the Durbeyfields, but when, following the disaster, she is filled with self-reproach, 'which she continued to heap upon herself for her negligence', she is the daughter of her age. 'Nobody blamed Tess as she blamed herself' – in that phrase we have expressed that divisiveness of consciousness which separates her from her parents. With this criss-cross of feelings already established we cannot think of Marlott simply as life before the Fall.

It is a pattern of feeling which is to be enlarged considerably in Tess's relationship with Alec, when attitudes towards nature first become explicit. Place, as usual, establishes the dramatic key. Alec's house is surrounded by the Chase, 'a truly venerable tract of forest land, one of the few remaining woodlands in England of undoubted primaeval date, wherein Druidical mistletoe was still found on aged oaks'. We have nature as something given, beyond the memory of man, promising, in the mistletoe, fertility, a continuing life. Closer to the house, 'nature' is very different: 'Everything on this smug property was bright, thriving, and well-kept; acres of glass-houses stretched down the inclines to the copses at their feet. Everything looked like money – like the last coin issued from the Mint. . . . On the extensive lawn stood an ornamental tent, its door being towards her.' Nature now is nature methodised, the province of man, bought, designed, forced, mastered.

In a brief but vivid scene, these senses of nature are lightly caught up and dramatised in a way anticipatory of the seduction scene. Alec offers Tess a specimen strawberry from his greenhouse – a conquest for nurture over nature:

> . . . he stood up and held it by the stem to her mouth, 'No – no!' she said quickly, putting her fingers between his hand and her lips. 'I would rather take it in my own hand.' 'Nonsense!' he insisted; and in a slight distress she parted her lips and took it in. They had spent some time wandering desultorily thus, Tess eating in a half-pleased, half-reluctant state whatever d'Urberville offered her.

'Half-pleased', 'half-reluctant', that conflict of emotions is an essential part of Tess's being. She is attracted, quite instinctively, to Alec, not just because of his charm and flattery, but because of what he is. In saying this, I am not trying to contend against the criticism that finds in him a lay figure of Victorian melodrama, with his 'full lips, badly moulded', his moustaches, and the idiom to match, 'Well, my beauty . . .'. But he is not only that, and I think Lawrence is right in claiming that 'he could reach some of the real sources of the female in a woman and draw from them!'[1] What Alec presents irresistibly to Tess is a sense of power. In spite of his crude and self-conscious role-playing he recognises her as a woman, and this gives to her, in a way that she has never experienced before, a sense of her *own* power, her own attraction. It gives her a new sense of her individuality and she is right to think that if she betrays that she imperils her own being; so that when the time comes she will have her own role to play as the avenging woman. In Alec, she senses both her creator and her destroyer. It is the attempt to do justice to the extent and range of these feelings that makes Hardy so calculatedly ambiguous about the nature of their encounter in the Chase; it is both a seduction *and* a rape. If it were merely a rape, then there would be no sense in Tess's profound feeling throughout the novel that her whole being has been invaded by Alec, so that in one sense she feels she 'belongs' to him, belongs because he brought to consciousness her own sexuality. If it were simply a seduction, then there would be no sense in Tess's equally profound feeling that her past with Alec is a nullity. We could say that as a woman, Tess feels it to be a seduction in the way the strawberry scene hints at; as an individual person, she knows it was rape, 'There were they that heard a sobbing one night last year in The Chase.'

Tess's education at Trantridge at the hands of Alec throws into fresh conflict her relationship with her family, a conflict which for them is needless. Hardy makes the kind of tension explicit in the concluding sentence to the whole phase:

> As Tess's own people down in those retreats are never tired of saying among each other in their fatalistic way: 'It was to be.' There lay the pity of it. An immeasurable social chasm was to divide our heroine's personality thereafter from that previous self of hers who stepped from her mother's door to try her fortune at Trantridge poultry-farm.

'It was to be', 'an immeasurable social chasm' – the conflict between

---

[1] D. H. Lawrence, 'Study of Thomas Hardy', *Phoenix*, I, p. 484.

the generations is there, but the phrases stand in need of a gloss. For Tess's 'own people' the sheer occurrence of event involves a passive acceptance of good fortune as well as bad, a kind of acceptance, the author implies, now only possible in 'engirdled and secluded regions'. It can give rise to a 'dreaminess' which is self-forgetful. But for Tess such a dreaminess gives rise to self-consciousness, to speculations, which she feels divide her not only from the world outside her, but within her own being. As the narrator says, she has come to feel 'the ache of modernism', she no longer has access to the feelings which the field-workers display as they return to Trantridge after dancing away the night hours:

> Then these children of the open air, whom even excess of alcohol could scarce injure permanently, betook themselves to the field-path; and as they went there moved onward with them, around the shadow of each one's head, a circle of opalized light, formed by the moon's ray upon the glistening sheet of dew. Each pedestrian could see no halo but his or her own, which never deserted the head-shadow, whatever its vulgar unsteadiness might be; but adhered to it, and persistently beautified it; till the erratic motions seemed an inherent part of the irradiation, and the fumes of their breathing a component of the night's mist; and the spirit of the scene, and of the moonlight, and of Nature, seemed harmoniously to mingle with the spirit of wine.

It is a hymn to sensual beauty, to a happy congruence of feeling between man and 'the spirit of the scene'; in a sense, it is Hardy's last tribute to the glory that was Wessex. The dramatic significance of the scene lies in its placing, the final paragraph in the chapter immediately before Tess's seduction. It establishes a perspective within which we can see that incident. For Tess there is no such possibility of the harmony which is known to the 'children of the open air'. They share the passive acceptance that typifies her family. That is an acceptance which her own consciousness can never make, and if later she is to say 'I am ready', the feeling will be of a quite different order. She is to be a true inheritor of the modern world and to receive what for Hardy is its distinctive legacy, that interior conflict which he describes as 'the mutually destructive interdependence of flesh and spirit'. If she is to overcome her self-estrangement she will have to find within herself the strength of selfhood which will allow her to make her peace with the past – to find a route whereby Tess Durbeyfield can achieve the inviolable identity of Tess of the D'Urbervilles.

'Well, we must make the best of it, I suppose. 'Tis nater, after all, and what do please God!' The authentic accents of Joan Durbeyfield are there to greet Tess on her return to Marlott. But 'nater' is now something that Tess feels herself at odds with as she steals out at that time of day when 'the light and the darkness are so even balanced', and 'the plight of being alive becomes attenuated to its least possible dimensions'. The line which separates 'the world' from her consciousness of the world becomes difficult to draw, 'natural processes . . . seemed a part of her own story . . . the world is only a psychological phenomenon, and what they seemed they were'. Her habit of reverie, of self-withdrawal is now carried to an extreme. Her baby is born, she takes work as a field-woman, 'living as a stranger and an alien here, though it was no strange land that she was in'. For most of this phase, 'Maiden No More', Tess is present as a suspended consciousness, unseeing, numb within, instinctual in movement. Around her, 'the children of the open air' continue their unperturbed lives, feeling, on occasion, a pang of sympathy for 'the alien', ' 'twas a thousand pities it should have happened to she, of all others', and then they recall the ballad of the maid 'who went to the merry green wood and came back a changed state'. The gap which has always existed between Tess and 'the world of Marlott' is now at its greatest, and yet it is precisely at this point, when she reaches her most extreme isolation with the death of her baby, that Tess begins her recovery. The emotional as well as the physical release which the baby's death brings to Tess is to make her contemplate her own life more detachedly, and this time her speculation brings with it a renewed vitality:

> Almost at a leap Tess thus changed from simple girl to complete woman. Symbols of reflectiveness passed into her face, a note of tragedy at times into her voice. Her eyes grew larger and more eloquent. She became what would have been called a fine creature . . .

This is an important reflection to remember as we accompany Tess to the Valley of the Great Dairies, the reflection that it is tragedy, and the pondering upon it, which has helped to create the beauty of the milkmaid. Similarly, when Hardy talks now of 'the recuperative power which pervaded organic nature', and 'the invincible instinct towards self-delight', this movement has behind it the desolations of The Chase. The pendulum begins its upward swing, and though 'the harmonies' of 'the children of the open air' are not for her, her reflectiveness is now to know a keener joy than theirs.

It is arguable that in the next three phases of the novel – 'The Rally', 'The Consequence', 'The Woman Pays' – Hardy reached his high-water mark as a novelist. His touch hardly falters, Tess is continually before us, a poignant presence, and yet hardly to be thought of apart from the varied landscapes which surround her. Above all, there is conveyed with an intensity which is never mawkish, a sense of compassionate feeling which pervades all three sections and gives a fresh dimension to our understanding of what writing that is 'deeply felt' can be. Passion, as I have tried to show throughout this study, is an integral element in all of Hardy's major novels, but nowhere is it given such extended treatment as it is in these sections, and nowhere, we have to go on to add, is Hardy more sure in his presention of it, when in isolation from our total sense of self, as a source of consuming pleasure and fearful illusion.

It is that calculated ambivalence which lies deep within these sections of the novel and, particularly in those dealing with the development of the relationship between Angel and Tess. There is a genuine ambivalence to which I feel adequate justice has not always been done in the varied critical accounts which have been given of life at the Dairy. Either it is seen in terms of a lyrical intensity impossible for human beings to sustain, or as a sardonic comment on the blindness of love. I would like to argue that from the particular vantage-point from which Hardy writes, both these reactions are too extreme, and he continually writes in subtler and gentler terms. Two particular episodes can be made to serve as illustrations.

The first one has been the subject of considerable debate and occurs at that moment when Tess walking in the garden alone overhears Angel playing his harp. Tess is fascinated and creeps 'like a fascinated bird' out of sight of the performer:

The outskirts of the garden in which Tess found herself had been left uncultivated for some years, and was now damp and rank with juicy grass which sent up mists of pollen at a touch; and with tall blooming weeds emitting offensive smells – weeds whose red and yellow and purple hues formed a polychrome as dazzling as that of cultivated flowers. She went stealthily as a cat through this profusion of growth, gathering cuckoo-spittle on her skirts, cracking snails that were underfoot, staining her hands with thistle-milk and slug-slime, and rubbing off upon her naked arms sticky blights which, though snow-white on the apple-tree trunks, made madder stains on her skin; thus she drew quite near to Clare, still unobserved of him.

Tess was conscious of neither time nor space. The exaltation which she had described as being producible at will by gazing at a star, came now without any determination of hers; she undulated upon the thin notes of the second-hand harp, and their harmonies passed like breezes through her, bringing tears into her eyes. The floating pollen seemed to be his notes made visible, and the dampness of the garden the weeping of the garden's sensibility. Though near nightfall, the rank-smelling weed-flowers glowed as if they would not close for intentness, and the waves of colour mixed with the waves of sound.

Some years ago, John Holloway drew attention to this passage, claiming that it was 'almost uniquely significant' in an understanding of Hardy, 'among the most intensely realised the author ever wrote' and he used it as a central illustration in a general argument about the multiplicity of Hardy's universe.[1] David Lodge writing later about Holloway's comment, remarked on its perceptiveness, but argued that 'it was a slightly tame account of a passage so centrally important.'[2] He then proceeded to his own reading in which he pointed out, rightly in my view, that though the garden was 'unpleasant', nevertheless, there was at work within the passage, descriptive elements which countered it, and the total effect was one of rich confusion. Lodge then went on to examine the whole passage in interesting detail, and if I take issue with his analysis, it is not with the details, but with his conclusions. What makes this

[1] John Holloway, *The Victorian Sage*, p. 263.
[2] David Lodge, *The Language of Fiction*, p. 181.

a critical exchange worth pursuing is that what is at stake here is not just a matter of interpretation of an individual passage, even if it is 'almost uniquely significant', but rather it enables us to catch, in slow motion as it were, the way Hardy is being read; and this shapes, of course, our whole critical account.

Lodge's reading derives from a close look at what we might call the texture of the passage, its profusions, its contrary impulses, and he concludes that there is confusion here rather than complexity: 'It is as if Hardy, bewildered by the rich possibilities of the scene, has confused himself and us by trying to follow out all of them at the same time'.[1] Where Lodge sees confusion I see a calculated ambivalence, and I see it emerging not from the individual paragraph, but in the relationship set up in the movement from one paragraph to the next. It is the difference between seeing 'stills' from a film and seeing that film in motion.

In the first paragraph we have what Lodge rightly describes as an image of unconstrained nature. This is 'the nater' which has been made familiar to us by the Durbeyfield family, by 'the children of the open air' at Trantridge – profuse, vital, colourful, above all, heedless. In a sense, as we have seen, Tess 'belongs' to that unculti-vated garden, but *she passed through it*, stained certainly, but only on her skin. She proceeds intent and unaware. She is able to do this because of her innate dreaminess, her soul can move outside of her body, that 'exaltation which she had described as being producible at will by gazing at a star'. Her fantasies transform the garden, it becomes an indistinguishable part of her, clinging to her skirt, her hands, her feet, her arms, the 'harmonies passed like breezes through her, bringing tears into her eyes. The floating pollen seemed to be his notes made visible, the dampness of the garden the weeping of the garden's sensibility.' Her tears and the tears of the garden become one; we are reminded again of 'her whimsical fancy [which] would intensify natural processes around her till they seemed part of her own story'. The movement between the two paragraphs dramatises the fatal dislocation that exists within Tess between the world as an obdurate reality, making 'madder stains on her skin', and her apprehension of that world, which so exaltedly 'dissolves

---

[1] Lodge, op. cit., p. 187.

time and space'. What is writ small in these paragraphs is writ large into her whole relationship with Angel Clare.

The second episode that I would like to draw attention to is the meeting in the half-light of dawn between Angel and Tess:

> The spectral, half-compounded, aqueous light which pervaded the open mead, impressed them with a feeling of isolation. . . . She looked ghostly, as if she were merely a soul at large. In reality her face, without appearing to do so, had caught the cold gleam of day from the north-east; his own face, though he did not think of it, wore the same aspect to her. It was then, as has been said, that she impressed him most deeply. She was no longer the milkmaid, but a visionary essence of woman . . .

Tess perceives, or at the least senses, this attitude in Angel, and knows that 'a visionary essence of woman' can have no 'past'; it is her function simply to be. And if she fails to tell Angel of her relationship with Alec, this is not because of some malign fate operating against her, but rather of her intuitive knowledge that, so far as Angel is concerned, such a revelation would make – as she says in her 'Lament' with a slightly different emphasis:

> My doings be as they were not,
> And gone all trace of me![1]

One of the subsidiary ironies that runs throughout 'The Rally' is that in repudiating the stereotype of the farming community as a creation bearing the name of 'Hodge', Angel recognises keenly enough the importance of human particularity, and indeed, when reflecting on Tess he reminds himself 'the consciousness upon which he had intruded was the single opportunity ever vouchsafed to [her] . . . her every and only chance'. When he is in the actual company of the farm-workers, however, they become for him creations of Rousseauistic fancy, just as in the company of Tess, he sees her as 'a whole sex condensed into one typical form'. The co-existence in Clare of 'the man of advanced ideas' and the man of conventional behaviour, splinters his consciousness, dividing him against himself, very much, in a way, as Tess herself is divided. Her inability to reveal her past to him, his inability to sense that she

[1] Hardy, 'Tess's Lament', *Collected Poems*, p. 162.

has something to say, proceed from deep uncertainties within themselves, protective devices against the kind of truth which the confession scene makes plain.

We should say at once that that truth is not of a simple 'moral' kind – the erring wife, the unforgiving husband. Hardy's concern is with something much more elemental – the reassurance which, in their various ways, both Tess and Angel stand in need of, the reassurance of self-identity. Tess has no difficulty in 'forgiving' Angel his past, because she has never presumed to know him in that way; he is not a man with a biography, he is an occasion of awe. And it is of course because of this that she shrinks from telling him her past. If she felt that he was a man capable of erring himself, she might risk his condemnation in the hope of winning his magnanimity. But for her, Angel is not flesh and blood in that kind of way, he is Justice itself and such Justice will surely not just see her, it will see *through* her, and this she cannot bear. She longs to continue simply to be.

For Angel too, 'forgiveness' is an irrelevance, and for reasons not so very different from Tess's. It is the conclusion that he draws that is so fatally different. Angel is right in saying that so far as he is concerned 'forgiveness does not apply to the case'. That would imply a continuity in his apprehension of Tess, a way in which past and present might be made to come together. But 'a visionary essence' does not belong to such a time scale and he speaks in sober truth when he remarks:

'I repeat, the woman I have been loving is not you.'
'But who?'
'Another woman in your shape.'

Indeed, he merely confirms the truth of Tess's own insight on her wedding day:

'O my love, my love, why do I love you so!... for she you love is not my real self, but one in my image; the one I might have been.'

The imaginative drive throughout these phases of the novel, 'The Rally' and 'The Consequence', has been to create a state of intense mutual feeling, feeling enclosed by the pure moment, cut off from the past, from all memory. Outside that feeling, the world loses clarity in the half-lights, mists and heat hazes prevail, there is an overwhelming sense of deliquescence, of strange, shifting perspectives, where sun and moon, water and land, come strangely together, as in that moment when Tess and Angel make their way across the meadows:

> Looking over the damp sod in the direction of the sun, a glistening ripple of gossamer webs was visible to their eyes under the luminary, like the track of moonlight on the sea.

The web screens their visions both of the world which surrounds them and of each other. In *Tess*, more emphatically than in *The Woodlanders*, that web is now in Pater's phrase 'woven through and through us'. It is Hardy's triumph to find in the life at the Dairy a means of registering the intensity and subtlety of the relationship between Angel and Tess, so that when the heart is finally laid bare in the confession scene, we already feel the consequence to be in our possession. It only remains for Angel to 'bury' that self which died at the moment of revelation, and this he does when, walking in his sleep, he lays Tess in the empty stone coffin in the near-by abbey.

If, in evoking life at the Dairy, Hardy has been preoccupied with spinning a web of illusion and dream, the life to be revealed at Flintcomb-Ash is, in every way, the reverse. Physical hardship, the obduracy of the earth, thrusts its way into the reader's consciousness; Tess at work in the fields is barely distinguishable from the land, or the land from her:

> The swede-field in which she and her companion were set hacking was a stretch of a hundred odd acres. . . . Every leaf of the vegetable having already been consumed, the whole field was in colour a desolate drab; it was a complexion without features, as if a face, from chin to brow, should be only an expanse of skin. The sky wore, in another colour, the same likeness; a white vacuity of countenance with the lineaments gone. So these two upper and nether visages confronted each other all day long, the white face looking down on the brown face, and the brown face looking up at the white face, without anything standing between them but the two girls crawling over the surface of the former like flies.

Nothing could be more reductive of the size and significance of the human being, trapped between the blank impersonal gaze of earth and sky. It sets the mood and significance of the phase 'The Woman Pays' as surely as 'the oozing fatness and warm ferments' set that or 'The Rally'. Illusion too is present, though in a distinctively different manner, this time associated not with mists and hazes of the valley, but with the winds and snow which drive across the upland farm, numbing feeling, enclosing Tess ever more tightly within herself. A sharp light is thrown on this in that striking moment when Tess and her companions begin to notice 'strange birds . . . gaunt spectral creatures with tragical eyes – eyes which had witnessed scenes of cataclysmal horror in inaccessible polar regions of a magnitude such as no human being had ever conceived. . . . These nameless birds came quite near to Tess and Marian, but of all they had seen which humanity would never see, they brought no account. The traveller's ambition to tell was not theirs, and, with dumb impassivity, they dismissed experiences which they did not value for the immediate incidents of this homely upland. . . .' This provides a precise comment on the kind of suffering which Tess undergoes at Flintcomb-Ash. For a time her way is that of the polar birds; she sinks into 'a dumb impassivity', totally preoccupied with 'the immediate incidents' of the work. But then, Tess begins to re-assert herself; she, unlike the birds, must seek to give 'an account'. If life in the Valley of the Great Dairies has exploited the divisiveness in Tess's consciousness, by tempting her into the world of reverie and illusion, life at Flintcomb-Ash has threatened to make her repudiate reflection in the grinding actuality of her hardships. But if she is destined to suffer it will be a human and not an animal suffering, she will not remain in 'dumb impassivity', but rather share the traveller's ambition to tell, and in the telling seek to understand.

Her first attempt to tell is frustrated. She attempts to see Angel's parents, but is deflected from her aim by a 'feminine loss of courage at the last and critical moment through her estimating her father-in-law by his sons'. And Hardy goes on to suggest, gently, that it is Tess's judgement which is at fault here, working – like her husband's – in terms of typicalities, whereas, 'Her present condition was precisely one which would have enlisted the sympathies of old Mr. and

Mrs. Clare.' As she turns to make her way home, humiliated by Mercy Chant's unwitting removal of her walking-boots, Tess is blinded by her tears, but they are tears of self-criticism as well as self-pity. 'She knew it was all sentiment, all baseless impressibility, which had caused her to read the scene as her own condemnation. . . .' It is an insight precariously held and it battles with her sense of 'these untoward omens', but it is also her first tentative beginning to accept herself wholly, to join her past with her present. And so in the last two phases of the novel, 'The Convert', and 'Fulfilment', she faces again situations involving, first Alec, and then Angel, but this time in a way which is wholly committed and self-aware – a sense which later Hardy, reading over his completed novel, felt he wished to describe as 'pure'.

Alec's world, the world of the Stoke-D'Urbervilles, is inseparable from nineteenth-century *laissez-faire* capitalism, it is the triumph of the individual bourgeois ethic, what is wanted can be bought. So it is now – and really for the first time – that Hardy introduces in a sustained and explicit way the agricultural and economic crisis that has overtaken Wessex, and turned families like the Durbeyfields, into migratory 'labour'. The wider world is now forcing itself in upon Tess, and the last phases are to be dominated not by the individual consciousness and its correlative, landscape, but by money, changing methods of work, migration of families, 'a fashionable watering place', and the law. Social institutions, economic processes, these are to give a fresh definition to Tess's consciousness, and in its turn, that consciousness is to put such processes under judgement.

The threshing-scene at Flintcomb-Ash serves as a microcosm of Tess's renewed relationship with Alec. The field in which Tess is working is dominated by a nameless figure who calls himself simply 'an engineer', together with his steam threshing-machine. 'He was in the agricultural world, but not of it. He served fire and smoke; these denizens of the field served vegetation, weather, frost, and sun.' For Tess, as for the Wessex world in general, the old 'service' is being gradually replaced by the new, that of a world held together by an increasingly impersonal power: 'The long strap which ran from the driving-wheel of his engine to the red thresher under the rick was the sole tie-line between agriculture and him.' Work continues, and because he sees she is quick and efficient, the farmer keeps Tess on the platform of the machine. Alec D'Urberville enters the field, now wholly intent on winning Tess back to him, having abandoned his preaching and resumed 'the old jaunty, slap-dash guise under which Tess had first known her admirer'. The parallel forces begin to enclose Tess; the nameless engineman driving the shaking platform on which she is forced to work, the seducer renewing his temptation. Economic and physical possession is the object of both, money the common means. The offer to exchange one situation for the other is now made explicit:

'. . . Tess, my trap is waiting just under the hill . . . you should be willing to share it, and leave that male you call your husband for ever.'

One of her leather gloves, which she had taken off to eat her skimmer-cake, lay in her lap, and without the slightest warning she passionately swung the glove by the gauntlet directly in his face. It was heavy and thick as a warrior's, and it struck him flat on the mouth. Fancy might have regarded the act as the recrudescence of a trick in which her armed progenitors were not unpractised. Alec fiercely started up from his reclining position. A scarlet oozing appeared where her blow had alighted, and in a moment the blood began dropping from his mouth upon the straw. . . .

'Now, punish me!' she said. . . . 'Whip me, crush me; you need not mind those people under the rick! I shall not cry out. Once victim, always victim – that's the law!'

The gauntlet is literally thrown and, in that action, Tess challenges Alex with the whole of her being; she sees in him not just her seducer, but a whole complex of interrelated forces. Likewise, she challenges him, not as a single wronged girl, but as someone who now accepts her own past and draws strength from her whole inheritance. It is the beginning of that crucial re-registration, Tess Durbeyfield into Tess of the D'Urbervilles.

If Alec is now to achieve a victory over her it will have to be the same kind of victory as the engineer's – as a body and not as a person.

Such a 'victory' will make plain the meaning of his initial seduction, and she will be literally 'a kept woman'. Tess is to accept this division within herself to such an extent that, when Angel meets her at Sandbourne, he feels 'that his original Tess had spiritually ceased to recognize the body before him as hers – allowing it to drift, like a corpse upon the current, in a direction dissociated from its living will'. Alec has mastered her twice – the first time by exploiting a fatal division within her own consciousness; the second time, by her own consent, ratifying her own acknowledgment of that division. It is a movement in time which brings out the difference between Tess as unwitting victim of her own nature, and Tess as tragic heroine, throwing down the gauntlet, seeing her life in a context which moves back to include her ancestors and forward to the economic pressures which have helped to create the conditions, which have made a 'victory' for Alec possible.

It is outside Wessex that Angel has access to that wisdom which makes him re-view his behaviour towards Tess. He encounters a traveller in Brazil who makes him reflect on

> the old appraisements of morality. He thought they wanted re-adjusting. Who was the moral man? Still more pertinently, who was the moral woman? The beauty or ugliness of a character lay not only in its achievements, but in its aims and impulses; its true history lay, not among things done, but among things willed.

In some ways the passage is misleading because, quoted in isolation, it gives a much sharper emphasis to the word 'moral' than is called for by the wider context. It helps to give a severe didactic restriction to the famous subtitle, 'A Pure Woman'. The passage looks like an epigraph in support of situational ethics but, as the drift of the novel makes plain, Hardy is not entering rival claims for 'intentions' as opposed to deeds, but contending for the involvement of the total self in matters of moral judgement. It is a contention that in so far as Angel loved Tess, he must love her as a person with a past as well as a present, not as an image kept in being through the sheer intensity of his own immediate feelings. It is for Tess as a missing person that he begins to search, not for a revival of 'the visionary essence of woman'.

If Tess is to live out in the end the truth of her relationship with Alec, there is also a truth to be lived out in her relationship with Angel. It is not a truth which Alec can recognise, and a failure here brings about his death. Tess escapes to join Angel and they succeed in enjoying a brief idyll in a large deserted house. She resurrects her buried image:

> In the small hours she whispered to him the whole story of how he had walked in his sleep with her in his arms across the Froom stream . . . and laid her down in the stone coffin at the ruined abbey.

In that house, Tess's relationship with Angel reaches its fulfilment, but she knows it cannot last. It exists, momentarily, outside time, outside society, and when it is over, she is ready to accept her fate in the place of ritualistic sacrifice:

> 'I like very much to be here,' she murmured. 'It is so solemn and lonely – after my great happiness – with nothing b .t the sky above my face.'

She is aware that such an isolation is not for her, and that her fate can only be decided within the social law:

> 'What is it, Angel?' she said, starting up. 'Have they come for me?'
> 'Yes, dearest,' he said. 'They have come.'
> 'It is as it should be,' she murmured. 'Angel, I am almost glad – yes, glad! This happiness could not have lasted. It was too much, I have had enough; and now I shall not live for you to despise me!'
> She stood up, shook herself, and went forward, neither of the men having moved.
> 'I am ready,' she said quietly.

With a passage like this before us, we can see why Hardy entitled the final phase of his novel 'Fulfilment'. It is a description which has behind it the full weight and movement of the novel and, as we could expect, it contains within it that calculatedly ambivalent play on 'nature' which runs throughout the novel. From one point of view 'fulfilment' is the completion of 'nature's plan', and we can imagine Joan Durbeyfield echoing her sentiments about Tess's earlier tragedy and saying, 'It had to be.' From another point of view, it is Tess's own acceptance of herself: 'It is as it should be ... I am almost glad – yes, glad!' Here the appropriate comment is not Joan Durbeyfield's so much as Hamlet's: 'If it be now, 'tis not to come; if it be not to come, it will be now; if it be not now, yet it will come – the readiness is all.'[1] She has vindicated herself, she has fused for Angel the image he adored with the woman he rejected, she has revealed the endurance, the patience and the forgiveness of which the human spirit is capable: she is, genuinely, 'fulfilled'.

In the last, notorious paragraph of the novel all the resonances of the novel are heard:

> 'Justice' was done, and the President of the Immortals, in Aeschylean phrase, had ended his sport with Tess. And the d'Urberville knights and dames slept on in their tombs unknowing. The two speechless gazers bent themselves down to the earth, as if in prayer, and remained thus a long time, absolutely motionless: the flag continued to wave silently. As soon as they had strength they arose, joined hands again, and went on.

How often the opening sentence of that paragraph has been quoted in isolation, and made to serve as 'the conclusion' to the novel, whereas Hardy, true to his practice, makes his conclusion multiple in emphasis. The first sentence is a sombre acknowledgement of forces in the world over which we would seem to have little or no control. It is followed by a sentence which shifts from metaphysics to history, proclaiming the serene indifference of the past to the present. These two sentences are followed by two others which indicate contrary possibilities. We see an intimation of human resilience in 'the speechless gazers' who seek in the earth itself, in the conditions of man's terrestrial existence, notwithstanding his mutability, hope and not despair. In the last sentence hope turns into strength, strength to affirm the human bond and to give direction to action, 'they ... joined hands again, and went on'. It is a sentence which recalls, in its rhythm, the sadness – and the resolution – present in the final lines of *Paradise Lost*:

[1] *Hamlet*, V, ii.

> They hand in hand with wandring steps and slow,
> Through *Eden* took their solitarie way.

It would be as foolish to isolate Hardy's last sentence and see the final emphasis of the novel to lie there as it would be to isolate the first. For him, it is the four sentences taken together which constitute a human truth, by catching in varying lights our condition, flux followed by reflux, the fall by the rally; it is this sense of continuous movement which suggests that the fiction which records it should be described as 'a series of seemings'.

That last phrase brings us back, as it has done so often, to the nature of the novel as Hardy conceived it, and it allows me in consequence to return to the critical issue with which I began this account of *Tess* – the crucial relationship between 'character' and 'ideas' within the novel. My account has been shaped by implicit assumptions about that relationship as far as *Tess* is concerned; I would now like to make the relationship explicit. Or, to put it concretely, I would like to provide, by way of a conclusion, the wider context for reading the final paragraph in this novel.

From the viewpoint which finds the 'ideas' in *Tess* an unfortunate intrusion and the strength of the novel to lie in the presentation of the main character, the description I have given of the final paragraph will read as one of evasion, if not actual confusion, on the part of the author. I want to suggest that that criticism proceeds from a very precise aesthetic, which seeks to find in the individual paragraph a harmony of attitudes, a homogeneity of feeling, and which also reflects wider assumptions about the autonomy of the individual work of art and the relationship of the artist to his work. In the first chapter of this study I have tried to characterise and assess the general implications of this attitude so far as Hardy's novels as a whole are concerned; I want here to take up these implications in relation to *Tess*, because this novel draws attention to them in a particularly forceful way. The last paragraph of the novel exhibits in miniature a structure of feelings, writ large throughout the whole work – a structure which can be most easily characterised first in terms of the movement in a Hardy novel, and second in the way the author or narrator is present in his tale. And, as I have tried to indicate in my opening chapter, these seemingly disparate considerations are, in fact, intimately related.

To take the question of movement first. I remarked at an earlier stage in this chapter that the sentence, 'So do flux and reflux – the rhythm of change – alternate and persist in everything under the sky' could well stand as an epigraph for both the manner and the matter of this novel. I plotted my analysis in terms of Tess's fractured consciousness and the precarious image she entertained of herself, and developed that plotting through the six phases of the novel. In isolation, each phase establishes a characteristic mood; taken in sequence, that mood takes on a wider significance.

In the first phase, particularly in its dealing with life at Marlott, there is present a constant sense of unease between the dying world of peasant custom, with its superstitions, its seediness, and the encircling world of money and business. In the contrasting reactions of the Durbeyfields, the Marlott world receives its definition: Jack obsessed by his possible connection to a noble family, Joan seeing in the connection a lifeline to a brighter economic future through the marriage of her daughter. Past and future hold them respectively in thrall. It is left to Tess to feel the sharp sting of the present. In this first phase of the novel she is, in comparison with her later development, little more than a passive register. Perhaps because of this, this first phase seems by far the weakest in the novel, with the plot moving rather cumbrously, and the pressure of a stereotype situation – the poor young girl seduced by the raffish young landowner – uncomfortably close. The reason for this lies chiefly in Hardy's presentation of Alec, who at this stage of the novel at any rate, is little more than a cut-out figure of Temptation, beside whom characters like Troy, Fitzpiers, and even Wildeve, have, we feel, engaged the author's imagination much more completely.

The crucial turn in the book, the moment when it establishes in the reader a confidence that this, in fact, is going to be a very considerable novel, comes, I would say, in the closing pages of the second phase, 'Maiden No More', when for the first time, Hardy shifts our attention to 'the recuperative power of nature', 'the invincible instinct towards self-delight'. I would like to stress the word 'turn' here because, brilliant and overwhelmingly imagined as the next phases are to be, they derive a considerable part of their power from the way in which they fit into the unfolding pattern. It is the pervasive sense of Tess's past throughout 'The Rally', a past which is now the reader's also, which gives poignancy and lyrical fragility to the emotions which that section evokes so finely.

A significant thing about the central dramatic incident of the novel – Tess's confession to Angel – is its omission. We might argue that the repetition of events, already known to the reader, would be redundant. This is true, but it misses an important point in our reading experience of the novel, as we move across the blank page which separates the fourth from the fifth section. The fourth section ends:

> . . . pressing her forehead against his temple she entered on her story of her acquaintance with Alec d'Urberville and its results, murmuring the words without flinching, and with her eyelids drooping down.

The fifth section opens – 'Her narrative ended'. For Tess, 'her story' has continuity, it is very much *her* story. The tale and the teller are one. For Angel, however, the gap which divides the beginning of her narrative from its end is total, so that he can only murmur numbly, 'You were one person; now you are another.' In one sense, Tess agrees with him, in that for her, her relationship with Alec is a genuine blankness, a nullity in her life, as she makes clear when she is moved to say later, 'What was the past to me as soon as I met you? . . . I became another woman . . .' But for him, the narrative itself is not a nullity, it marks the place where an image died. In the reader's experience of the movement from the fourth phase to the fifth, with the blank page marking the absent 'story', there is this duality of impression. For Tess, the story is no longer there, for her it is a mere recital of events belonging irretrievably to the past; for Angel, the story is not there in its substance, only in its effect, which is to destroy the Tess he thought he knew.

As I tried to bring out in my earlier description of the novel, Tess moves, or is forced to move, from the luxuriant world of fancy which dominated 'The Rally', to the mute insensate world of deprivation which reaches its climax at Flintcomb-Ash, a phase which shifts direction when suffering turns to action and she makes her abortive visit to Angel's parents at Emminster. These phases are complementary, in that they are coextensive states of feeling, but we do not experience them in that static way, because they are continuously interrupted by an element which, perhaps more than anything else in the novel, contributes to its sense of movement; and that is the journey.

The traveller on the road, alone or in company, is an integral part of Hardy's fictional world, and again and again we have encountered him as we have examined the various novels. Oak walking across the fields 'on a certain December morning'; Captain Vye with his silver-headed walking-stick and 'Before him stretched the long, laborious road, dry, empty, and white'; Susan Henchard, accompanying her husband, although 'Virtually she walked the highway alone, save for the child she bore'; the rambler tracing the forsaken coach-road in *The Woodlanders* – all these moments help to create the distinctive world in which these novels take their origin, but in none of Hardy's novels is the actuality of the journey so persistently maintained, so woven into the substance of the narrative, as it is in *Tess*.

Dorothy Van Ghent describes this element in *Tess* very effectively when she refers to 'the long stretches of earth that have to be trudged in order that a person may get from one place to another, the slowness of the business, the irreducible reality of it (for one has only one's feet), its grimness of soul-wearying fatigue and shelterlessness and doubtful issue at the other end of the journey where nobody may be at home'.[1] Miss Van Ghent's emphasis is on the hardship and possible disappointments of this constant journeying, but I think we must take along with this the energy and sense of purpose that these journeys evoke in the mind of the reader.

'The tape-like surface of the road diminished in his rear as far as he could see, and as he gazed a moving spot intruded on the white vacuity of its perspective. It was a human figure running. . . .' The last journey begins in Tess's reunion with Angel, and its start suggests the mood of the last phase of the novel. It is a phase dominated by pursuit, as Tess is followed first by Alec and then by Angel;

[1] Dorothy Van Ghent, 'On Tess of the D'Urbervilles', *The English Novel: Form and Function*, p. 201.

and as the migratory carts crowd the lanes on Lady Day, we feel the last convulsions of the Wessex world. But if this last phase is one of pursuit, it is also one of counter-action, Tess no longer moves in the emotionally screened worlds, whether of happiness or of isolating endurance, that marked her life in the Dairy and on the upland farm. There is a continual oscillation of mood, so that if in my earlier account of the threshing scene, I put the emphasis on Tess's acceptance of Alec's challenge, her attitude of defiance, it is an emphasis which has to be counter-balanced by her sense of daze, of drift: 'Then the threshing-machine started afresh; and amid the renewed rustle of the straw Tess resumed her position by the buzzing drum as one in a dream, untying sheaf after sheaf in endless succession.' Both these moods receive their starkest dramatic expression in her murder of Alec, at once an act of blind impulse, and an act which her whole being endorses, as she ratifies the gesture of the thrown gauntlet.

'All is trouble outside there; inside here content.' Tess's reflection on her brief interlude in the deserted house with Angel comes close to describing, in more general terms, her mood at the end, and it enables her to find within herself the strength ot see Angel's life continuing without her. Life has become so precious to her that, paradoxically, she cannot think of confining it to her individual existence, and in her sister she sees an extension of that life, 'She has all the best of me without the bad of me; and if she were to become yours it would almost seem as if death had not divided us. . . .' And so in a delicate and gentle way, 'the rally' begins again. The movement of the novel, the flux and reflux, is misread if this final emphasis is not taken. That the pendulum should begin to swing is not an intrusion on the author's part of an unassimilated belief in 'evolutionary meliorism', affixed to a narrative quite alien to that idea, it is implicit within the whole oscillating structure of the novel. It is in fact Hardy's own way of paying tribute to the kind of strength he sees in Tess, a strength which seeks to go beyond the sufferings of one individual: her seeing herself, neither as 'a soul at large', nor as a fly trapped between the blank gaze of earth and heaven, but as a person who can, with full consciousness of purpose and with no self-diminution, give herself to forces outside her and say 'I am ready'. That 'readiness' is built into the hope which Angel and 'Liza-Lu draw from the earth and which in turn gives them their strength. And it is with the phrase 'and went on' that the novel ends.

In establishing a wider context for the reading of the final paragraph of the novel, I have tried to indicate that in its movement, in its shifts of emphasis, it enacts the movement of the whole novel which precedes it. What is left out of such a description is that it bypasses the question: what is it that prevents such a structure of feeling from disintegrating the coherence and unity of the novel? And it is here that we face directly the role that 'ideas' have to play, as well as the presence of the narrator. These two elements are aspects of the same thing, because it is in 'the intrusion' of ideas that the narrator makes his presence most clearly felt.

It is perfectly possible to go through *Tess* and isolate a whole series of comments which, taken together, would seem like a consistent philosophical attitude. We could go further and say that such comments would be, more likely than not, pessimistic, sardonic, even embittered in their intent. We might then feel very much as Lionel Johnson did when he remarked that he was reminded of the marginal glosses in *Pilgrim's Progress* and *The Ancient Mariner*: 'Here Tess illustrateth the falling out betwixt Nature and Society', or 'to this place did Angel mock at Giant Calvinist, for that he taught an untenable redemptive theolatry'.[1]

Johnson's remark is a useful one because it reminds us that those marginal glosses of Bunyan and Coleridge are an integral element in our experience of reading those works, typographically in the margin, aesthetically part of the text. So far as Hardy is concerned we say that the dramatic function of 'the glosses' lies in their constant tension with the narrative. The latter acts as the ruthless commentator on the metaphysic, now sceptical, now approving; the metaphysic, on the other hand, gives to the narrative a gravity, a personal urgency, which keeps altering the relationship between the reader and the text.

Given Hardy's particular ideas, however, we can be more precise in plotting this dramatic interplay between the teller and the tale.

[1] Lionel Johnson, *The Art of Thomas Hardy*, p. 219.

Whether we think of those ideas in terms of the images which I have used in this study – the great web, the fall and the rally – or choose some other description, we can see that, with that profound sense of process which is integral to the fiction, the narrator himself will undergo the shifting experiences of his tale in a way not markedly different from that of the characters. There is common tissue between his reflections and theirs, his plotting and theirs. And if the substance of his narrative is as ambivalent as I have attempted to suggest it is, there will be a constant challenge to any authorial commentary which seeks to claim rights of privilege. It was Lawrence, who created a very similar kind of fiction, who delivered the famous admonition, 'Never trust the artist, trust the tale', a remark whose weight only becomes clear in a context of this kind. Unquestionably there is an impulse in Hardy, and perhaps a dominant one, that makes him want to view Tess's story through the eyes of the President of the Immortals; but the narrative cannot leave that unchallenged, it demands a contrary voice, and the author is too honest to deny it. The plurality of meaning in this kind of fiction is always manifest.

To leave the matter in these abstract terms would be to falsify it, it is too instinctual for that. What harmonises the dialectic within the novel, what gives direction to its movement, is not just a reconciliation of contraries within the mind of the author, it is the feeling which encompasses both 'character' and 'idea'. And in Hardy that feeling is an overwhelming compassion, which virtually never fails him. Of no other novel in the present study is this truer than of *Tess*. In his novel, it is Tess herself who releases in Hardy a feeling that we can only describe as love – a love prompted, at least, by the fact that Hardy finds woman expressive, in the purest form, of the human capacity for endurance and the steadfast refusal to be overcome. But, as I have tried to show throughout this study, and in particular in my commentary on this novel, to think of Tess as 'a character', who can be extracted either from the world she inhabits or from the reflections which her life gives rise to, is to impoverish the whole fiction and to misunderstand the reasons for its imaginative power. In her, Hardy has invested his whole imaginative capital. What is history, what is fiction, what is an idea, what is character? – these distinctions hardly seem to make sense any more to the author as we see him pondering his title page, amending 'faithfully depicted' to 'faithfully presented', inserting a subtitle, 'A Pure Woman', looking again at the title and finding in Shakespeare an epigraph which will finally obliterate the gap between the teller and his tale, and make the creator one with his creation:

> . . . Poor wounded name! My bosom as a bed
> Shall lodge thee.

7
An End and a Beginning
Jude the Obscure (1895)

More than any other of his novels Hardy's last work draws our attention to the form it takes. Hardy realised this and in a characteristically depreciatory and laconic remark observed about *Jude*: 'The book is all contrasts – or was meant to be in its original conception. Alas, what a miserable accomplishment it is, when I compare it with what I meant to make it! – e.g. Sue and her heathen gods set against Jude's reading the Greek testament; Christminster academical, Christminster in the slums; Jude the saint, Jude the sinner; Sue the pagan, Sue the saint; marriage, no marriage; etc. etc.'[1]

From such a description we might well conclude that 'form' was a very external thing for Hardy, a self-conscious designing into effective shape of material already present to his imagination. But our sense of the form of the novel in reading it, is of something much more turbulent, a sense not of imposed design but of vexed movement, as if Hardy, in leaving the Wessex novels behind him, had mined a new power within himself, but a power no longer always under his own control. If the novel is 'all contrasts', this is indicative of the way in which the tension which I have described as a central element in the substance of the Wessex novels has now worked its way into the very structure of his fiction. In the chapter that follows I would like to argue that in *Jude* we see Hardy driving his fiction to its furthest extreme, and discovering as he does so, new territories for himself, but territories which only a later kind of fiction will be able to explore satisfactorily.

Perhaps the most obvious sign which indicates the variety of pressures at work in the novel is the difficulty we have in saying, however baldly, just what the novel is 'about'. It seems, almost ostentatiously, to be 'about' so many things – a malevolent universe, an outworn system of education, the rigidity of the marriage laws, or, as one of its most recent critics has put it, 'the sheer difficulty of

[1] *Life*, pp. 272–3.

human beings living elbow to elbow and heart to heart; the difficulty of being unable to bear prolonged isolation or prolonged
closeness; the difficulty, at least for reflective men, of getting through
the unspoken miseries of daily life'.[1] There is no reason why a novel
should not be about all these things and achieve its own formal unity
– but in the case of *Jude* we do feel a genuine disparateness of theme,
a constant oscillation of interests. The total effect the novel makes
is of massive coherence, a coherence arising less, however, from the
substance of the book than from its mood and tone.

We can put the matter in more historical terms. From one point
of view we feel that *Jude* is the work of a man for whom the universe
makes – or ought to make – rational sense; it is something 'out
there' to be interrogated, pondered over. And the interrogator,
though he may be sceptical in his enquiry, frustrated and dis-
appointed by his conclusions, is never in doubt about the validity or
the importance of his undertaking. An entry in Hardy's journal for
January 1890, catches the mood: 'I have been looking for God for
50 years, and I think that if he had existed I should have discovered
him. As an external personality, of course – the only true meaning
of the word.'[2] It is the note of a detective in search of a Missing
Person, confident that nothing has been overlooked and with no
doubt as to the 'true meaning' of clues. But it is not the particulars
of Hardy's scepticism that make us think of *Jude* as a nineteenth-
century novel, so much as the more generalised feeling that the
novelist, with all his assurances and doubts, hopes and fears, is
present in his work in a very direct way, and yet in a way which
quite forbids us to confuse fiction with autobiography. There is a
grandeur of conception, a completeness of commitment, a quality of
caring, which has all been transmuted into art, and yet which we
feel impelled to describe in personal terms; for the integrity of the
art has about it a transparency which makes the integrity of the
artist an inseparable part of our reading experience. With this kind
of fiction before us we have no difficulty in understanding the positive quality there might be in the description 'the novelist as sage'.
Nevertheless, it is this element which marks out *Jude* as not of our

[1] Irving Howe, *Thomas Hardy*, p. 135.
[2] Hardy, *Life*, p. 224.

own time, and of course it is a quality which extends into every detail of the fiction.

Within this firm and articulated structure, however, there glimmers another kind of novel which could only be described in terms very different from these we have been using. Far from the characters in *Jude* seeming fixed, they are seen in constantly shifting emphases and depths, taking themselves – and us – by surprise; the plot is less a narrative line made up of interlocking events, than a series of significant but isolated moments: the ideas debated seem integral to the characters rather than on loan from the author. Though the novel is structured in terms of places, they hardly seem to matter, and as the characters move restlessly from one place to another, the world of the novel seems to be less in Wessex than at the nerves' end. Above all, the novel is conceived in terms of rhythm, markedly seen in the elaborate contrasting and counterpointing of character and incident, but even more significantly felt in the rhythm of the whole, where in the evolving relationship of section to section, the central themes gradually reveal themselves. If *Jude* prompts us to think of 'the novelist as sage', it prompts us no less to think of 'the novel as process', and with that description we think of the fiction of our own time, with its multiplicity of techniques, its interior landscapes, its careful irresolutions.

Implicit in this dualistic impression which the novel makes is a tension, but unlike the tension present in the Wessex novels, it is now present in the very form the novel takes. From one point of view, it is quite clear that in *Jude* Hardy wanted to evoke a sense of cosmic tragedy, with a novel claiming epic status; from another point of view, however, that is by no means so clear, if we see it, not in its compositional totality, but as an unfolding process. Here the sources of the tragedy are more complex, the ironies more subtle, the tone more wry and more detached.

In the pages that follow I would like to argue that the power of Hardy's last singular achievement was shaped by a conflict between a kind of fiction which he had exhausted and a kind of fiction which instinctively he discerned as meeting his need, but which, imaginatively, he had no access to.

♣ II ♣

There occurs an incident in Jude's boyhood which both focuses this duality of emphasis and provides an image which serves to introduce a reading of the novel as a whole. Jude, pursuing his dream of learning, has sent to Christminster for some Greek and Latin grammars:

> Ever since his first ecstacy or vision of Christminster and its possi-bilities, Jude had meditated much and curiously on the probable sort of process that was involved in turning the expressions of one language into those of another. He concluded that a grammar of the required tongue would contain, primarily, a rule, prescrip-tion, or clue of the nature of a secret cipher, which, once known, would enable him, by merely applying it, to change at will all words of his own speech into those of the foreign one . . . He learnt for the first time that there was no law of transmutation, as in his innocence he had supposed . . .

'He learnt for the first time that there was no law of transmutation' – this is a lesson which is to preoccupy Hardy, no less than Jude, as the novel develops. The language in which men seek to make clear to themselves their metaphysical questions, their educational needs, their emotional longings, is in constant need of interpretation. One idiom must be found to complement another. To feel as Jude does that here is some 'secret cipher, which, once known, would enable him, by merely applying it' to master his problem, is a dangerous illusion – whether that illusion finds expression in the prophesyings of Aunt Drusilla, the cynical pragmatism of Arabella, or the fervent idealism of Sue. The incident of the grammars initiates Jude into a life-long education in which he is to learn that there is no simple law of transmutation by which one kind of experience can be simply translated into another, there is only 'a series of seemings' – a phrase which directs us both to the manner and the matter of his novel.

One of the most remarkable things about *Jude* is the tone of the first part – 'At Marygreen'. It is a tone intimately related to the pace of the narrative, uncomfortably reminiscent at times of early silent films. At the still centre is Jude – lying in a field looking through the interstices of his straw hat at 'something glaring, garish, rattling, and the noises and glares hit upon the little cell called your life, and shook it, and warped it.' 'Events did not rhyme quite as he thought' – that sentence could well stand as an epigraph for the section as a whole. Unlike the Wessex novels, which generally build up gradually, *Jude*, plunges us directly into tragedy, or at least the potentialities of tragedy, *con brio*. From the opening pages, Aunt Drusilla reminds us of Jude's luckless existence, 'It would ha' been a blessing if Goddy-mighty had took thee too, wi' thy mother and father, poor useless boy'; we have Jude deserted by Phillotson, his only friend, thrown out of his job by Farmer Troutham, deceived by Vilbert – so that long before he has even met Arabella he has felt 'his existence to be an undemanded one', and indeed wished 'that he had never been born'. The second half of this opening section drives home these feelings without pause – he meets Arabella at the point when his self-education is beginning to take shape, she tricks him into marriage, they have a brutally short and cynical life together, and then she leaves him. We are hardly surprised that Jude – knowing him as we do – walks out to the centre of a frozen pond and seeks to drown himself. From the moment of his arrival at his aunt's house, orphaned and alone, to the moment when Arabella deserts him some seven or eight years later, he would hardly seem to have known more than the most fleeting moments of happiness. Looked at simply in the light of events and the speed with which they succeed each other, the whole opening section is so relentless that it operates dangerously near the area of black farce.

And yet, as we read, it does not strike us in this way. The reason is not far to seek. It is because we find in Jude, playing directly against the force of these events, an instinctive resilience: 'Like the natural boy, he forgot his despondency, and sprang up' – that too is the note struck by the first section, and if the background contains the Clytemnestra-like tones of Aunt Drusilla, there is also the persistent glow of Christminster on the distant horizon with its promise of a life elsewhere. Perhaps what is so striking about the Marygreen section of the novel is the way in which everything is pushed to extremes – the ugliness of the immediate scene contrasted with the city of light glimpsed through the surrounding mists, Jude's absorption with the birds and the clout from the Farmer, and most of all, the juxtaposition of Jude's dream of learning 'Livy, Tacitus, Herodotus, Aeschylus, Sophocles, Aristophanes –' with the sounds on the other side of the hedge, 'Ha, ha, ha! Hoity-toity!' What is interesting to note however is that, while the substance of this first section may not seem uncharacteristic of Hardy, it is all accelerated in such a way that the impression it makes is laconic, faintly off-hand, as if Hardy feels that these extremities of tragedy and un-focused aspiration are much too simple a rendering of experience. 'Events did not rhyme as he had thought', this theme is to be caught again and again in the novel, but in a way which makes us increasingly aware that the apocalyptic tones of the opening will become subdued, as Christminster transforms itself from 'a glow in the sky', an ideal to be lived for, into buildings, streets, people.

'It was a windy, whispering, moonless night. To guide himself he opened under a lamp a map he had brought' – and so Jude begins his exploration of Christminster. His first encounter is not with the present of Christminster, but with its past; and as he wanders through the deserted streets in the moonless night he hears the voice of the university in the accents of Addison, Gibbon, Peel, Newman and, most clearly, in Arnold's famous apostrophe, 'Beautiful city! so venerable, so lovely, so unravaged by the fierce intellectual life of our century, so serene!' The clash intimated by Arnold, between the serenity of Oxford and its remoteness from contemporary intellectual concern, foreshadows the stance to be taken by Sue and indeed it is ironically caught in Jude's first glimpse of her at work in the Anglican bookshop – 'A sweet, saintly, Christian business, hers' – while her thoughts dwell on the pagan deities she has bought to decorate her room and the books of Gibbon and Mill which provide her nightly reading. But for Jude, it is not the intellectual remoteness but the social remoteness which strikes him. 'Only a wall divided him from those happy young contemporaries of his with whom he shared a common mental life: . . . Only a wall – but what a wall!' That is the note which is struck throughout this section, and when Jude eventually comes to write to the Master of one of the colleges, the reply expresses in its address the reason for rejection, 'To Mr. J.

Fawley, Stone-mason.' For the Master, Jude is not there as a person but as a trade, a trade which should not seek to go beyond the walls it is committed to restoring. The social criticism of this section is direct and unequivocal, and the authorial sentiment none the less trenchant for its familiarity: 'here in the stone yard was a centre of effort as worthy as that dignified by the name of scholarly study within the noblest of the colleges'. But the criticism of Christminster goes beyond a defence of the dignity of labour, it extends to its self-conscious medievalism 'as dead as a fern-leaf in a lump of coal?' The social astringencies of this section, while they are not remarkable in themselves and, are, indeed, commonplaces in the social writings of critics like Arnold, Ruskin and Morris, nevertheless evoke a very different mood from the first section of the novel with its large metaphysical gestures, its sustained air of cosmic gloom. While this is a mood in which precise social criticisms are emphatically made, nevertheless other notes are being struck in a quiet way which subtilise that criticism. There is a *naïveté* about Jude which is difficult to gainsay. While he might have failed to recognise that 'mediaevalism was as dead as a fern-leaf in a lump of coal', he might have made a more effective communication with the colleges if he had chosen a more profitable method of selection than walking the city looking for the heads of colleges and then selecting 'five whose physiognomies seemed to say to him that they were appreciative and far-seeing men. To these five he addressed letters. . . .' This does not blunt the edge of criticism about the attitude of the colleges, but it gives an additional nuance to the epigraph which prefaces the section, 'Save his own soul he hath no star'. The exclusiveness of that statement is something that Hardy is to look at several times in the course of the novel, but here it is offered in its simplest form. Jude's *naïveté*, while being related to a fundamental honesty, is also disabling in that it prevents him from taking an adequate measure of the situation in which he finds himself. So that as the section concludes with Jude seeking solace for his rejection in a Christminster pub and being challenged to recite the Nicene Creed to a public for whom it might as well have been 'the Ratcatcher's Daughter in double Dutch,' our response is not simply that the Christian creed is incomprehensible to 'the real life of Christminster', but that Jude himself has a great deal to learn about himself and the world in which he lives.

Is it right to equate education with formal learning? Might an education not be found in a vocation pursued away from the college world of Christminster? It is with questions like these in mind that Jude goes to Melchester to the theological college, with a vague intention to enter the Church, but primarily to be near Sue.

Up to this point Sue's role, lightly sketched in as it has been, would seem clear and unequivocal. She is, among other things, the sceptical voice of the present age, at ease in Christminster, but scornful of its social exclusiveness and even more of its attachment to a creed outworn. The pieties she respects are those of the free spirit; she is wary of the dead hand of the past, sensitive and open to change. For her, Jude is enslaved to a false dream of learning and an idle religious superstition. The kind of conflict which exists between them is succinctly expressed in this exchange:

'Shall we go and sit in the Cathedral?' he asked, when their meal was finished.

'Cathedral? Yes. Though I think I'd rather sit in the railway station,' she answered, a remnant of vexation still in her voice. 'That's the centre of the town life now. The Cathedral has had its day!'

'How modern you are!'

'So would you be if you had lived so much in the Middle Ages as I have done these last few years! The Cathedral was a very good place four or five centuries ago; but it is played out now. . . .'

The unhesitating sharpness of Sue's replies might perhaps alert us to an authorial irony here, but it is a measure of the feeling of the novel that, at this stage, it is Jude's reactions which take our attention. With our reading of the Christminster section behind us, he would still seem to be the victim of a romantic *naïveté*, a nostalgic addiction to the past. And so when sometime later Sue says, 'the mediaevalism of Christminster must go, be sloughed off, or Christminster itself will have to go,' we feel that diagnostic confidence evokes sympathy in the author. When Sue falls foul of the rules governing her training college, we suppose that the kind of criticism against educational institutions operative in the Christminster sections is simply being extended here – the intellectual rigidities of the one being replaced by the moral rigidities of the other.

But it is just here, at the centre of the Melchester section, when the pattern of authorial feeling would seem to be becoming increasingly defined, that the novel begins to change tack in an extremely interesting and unexpected way.

Sue having escaped from the confining discipline of the college takes refuge with Jude, and begins to recall her past: 'My life has been entirely shaped by what people call a peculiarity in me. I have no fear of men, as such. . . .' For the first time we are given a perspective on Sue other than that of the free spirit, the devoted Hellene, the admiring follower of Mill. This new impression is developed quickly, so that when she says to Jude, 'You mustn't love me. You are to like me – that's all,' we feel a vibration here which is not that of Sue delicately preserving her commitment to Phillotson, but rather that of her inability to achieve a commitment of any kind. The 'freedom' she has been at such pains to assert, and which up to this stage in the novel would seem to have provided an unequivocal point of vantage for criticising Jude's dream and the institutions which thwart it, is now seen as something much more ambivalent, a nervous self-enclosure, the swift conceptualising, safeguarding the self against the invasions of experience. Sue's scrutiny is keen, but it is judiciously angled. The effect of this interplay between her public and private self emerges in this exchange:

'At present intellect in Christminster is pushing one way, and religion the other; and so they stand stock-still, like two rams butting each other.'

'What would Mr. Phillotson—'

'It is a place full of fetichists and ghost-seers!'

He noticed that whenever he tried to speak of the schoolmaster she turned the conversation to some generalizations about the offending University.

This is an interesting passage because we can gauge the effect of the personal pressures being exerted on Sue. Her opening remark is of a piece with her general criticism about the intellectual sterility of Christminster and the simile exhibits the familiar self-confidence in her analysis. The effect of Jude's mention of Phillotson is immediately to make that analysis shrill and strained, 'it is a place full of fetichists and ghost-seers'. Gradually we begin to see that for Sue the pursuit of the idea becomes a surrogate for the presence of personal feeling. The effect of this is not to invalidate the idea, but to make us increasingly aware that, by the end of the Melchester section, the centre of Hardy's interest has moved from the world Jude sees – and with it the criticism provoked by that world – to Sue and 'that mystery, her heart'.

At the very end of the Melchester section there occurs an incident, insignificant in the general development of the novel, but which expresses in a modest but beautifully precise way the 'series of seemings' which the novel as a whole is building up. Greatly moved by a hymn being sung that Easter, 'At the Foot of the Cross', Jude feels that the composer is a man who will understand the problems that beset him, and characteristically, resolves to pay him a visit. The meeting is a crushing disappointment – the composer is interested only in his royalties and has turned to the wine trade for greater financial comfort. The ironies are strident and would seem a further variant on the deceptions of appearance, and generally to be taking up the kind of social criticism present in the Christminster section; there is, besides, a gentle deflating of Jude's *naïveté*. The episode however is to have further implications.

Settled in Shaston – 'the ancient British Palladour . . . the city of a dream' – Sue prepares to meet Jude for the first time as Mrs. Phillotson. The afternoon is growing dark and Jude makes his way to the schoolroom where he expects to find her. Seeing it empty he proceeds to play idly on the piano the opening bars of 'At the Foot of the Cross':

> A figure moved behind him, and thinking it was still the girl with the broom Jude took no notice, till the person came close and laid her fingers lightly upon his bass hand. The imposed hand was a little one he seemed to know, and he turned. 'Don't stop,' said Sue, 'I like it. I learnt it before I left Melchester . . .'

Jude then asks her to play it for him:

> Sue sat down, and her rendering of the piece, though not remark-

able, seemed divine as compared with his own. She, like him, was evidently touched – to her own surprise – by the recalled air; and when she had finished, and he moved his hand towards hers, it met his own half-way. Jude grasped it . . .

It is the renewal of the relationship which is to culminate in Sue's leaving Phillotson and going to live with Jude. The darkening room and the rich melancholy music conspire to weave the spell which enables their relationship to take on an added intensity, an intensity made possible by the fact that the music succeeds in awakening Sue's emotions, but at the same time provides a suitably 'spiritual' mode of expression. This episode, coming at the beginning of the Shaston section, initiates an ever-increasing concern with Sue which is to dominate the remainder of the novel.

'We were too free, under the influence of that morbid hymn and the twilight.' Sue's self-reproach and resolution to withdraw from Jude's company has a fugitive life, and at Shaston we see the break-up of her marriage with Phillotson and the elopement with Jude. When we look at the series of conversations with Phillotson we can see how far Hardy has now taken us into the area of personal relationships. We can catch it revealingly in this exchange, where Sue is attempting some kind of defence of her marital attitudes to Phillotson:

'But it is not I altogether that am to blame!'
'Who is then? Am I?'
'No – I don't know! The universe, I suppose – things in general, because they are so horrid and cruel!'
'Well, it is no use talking like that.'

That Sue's reference to 'the universe' should come over as limply rhetorical – an unfocused irritation – and Phillotson's pragmatism as both just and solicitous, is an index of the change in mood and direction since the opening sections of the novel. Sue's critical intelligence may still be on display, but we feel that she is now very much its victim, in the sense that having announced her wish to leave Phillotson and live with Jude, she quotes Mill by way of justifying her action: 'J. S. Mill's words, those are. I have been reading it up. Why can't you act upon them? I wish to, always.' If this was not so clearly dictated by emotional desperation, it would simply strike us as callow and grossly insensitive to the situation in which she finds herself. This is enforced by the increasing sympathy with which Phillotson is presented throughout the section. The account of his final evening with Sue is one of the most deeply felt passages in the novel, and all the more so for the restraint and delicate precision of its feeling.

If Jude formally commits himself to Sue now, he does so with an increasing awareness of her enigmatic nature. And Phillotson's generous farewell tones 'You are made for each other', echo hollowly in the railway carriage as Sue leaves her husband, only to tell Jude that they are not to be lovers in the way he anticipated. He sees her now in a way that he has not seen her before, and though this does not affect his love, a new sharpness of insight is unquestionably present: 'Sue, sometimes, when I am vexed with you, I think you are incapable of real love'; 'under the affectation of independent views you are as enslaved to the social code as any woman'; 'you spirit, you disembodied creature, you dear, sweet, tantalizing phantom – hardly flesh at all; so that when I put my arms round you I almost expect them to pass through you as through air.' And characteristically, Sue's supreme moment of committing herself to Jude is to enter her hotel room – alone.

The deepening analysis of Sue, this is the main preoccupation and drive of this section of the novel, but if we are to understand the remainder of the novel it is important to see that analysis in its context. And it is a context which is increasingly concerned to ponder the meaning of 'freedom'. All the characters in the Shaston section are, in one way or another, asked to ponder this, Sue, Jude, Phillotson and Gillingham. And this meditation is given sharp emphasis by the incident of the rabbit caught in the gin and mercifully killed by Jude. When Jude comes to reflect on his ruined career at the hands of two women, he uses precisely this imagery: 'Is it that the women are to blame; or is it the artificial system of things, under which the normal sex-impulses are turned into devilish domestic gins and springes to hold back those who want to progress?' 'The artificial system of things' – it would seem precisely that which Sue, Jude and Phillotson are brought to recognise in

Shaston and to be able to set aside. Phillotson gives Sue her freedom', first to be able to go and live with Jude, and then, if she
desires, to marry him. Sue begins a life with Jude and appears to be
able to call the terms on which it will be lived. Jude formally turns
his back on his ambitions, burning his books, and going to live with
the woman he loves. Arabella, by marrying again, removes any
obstacle about his remarriage to Sue. Connections with the past too
are formally severed as Aunt Drusilla dies, and with her the old
Wessex of legend and 'the family curse'. In Shaston then, Hardy
would appear to wipe the slate clean, to give the characters precisely
that freedom of decision they have constantly desired and that
definition of self they have longed for. Even in the case of Phillotson,
where unhappiness has prompted his action, there is a power of
resolution, a revelation of self-knowledge which previously had not
been open to him. 'The artificial system of things' has now been
openly challenged and a fresh significance is given to human decision. It is significant that Aunt Drusilla dies in this section of the
novel, because it marks the opposite pole from the doom-laden
world of Marygreen; it is the moment when the free and untram-
melled self seems triumphant.

This then is the context in which we must see the deepening
analysis of Sue – that fine instance of 'freedom', the supremely
individual case. With her we find displayed the consciousness of
self, the innate uncertainties, the psychic disturbance with which the
fiction of our own day is to make us so familiar. And the end of the
Shaston section of *Jude* is the ending of a characteristically modern
fiction. The wounded rabbit has been set free from the gin, the
artificial system of things has been challenged, the individual will
has been triumphantly exercised and, though the past may be painful
and the future unknown, the self has been validated.

But for Hardy that picture would be radically incomplete. He
does not share the views of a later age. Lawrence voiced the representative twentieth-century criticism when he remarked that
Hardy's characters were all cowed by 'the mere judgement of man
upon them, and when all the while by their own souls they were
right'. That antithesis would have been alien to Hardy, and the last
two sections of *Jude* are there to show that 'the mere judgement of

man' is for him an inextricable part of man's soul. They enable us to look at 'the artificial system of things' from an aspect different from any we have had so far – to draw a distinction between the tragedy of a rabbit and the tragedy of a man. The epigraph to the fifth section establishes the emphasis of the section:

> Thy aerial part, and all the fiery parts which are mingled in thee, though by nature they have an upward tendency, still in obedience to the disposition of the universe they are overpowered here in the compound mass the body.

'The aerial part', 'the body', this is the dichotomy to be explored, and with the Phillotson decree made absolute and Arabella marrying again, Sue and Jude are in her words, 'just as free now as if we had never married at all'. For Jude this has its own significance: 'Now we'll strut arm and arm like any other engaged couple. We've a legal right to.' But for Sue, such legality is inimical to the freedom she has just painfully re-acquired – it implies a gesture of public commitment which she, and in effect Jude too, are reluctant to make. Her aversion to marriage has nothing to do with uncertainty about her feelings for Jude, but she fears that those feelings will be debased by 'the government stamp', by a construct which is no more than 'a licence to be loved on the premises'. Faced with the idea of a marriage ceremony, she can see only a sequence of external gestures from which all inner significance has been drained. It marks the high points of her self-enclosure – a self-enclosure not disturbed by the widow Edlin's sardonic reminders of a world beyond herself: 'Nobody thought o' being afeard o' matrimony in my time, nor of much else but a cannon ball or empty cupboard! Why when I an my poor man were married we thought no more o't than of a game o' dibs!'

Two events however do conspire to modify it. The first is the arrival of Arabella, when feelings of jealousy precipitate Sue into sharing her bed with Jude. The second is more far-reaching – the arrival of Father Time, the natural son of Arabella and Jude, and it is with this figure that Hardy gives his narrative the last decisive shift.

From his introduction Father Time stands apart from the narrative, and of course at the level of realistic presentation he is very awkwardly accommodated indeed. But Hardy leaves us in no doubt that his role is to be choric: 'He was Age masquerading as Juvenility, and doing it so badly that his real self showed through the crevices.' And as he sits in the railway compartment he 'seemed to be doubly awake, like an enslaved and dwarfed Divinity, sitting passive and regarding his companions as if he saw their whole rounded lives rather than their immediate figures'. It would be foolish to deny that the attempt to integrate Father Time into the novel is not a success; Hardy has set aside the conventions of realism too easily, so that the child appears to have strayed into the novel from another art form, Lady Macduff's son unnervingly encountered on 'The Great Western'. But that Hardy should be prepared to risk so much with him is an indication both of the necessity of what he is trying to say at this stage of the novel and of his difficulty in finding a satisfactory way of saying it. In a phrase, he is introducing with Father Time the processes of history into the lives of Jude and Sue – his sorrowful contemplative eyes become ours as we watch them desperately attempting to cheat time, repudiating the past, evading the social commitments of the present, indifferent, with their ever increasing family, to the demands of the future. With Father Time their 'dreamless paradise' fades into the light of common day.

This is poignantly revealed in the visit which Jude and Sue pay to the Great Wessex Agricultural Show. It is one of the rare moments when happiness seems to prevail, and it is also one of the rare moments when we see Jude and Sue through the eyes of others, in this case those of Arabella and Cartlett. The effect is that of a brightly lit picture, darkly framed. Wessex, once a whole way of life, is now present merely as 'a show' for itinerant observers. Jude and Sue arrive by excursion and wander through the exhibition ground. Entirely lost in each other's company, they are oblivious of the people around them:

> 'Happy?' he murmured.
> She nodded.
> 'Why? Because you have come to the great Wessex Agricul-tural Show – or because *we* have come?'
> 'You are always trying to make me confess to all sorts of

absurdities. Because I am improving my mind, of course, by seeing all these steam-ploughs, and threshing-machines, and chaff-cutters, and cows, and pigs, and sheep.'

What was once a way of life, a history, has now become an inventory for 'the improvement' of the mind, and a mind exercised not by things in use, but by things exhibited. Jude, trying to find in the event a crystallisation of his feelings, only moves Sue to a character-istic withdrawal of hers as she marks out, with firm lines of demarca-tion, the observer from the world observed. If the world observed is to extend her feelings, then it must not be through a shared experi-ence, but through one in which she participates alone.

And so we find her pausing to admire the roses, 'I should like to push my face quite into them – the dears!' Like Miriam in *Sons and Lovers*, she can encounter the sensual world only when she can im-pose herself upon it, when it cannot make reciprocal demands, but is simply there to feed the contemplative soul. Such a moment cannot be sustained, and Father Time reflects that in a few days the flowers will all be withered.

The moment of joy is precarious and the shadows of Arabella and Father Time, cast emblematically at the Show, begin to acquire a social reality. Ironically, Jude's and Sue's trouble begins with a return to the law which they have both, in their various ways, tried to set aside – a law at once human and divine. Jude, commissioned to re-letter the Ten Commandments in a nearby church, causes a scandal when he is joined in his work by the pregnant, unmarried Sue, and is duly dismissed. His life of wandering now begins, his home is uprooted for the second time, his goods are sold. Father Time asks why they must go, and Jude replies sardonically, 'Be-cause of a cloud that has gathered over us; though "we have wronged no man, corrupted no man, defrauded no man." ' To which Father Time might have added that they have sought to meet no man either. They have neglected 'the disposition of the universe', and in consequence the 'aerial part' and 'the body' have been kept at war.

In Jude's decision to return to Christminster we find a summon-ing of will and a recognition of the disposition of the universe which has never been present in Sue. For Sue the place still remains what it has always been, 'a nest of commonplace schoolmasters whose characteristic is timid obsequiousness to tradition'. But for Jude, though he recognises himself as permanently excluded from it, 'it is still the centre of the universe. . . . Perhaps it will soon wake up, and be generous'. This acceptance of possibilities, of change, is a note which characterises Jude throughout the last tragic section of the novel, a section drawing out a radical difference in response, as Jude and Sue become increasingly enmeshed in the society they have sought to reject.

Once again the epigraph catches the main emphasis, 'And she humbled her body greatly, and all the places of her joy she filled with her torn hair.' The 'aerial part' now seeks to annihilate 'the body', and the freedom it seeks is the last freedom of all – the freedom of self-destruction. But 'the body' can no longer be thought of as 'the individual body', and in destroying herself, Sue destroys the lives of those around her. The full meaning of Father Time is to become clear in this last section where the social body and the individual body become inextricably united, a recall to Hardy's abiding theme that the human race is 'one great network or tissue which quivers in every part when one point is shaken, like a spider's web if touched'.[1]

Jude's attitude of mind in returning to Christminster is made clear in his speech to the crowd who have gathered for Remembrance Day. Though it is certainly not free from bitterness, it is clear in its emphasis:

> It was my poverty and not my will that consented to be beaten. It takes two or three generations to do what I tried to do in one. . . . Eight or nine years ago when I came here first, I had a neat stock of fixed opinions, but they dropped away one by one; and the further I get the less sure I am . . . I perceive there is something wrong somewhere in our social formulas . . . .

These sentiments give a suggestively defining edge to the way in which Jude has evolved throughout the successive stages of his life – the early metaphysical glooms, the unfocused intellectual and theological ambitions, the formal disavowals and the retreat into self, and now the attempt to come to terms with a social reality

---

[1] *Life*, p. 177.

which, harsh and forbidding as it might be, is resistant to prophecy and to judgement. As with the Greek and Latin grammars which he received as a boy, there is no simple law of transmutation, there is only a series of seemings. It is this view which Sue is to reject, and the extent of her negation will make plain what is at stake. In the last analysis, by a sad irony, assertions of the free spirit are to catch the inflexible tones if not the substance of Aunt Drusilla's curse.

The narrative now leads into the most terrible scene in Hardy's fiction, indeed it might reasonably be argued in English fiction – the killing of the children by Father Time. Although the scene is brutally disturbing in a way which the novel can hardly accommodate, nevertheless its animating purpose is rooted deep within the evolving structure of the novel, and it does not represent a deflection of Hardy's into a momentary despair, resulting in an episode more akin to *grand guignol* than realistic fiction. The scene is obviously an attempt at the same kind of choric effect as that represented by Father Time himself, a reaching out beyond the particulars of the narrative to an impersonal tragic dimension, a dimension where Time ceases to be a child and becomes 'the whole tale of their situation'. So that the author can go on to say: 'On that little shape had converged all the inauspiciousness and shadow which had darkened the first union of Jude, and all the accidents, mistakes, fears, errors of the last. He was their nodal point, their focus, their expression in a single term.' The scene is 'the action' of such a figure, the only action he is capable of performing.

To say this is not to argue for the success of the scene, but merely to suggest its nature. It also directs attention to the way in which it arises out of the previous narrative, though its relationship is more with the inner drama than with overt incident. And because it is a drama related to Sue rather than to Jude, it demands a new directness of treatment, now that the two characters are treading rather different paths.

To establish a context for the scene we might go back to a conversation at Shaston, referred to earlier, where Sue asks Phillotson for her freedom. To support her point she quotes Mill:

'She, or he "who lets the world, or his own portion of it, choose his plan of life for him, has no need of any other faculty than the

ape-like one of imitation." J. S. Mill's words, those are. I have
been reading it up. Why can't you act upon them? I wish to,
always.'

'What do I care about J. S. Mill!' moaned he.

The ironies cut deep. Hardy, like Sue a warm admirer of Mill,
chooses this passage – in which the variety and independence of
human behaviour are defended – to expose Sue's rigidities and in-
tolerance of opinions other than her own. And encompassing that is
her total inability to enter into Phillotson's feelings; her intellect is
at odds with her sensibility. The point is emphasised later when
having left Phillotson, she comes to visit him in his illness, though
she 'did not for a moment, either now or later, suspect what troubles
had resulted to him from letting her go; it never once seemed to
cross her mind . . .'

It is precisely this mixture of insensibility and forthright statement that she displays again in her conversation with Father Time
when they are frustrated in their search for lodgings at Christminster. He begins by asking:

> 'Can I do anything?'
> 'No! All is trouble, adversity and suffering!'
> 'Father went away to give us children room, didn't he?'
> 'Partly.'
> 'It would be better to be out o' the world than in it, wouldn't
> it?'
> 'It would almost, dear.'
> ' 'Tis because of us children, too, isn't it, that you can't get a
> good lodging?'
> 'Well – people do object to children sometimes.'
> 'Then if children make so much trouble, why do people have
> 'em?'
> 'O – because it is a law of nature.'
> 'But we don't ask to be born?'
> 'No indeed.'

She then goes on to tell the boy that there is to be another baby, but,
through a mistaken sense of delicacy, does nothing to remove his
impression that she has deliberately sought its arrival. The effect of
this on the child – the combination of the indifference of nature's

law with the apparent indifference of his mother – is overwhelming. Just as in her previous conversation with Phillotson, Sue is blind to the effect her words will have, and she makes no attempt to go behind the letter of what she is saying. For her, words alone seem certain good.

The situation is now set for the tragedy, and however grotesque the actual incidents that follow, Sue has established a structure of feeling which the boy will carry to a remorseless conclusion, exchanging in his pencilled note of explanation, 'Done because we are too menny', literalism for literalism. 'The letter killeth' has been made fact. In the icy language of that 'explanation', Sue reads her own indictment, and her world is shattered. But imprisoned within extremes, she can only exchange the letter of freedom for the letter of renunciation, and though she recognises that her literalness has provoked the boy's action, she is unable to assimilate the recognition into behaviour, so that she remains unmoved by Jude's agonised response to her proposed remarriage to Phillotson, 'Sue, Sue! we are acting by the letter; and ' "the letter killeth"!'

The deaths of the children are a decisive point for her, driving her ever deeper into herself, so that although her behaviour is now in striking contrast to her previous conduct – the return to the church, the remarriage to Phillotson – her fundamental disposition is unchanged. 'The aerial part' and 'the body' are still held together only by a fanatical act of will, her 'enslavement to forms' of self-renunciation replacing her earlier enslavement to forms of self-assertion. Enclosed within herself, she seals herself off almost literally from human communication; 'clenching her teeth she uttered no cry' when Phillotson takes her into his bedroom, and when Jude leaves her for the last time she 'stopped her ears with her hands till all possible sound of him had passed away'. She has transformed herself into pure will.

To turn to Jude is to find that he has continued to move in a significantly different direction. Since his return to Christminster he has increasingly perceived his tragedy to be inextricably involved with time, place and person. 'Events did not rhyme as they should', that sentiment stands, but the cause is no longer abstract, metaphysical, nor as Aunt Drusilla said 'sommat in our blood'. It is Sue, the free spirit, who now voices that position:

'All the ancient wrath of the Power above us has been vented upon us, His poor creatures, and we must submit. There is no choice. We must. It is no use fighting against God!'

to which Jude replies:

'It is only against man and senseless circumstance.'

And that remains his attitude to the end. He recognises with perfect clarity his differences from Sue, that 'events which had enlarged his own view of life, laws, customs, and dogmas, had not operated in the same manner on Sue's', and more generally: 'Strange difference of sex, that time and circumstance, which enlarge the views of most men, narrow the views of women almost invariably.' His remarriage with Arabella is a black parody of Sue's with Phillotson, the one made possible only by will, the other through torpor. And it is Jude's remarriage that drives home his own personal tragedy. However much he has come to recognise his tragedy as contingent on circumstance, 'the time was not ripe for us! Our ideas were fifty years too soon to be any good to us'; however much he has sought to keep the letter informed by spirit, his own tragedy is stark and unrelieved. Truly, as Hardy says in his preface, Jude's is a tragedy of 'unfulfilled aims', and that unfulfilment is both public and private, educational and sexual. It is interesting to notice that in these closing pages Arabella for all her harshness and cynicism, gives us a sense of being a married woman in a way that Sue never does, and in Jude's refusal to let Sue visit him in his last illness, we feel that finally, he has come to recognise that she could never fulfil that need of his which, however tortuously and casually, is fulfilled by Arabella. His remarriage, of course, can hardly be said to exist at all in its own right, but it is capable nevertheless of casting a harsh retrospective light on Sue, and significantly, the last words of the novel are of Sue's self-deception, and they are spoken not by Jude but by Arabella.

Despite the harsh ironies that attend Jude's death – the cheers from the river sports counter-pointing his recital of verses from the Book of Job, Arabella already preparing herself a future with Vilbert – we feel that Hardy has now opened up perspectives which go beyond the individual tragedy, which reveal the individual as belonging to a wider history, and that it is Jude's singular achievement, despite his personal suffering, to have perceived this.

He never gives up the effort to translate his dream and, even when he returns to Christminster, having seen Sue for the last time, the place is still alive for him with figures of the past. For Arabella, the street is empty, 'There's neither living nor dead hereabouts except a damn policeman!' To Arabella, and to Sue in her very different kind of way, Jude's sense of history has no meaning. For the former, the only time is the present, for the latter, time is to be transcended, but for Jude the past is alive in the way that it was for his creator. For them both, things,

> That nobody else's mind calls back,
> Have a savour that scenes in being lack,
> And a presence more than the actual brings . . .[1]

In that 'presence more than the actual' Jude finds, however obscurely, his pledge for the future, and if he comes to reject a Power above us whether beneficent or malevolent, he senses in a recognition of the Spirit of the Years a clue to a proper humanity.

♣ III ♣

I would like to add a last perspective. In July 1914 we find Lawrence writing in a letter to Eddie Marsh:

'Have you got Lascelles Abercrombie's book on Thomas Hardy; and if so, could you lend it me for the space of, say, six weeks; and if so, do you mind if I scribble notes in it? And if you've got any of those little pocket edition Hardy's, will you lend me those, too? . . . I am going to write a little book on Hardy's people.'[2]

To come to that 'little book' after reading the Wessex novels is to find it a classical postscript. Classical, not in the sense of offering a judicious estimate of the novels – it is too turbulently involved for that – but classical in the sense that it expresses in a remarkably pure way the nature of creative literary influence. Lawrence discerns in Hardy's work elements he feels still inchoate, and through that

---

[1] Hardy, 'Places', *Collected Poems*, p. 332.
[2] *Letters of D. H. Lawrence*, ed. Huxley, p. 205.

discernment finds a sharper sense of his own fiction, his own meta-physic. By the end of 1914, 'the little book' has become 'a sort of Story of My Heart, or a Confessio Fidei'.[1] For the modern literary critic it is the workshop for *The Rainbow*; the way in which one kind of fiction becomes transformed into another.

If we read Lawrence's study with a primary interest in Hardy, then it will emerge differently. The critical discussion of Hardy is inset at intervals into Lawrence's own developing argument, and has the function of a series of images in relation to that argument. If we consider the critical discussion apart from its general context, we can see that Lawrence certainly perceived elements and tendencies in Hardy's fiction which remained opaque to the author, but we can also see in that fiction other elements, no less opaque to his critic. By way of illustration we can look at Lawrence's general judgement on the Wessex novels:

> There is a lack of sternness, there is a hesitating betwixt life and public opinion, which diminishes the Wessex novels from the rank of pure tragedy. It is not so much the eternal, immutable laws of being which are transgressed, it is not that vital forces are set in conflict with each other, bringing almost inevitable tragedy – yet not necessarily death, as we see in the most splendid Aeschylus. It is in Wessex, that the individual succumbs to what is in its shallowest, public opinion, in its deepest, the human compact by which we live together, to form a community.[2]

As a description, the criticism corresponds to the case I have tried to argue in the present book, but what Lawrence sees as weakness, I have contended is strength. It is precisely the way in which Hardy's fiction moves away from a world where 'vital forces are set in con-flict with each other', as in *The Return of the Native*, to the world of the later novels where 'the human compact' is vividly created, that seems to me to constitute his development as a novelist. Lawrence makes the distinction he has in mind more starkly in a remark I quoted earlier, when he asks about the main characters: 'What was there in their position that was necessarily tragic? Necessarily pain-ful it was, but they were not at war with God, only with Society.

[1] *Letters of D. H. Lawrence*, I, ed. Moore, p. 298.
[2] D. H. Lawrence, 'Study of Thomas Hardy', *Phoenix*, I, p. 440.

Yet they were all cowed by the mere judgment of man upon them, and all the while by their own souls they were right.'[1] 'The mere judgment of man . . . their own souls . . .,' the nerve of the difference in outlook between Hardy and Lawrence lies exposed in that distinction. Hardy's imaginative effort, as his fiction progressed, was directed towards seeing the individual will and the judgement of others in a constant interplay. For Lawrence, that interplay was a friction diminishing the endless variety, the unfinished possibilities that existed within the individual self, and the novel, as 'the bright book of life', was there to testify to the reality of those possibilities. If, at the end, for Hardy, in *Jude*, man seems defeated, it is through the obduracy of the world about him, Wessex has faded into the world in which the author wrote.

If we turn again to the way in which *Jude* ends, we can bring Hardy's difficulty into focus, and at the same time see more exactly what is at issue between the novelist who is oppressed by the conflict between the individual soul and the judgement of man, and the novelist who would seek to reject the necessity of a conflict expressed in those terms.

Endings, as I have argued throughout this study, were always a source of difficulty for Hardy, because they implied unity where he sought plurality, they expressed finality where he sought continuity. Hence the variety of strategies he adopted to overcome these constrictions. But *Jude* was to provide him with a particular difficulty because, as I suggested at the beginning of this chapter, the plurality of meaning is expressed in the very form the novel takes, it is an inseparable part of its unfolding movement. There seems nothing within that movement which indicates a natural point of rest, 'an ending'.

Furthermore, Hardy would seem faced at the end of his novel with making two rather different statements about Jude: he wanted to express the end of his career in terms which are unequivocally and inherently tragic; and also to show that tragedy as contingent on human institutions, on Jude's own failure of temperament. In Lawrence's terms, he wants to combine 'the war with God' with the judgement of men. It is the plurality of views carried to its farthest

[1] D. H. Lawrence, op. cit., p. 420.

extreme. If, in the final analysis, Hardy fails in his attempt, then I think we should realise that in *Jude* he sought to express an apprehension of contraries so deep that his kind of fiction could no longer accommodate them without collapsing into radical ambiguity or incoherence. But if final success eludes him, his attempt to register this last 'series of seemings' is remarkable.

To do justice to the impression of Jude as tragic hero, ravaged and finally destroyed by implacable events, Hardy draws lavishly on the ironies of plot. Jude abandoned by Sue for Phillotson, following the death of the children; Jude tricked and made captive again by Arabella; Jude catching his fatal illness through an abortive visit to Sue in the forlorn hope that she might return to him; Jude dying, alone, reciting the curses of Job, while the university which rejected him is *en fête* outside his windows. It builds up massively into an impression of great poignancy.

For Hardy, however, that impression of the suffering of 'the individual soul' has to be offset by another, no less urgent, but much more difficult to convey, the impression of that soul under judgement. It is difficult because it relies on shifting the attitude of the reader to the narrative. And so, running alongside the ironies of plot, Hardy begins to establish what might be described as ironies of tone – ironies calculated to disengage the reader, not from Jude, but from the whole recital of events, so that we can encompass them, rather than become involved in them. The first act of disengagement is Father Time's killing of the children, which, overwhelmingly tragic as it is, is also grotesque, a black parody of certain attitudes of Jude's and Sue's. This sets up within the reader a certain resistance, which enables Hardy to place his central figures in a rather more critical light. Sue's return to Phillotson, however psychologically understandable, is treated in such a way that it borders on the grotesque, and her subsequent life with him serves to confirm that impression. The effect on the reader is that Sue moves away from being a figure of tragedy, into becoming a clinical 'case'. This, in turn, has its effect on Jude, who for all his increasing alienation from her, still seems helplessly bound to her, so sunk in torpor at her departure that he can even be remarried to Arabella and scarcely notice it. Set against the dead passivity of Sue and Jude, we have the unabated energy of Arabella, plotting with zest and ardour. This builds up into an impression which, pushed further, would not be far removed from the world of black comedy. That is to make the point too strongly, but we can see Hardy at work in these pages not so much redistributing our sympathies, as directing them towards the total situation, and away from the individuals who compose it. One character at least, Arabella, is admirably built to survive into a future beyond the novel, and it is to her that Hardy gives the last words in the book, words free from irony and sharp in their judgement of Sue and Jude: 'She's never found peace since she left his arms, and never will again till she's as he is now!' It would be foolish to deny that Hardy intends a harsh irony in the Christminster celebrations which accompany Jude's death and so make us feel the more keenly the desolations of his life. But I think we must also concede that Hardy expresses a sense of the necessary continuity in human living here, and that if Jude finds in the Book of Job a text for cursing, it is also possible to find there a text for endurance. I have no wish to minimise the tragic effect of Jude's death, but I think that there is present at the end of the novel a wider spectrum of feeling than identifying Hardy's 'ending' with his death would suggest.

If Hardy does not quite succeed in registering that spectrum with the reader, this is because in *Jude* he has crossed into territory which Lawrence, in particular, was to make peculiarly his own, a territory where the end of the novel points beyond itself and becomes a new beginning. Hardy wrote a fiction which presumed a commission to write about the world as he found it; Lawrence's fiction felt under no such obligation. The novel was the 'one bright book of life', its business was 'to reveal true and vivid relationships', its commission to make all things new. Whereas it is central to Hardy's purpose to show that Sue's tragedy is, in large measure, due to her failure to come to terms with a history at once public and private, it is central to Lawrence's purpose to reveal Ursula Brangwen's triumph as having behind it precisely that sense of history, but being able to find its climax in vision, which enables her to transcend her past. The generations of history give way to the regeneration of the individual. Such a kind of fiction is bound, by its nature, to be exploratory, with the author no longer content to interrogate the radical contraries *within* his fiction, but seeking always to embody the on-going creative impulse itself, beyond 'the end' of his fiction. In such a novel, there is a danger that fictional form will submit to the pressure of authorial testament: it is, at least, a question whether Ursula's vision is supported by the fiction which precedes it. The 'end' is less a conclusion, something felt for, expected, within the work itself than a new start, a sense of life awaiting fulfilment. Gerald Crich's remark towards the end of *Women in Love*, 'It's a complete experience . . . It's not finished', is Hardy's phrase 'a series of seemings' carried to an extreme undreamt of by its author, an extreme where the form of the novel has become *all* process. In *Jude* Hardy was still committed to a fiction which pressed for a conclusion, even though it was to be a conclusion shaken to the core by the pressure of contraries. Looking back, it is difficult to see how that last hard-won ending could have been anything other than the ending to his whole fictional journey. But looking forward, we can see how another novelist was to find a fresh creative impulse in the very difficulties which he saw as characterising that journey: where *Jude* ends *The Rainbow* begins.

INDEX